# Kentucky's Domain
# of
# Power, Greed and
# Corruption

# Kentucky's Domain
## of
# Power, Greed and Corruption

*Betty Boles Ellison*

Writers Club Press
San Jose  New York  Lincoln  Shanghai

Kentucky's Domain of Power, Greed and Corruption

Writers Club Press
an imprint of iUniverse.com, Inc.

For information address:
iUniverse.com, Inc.
5220 S 16th, Ste. 200
Lincoln, NE 68512
www.iuniverse.com

ISBN: 0-595-15991-5

Printed in the United States of America

In Memory of Logan, John and Rubye


Dedicated to Margaret, Sam and Bill

# Contents

# PREFACE

Referring to college athletics as amateur sports is as archaic as football's flying wedge that was outlawed almost a century ago. College athletics are all about multi-million-dollar programs, billion-dollar television contracts, corporate control and cronyism. Power, greed and corruption have turned the top athletic programs into money-making machines controlled as much by people outside the program as university presidents and athletics directors.

Few, if any, books written about college athletics closely examine the behind the scenes deal making, how lucrative contracts are awarded and the favored few who benefit. This book reveals how and why sports decisions were made at the University of Kentucky, one of the nation's top programs, how they were influenced by powerful elements who profited, sometimes by questionable legal and ethical tactics from these actions. Six years of solid academic research stands behind the facts revealed in this book.

Kentucky's athletics program was selected for this book for a number of reasons. During the late 1980s, when another athletics scandal was brewing on campus, I was doing graduate work at UK in sports history. In a graduate seminar on urban history, Dr. Humbert S. Nelli, my supervising professor who wrote his own book, *The Winning Tradition, The History of Kentucky Wildcat Basketball,* encouraged me to look at the program through the athletic administration of the university's seven presidents.

From the very beginning, it was evident the school's athletics program decisions were influenced more from without than within. There was a century of catering to the whims of downtown Lexington interests at the expense of the school's athletic program. Dr. Nelli cautioned me about my personal safety as I was researching a subject long considered sacred. Kentucky athletics involved millions of dollars and national reputations. Arrogance had so permeated the program that athletic officials considered themselves above accountability and, in doing so, perfected stonewalling to an art form. Intimidating a mere woman, most of their attitudes indicated, was a piece of cake.

There were other reasons for Kentucky's selection for this book. A $37 million budget placed the program among the tops in the country. The school had a checkered past of rules violations in whatever governing organization they joined. The National Collegiate Athletic Association leveled their first "sudden death" penalty against Kentucky in 1952 for illegal subsidization of players by influential forces outside the program. Six of their athletes were involved in the point shaving scandals of the 1940s and 1950s.

The legacy of Adolph Rupp, who still holds the highest winning percentage of any college coach, was a factor. Kentucky's fan base is so immense and dedicated that the NCAA usually sends the school to play in the largest venues. The loyalty of some fans is so intense they take their last journey in outfits and caskets of blue and white, the school's colors. National public opinion surveys of the 1990s indicated Kentucky's basketball team was considered "America's Team."

An abundance of research was available until I reached the 1969-87 administration of president Otis A. Singletary, known as "Dr. Jock." Despite an Open Records Act governing state institutions, university administrators were enforcing their own twenty-year reserve on previous presidents' papers. As a former journalist, I knew it was necessary to jump through all the bureaucratic hoops to gain access to the papers. I filed the required petition for access to the Singletary Papers, and Donald Clapp, the school's custodian of official records, stonewalled me for nine months despite repeated requests for an answer to my petition. After speaking with an attorney, I filed a nine-page request to examine documents in about 100 boxes of Singletary's papers. Clapp's first act, before giving me access, was to notify the former president the university had to make his papers available despite their twenty-year reserve. With a copy of my Open Records request, Singletary began examining the stack of boxes. After looking into three or four boxes of the papers he had carefully sorted, indexed and, in some cases, marked restricted, Singletary halted his perusal. Why he stopped at that point was unknown as he refused to answer my written requests for interviews.

Although his papers were obviously laundered, ample material remained to detail the abuses and corruption of the athletics program for nearly twenty years. After Clapp's departure, the legal counsel's office was most accommodating in providing the requested documents.

A strange sequel of events unfolded after I filed the Open Records Act request. Ten months earlier I'd received my master degree in Kentucky history from the university. When I received my degree there was no indication my work was lacking. I had no plans to pursue a Ph.D. from Kentucky for two reasons: (1) with two degrees from the university I planned to enroll in a program elsewhere; (2) considering the problems I created forcing the school to open their presidential papers, I doubted I would be admitted even with a high grade point average.

Because I wanted to finish the project of researching the athletic administration of the seven school presidents, I continued taking graduate history seminars under Dr. Nelli on a post-baccalaureate basis, a common practice. A letter from Dr. James Abisetti, the history department's director of graduate studies, demanded to know why I was continuing to enroll in the university when I had been "terminated" at the master's level. That was news to me. Abisetti informed me that I wouldn't be admitted to their Ph.D. program. Keep in mind, I hadn't applied for admission. An extended correspondence with Abisetti revealed two interesting facts. He sent me the original typed notice of my "termination" back dated to my December 1990 oral exam. The notice was signed by the history department secretary who later married the chairman of the department who suggested that I leave the campus when my master's work was finished. If that note existed in December 1990, why did Abisetti send the original instead of a copy? Abisetti repeatedly refused to provide a reason for my alleged "termination."

While the UK history department claimed to have "terminated" me, Kentucky's historian laureate Thomas D. Clark still selected me to research a history he was writing.

There are no apologies for the facts revealed in this book. If the reader is one of those intense, Big Blue fans, the details reported will be hard to accept. There will be a tendency to blame me, the messenger, for chronicling the behind the scenes details. However, those exploits were perpetrated by people who subverted the intent and ideals of the program. If the reader's interest is in college sports in general, the insights into the Kentucky program are duplicated, to some extent, in major universities across the nation.

Those programs function for power and influence, for fame and glory and a venal craving for money. Next to last in line for consideration were the athletes the school used to bring in as much money as possible. Ordinary fans came last.

In undertaking such an exhaustive, time consuming project, the contributions other people made were considerable and much appreciated. Many people, outside my family and close friends, should be recognized, but I am sure they know of my gratitude and will be more comfortable and their reputations and positions kept more secure if their names aren't mentioned. For those who spoke with me off the record, I have kept their confidences. There was one person brave enough to have her name mentioned, and that was Jan Baker who did an extensive and absolutely impressive job proofing and editing the final manuscript.

Would I undertake such a grueling and demanding project again? Absolutely, I have every intention of repeating the experience.

Betty Boles Ellison

Lexington, Kentucky

October 2000

# INTRODUCTION

*Kentucky's Domain of Power, Greed and Corruption* examines one of the nation's top college athletic programs, whose basketball team is considered "America's Team." The long established practice of the university's presidents caving in to pressure from boosters; how their particular management practices were developed; the origin of the almost incestuous relationship between the school and downtown Lexington that cost the institution millions of dollars; a consistent failure to follow the rules of whatever athletic organization they belonged to; the shady business dealings that continued for decades, and the influential power brokers whose deep pockets and family connections entrenched them into Kentucky athletics are all a part of the facts.

"In The Beginning" provides an overview of the athletics program from the time the early power brokers established generations of their families' involvement with the school's athletics. The connection between politics and athletics has always been there. The passion for combat, the sheer delight of pitting one's skills against another, was transferred from carving out a life on the frontier to a fledgling sports program.

That early environment continued to influence a young athletics program at a struggling land grant college. "A Stacked Deck" illustrates how, even in those days, athletic officials and faculty members involved would take the darker path when other options were available. The university president was driven to distraction by the good old boys athletic antics. Kentucky was hit with "sudden death-like" penalties long before the NCAA gave the school their first real one in 1952.

The unbroken pattern of athletic abuse and corruption continues in "But, We've Always Done It This Way." The "good old boys" forced the president to build a stadium and gymnasium that strained the school's resources. Creative accounting in the athletic buildings was amazing. Athletic officials attempted to excuse their fudging of the rules by referring to their infractions as "irregularities." Illegally supported and academic deficient players were used to fill the stadium to clear athletic debts.

Adolph F. Rupp is introduced in "The Combative Kansan" as college basketball's most successful coach. Rupp's percentage of victories at one college stands untouched a quarter of a century after his death. His method of recruiting the best, drilling them endlessly and demanding excellence established Kentucky's offensive style of race horse basketball. His records and the style of game he played was how succeeding coaches were measured. The politically (in)correct assumption the media began making in the 1990s about Rupp being a racist is shot down.

It was inevitable a clash would occur between Rupp and a new president who was determined to retire the coach. Otis A. Singletary, who followed the reform presidency of John W. Oswald, was a suave politician who wanted to be a national power in college athletics. That would be difficult with Rupp sitting across the campus. "Dr. Jock" provides a look into Singletary's political background, how he forced Rupp into retirement, abused him afterwards and established his own strangle-hold on the athletics program.

Singletary's political skills are showcased in "Strong Arm Politics" that details how he built the new stadium. His Texas side-stepping political ways fitted right in with the way good old boys play the game in Kentucky. He out-foxed most of his opponents while using some of their ideas.

Things were all going Singletary's way until he tangled with the Lexington establishment in "See What The Boys Downtown Will Have." They burned him good. Fresh off his victory in the stadium deal, he expected the same success in moving basketball games off campus into a municipal arena the school neither owned nor controlled. Before the boys downtown were finished they owned a sizable chunk of the school's basketball revenue costing the university millions of dollars.

After the arena debacle, Singletary talked about going back to Texas and interviewing for the job of Southern Methodist University's president. The good old boys thought athletic life as they knew it was ending! They discovered, in "Whose Trust Is It, Anyway," their athletic-minded president wanted more money. They raided a tax-free educational and charitable trust fund to create a personal fund for Singletary. The amount taken each year grew from $20,000 in 1975 to $60,000 in 1986.

While sitting on all those prestigious national athletics committees to discover the evils of college athletics, Singletary neglected his school's own program. Scandals abounded in both basketball and football. Recruiting and supervision ran amuck as characterized in "The Great Indiana Caper and Other Follies." The NCAA investigation found fifty-one violations, and probably missed three times that number. Kentucky received light penalties and probation.

Singletary deserves credit for playing the game to the hilt. He stalled the implementation of Title IX, equal facilities and programs for women athletes, for ten years after it passed Congress. "Boss of Building, Tycoon of Tickets" illustrates his determination to run his athletics program to please himself, his political involvement in athletic buildings and his control of football and basketball tickets. Providing special housing for athletes was against NCAA rules, but he approved building them for the football and basketball teams.

"Sweethearts, Contracts That Is" reveals the power the good old boys asserted in controlling lucrative contracts, some obtained by competitive bidding and others without any bids at all. For instance, Singletary gave away the basketball game program rights in his agreement to play in the municipal arena, and only one person was allowed access to produce them.

Sports medicine was the last place I expected to find deep-seated politics, but it's there in "Benign Neglect." Had he been successful, a UK medical center chancellor would have gutted his own orthopedics department to bring in an outside physician to establish a sports medicine program for Kentucky athletes. When that failed, he arranged for the athletes to be treated by that physician at a local hospital instead of the university's.

In 1985 Singletary's athletic empire came crashing down when the local newspaper ran a series of articles on subsidization of basketball players by the deep pockets recruited by the coach. "Black October" demonstrates how history repeated itself. Thirty-three years after the NCAA slapped Kentucky with their first "sudden death" penalty for overt subsidization of athletes, the school's acts were so brazen the organization couldn't look away. Singletary stonewalled the investigation until he retired and headed for tall grass.

David P. Roselle, almost totally Singletary's opposite in athletic management, had to cope with that scandal's resolution. It wasn't long before the faithful discovered their new president was more like Oswald than Singletary, and he expected athletics to obey the rules. "A New Beginning" outlines Roselle's idea of how college athletics should operate, and how they would run in his administration. He had a basketball coach and athletics director who had other ideas.

Athletics out of control, a lack-luster athletics director, academic fraud and the Emery envelope scandal make up "A Good Old Boy Loses Out." How Roselle dealt with them, by bringing in a special investigator/counsel, sealed his fate. The governor was after his hide, and he got death threats. To his credit, he cleaned up athletics by firing the athletics director and basketball coaching staff.

The media falls in love with his new athletics director, but they don't know the whole story. "Two of A Kind" displays the ugly side of college athletic management, special deals, vocal contracts and allowing a favored few to influence major decisions. One businessman established a national sports marketing empire with Kentucky athletics as the base, and nobody objected or talked about the fiscal drain.

Roselle conducted a secret audit of athletic finances, but found no irregularities. The audit, however, didn't include the deep pockets that were pouring thousands of dollars into the program. "Follow The Money" deciphers the sources of that money, and some have never before been revealed.

"Faked Out" follows the nasty chronicle of sports medicine to a conclusion, of sorts. Roselle ordered his athletics director to clean up the mess, but he was ignored. An internationally famous orthopedic surgeon, who developed the UK Sports Medicine practice, is forced to leave because of petty politics. Athletes' medical care took a back seat to egos until a canny Scot surgeon stood up to the establishment.

That nasty racism raised its ugly head in "Color Made A Difference." The NCAA's investigators and those from the university made a difference in how they treated parents of black players, and the deep pockets.

Sometimes it was difficult to determine who was trying the hardest to protect their reputations: the good old boys who for years had polluted the program and were determined to continue or Roselle attempting to institute reforms and bring integrity to Kentucky athletics. "Reputations on The Line" clears it up.

Because of Roselle's determination to do a creditable investigation of athletics, basketball in particular, Kentucky's program was saved from another disaster. "No Sudden Death" reveals just how close the NCAA came to slapping the school with that penalty for two years. Few of the faithful believed that Roselle actually saved their beloved basketball program from destruction. They couldn't wait to get rid of him.

With the continuing athletic scandals, the football coach decided to leave. Roselle said he could stay as long as he wanted with 6-5 season and his players graduating at a rate of ninety percent. "Changing of the Guards" revealed how the powerful deep pockets not only helped select new football coach, but attempted to sink Roselle's choice of a new basketball coach as soon as he arrived. When that failed, they contractually and fiscally abused and embarrassed him.

After Roselle's departure, the power brokers installed as president one of their own, but he failed to have Singletary's sharp political mind. The nation's most popular and successful college basketball coach was expendable when it came to a $25 million Nike contract for the school. "The More Things Change, The More They Stay The Same" delineates just how it happened.

The "Epilogue" brings everything up to date. Athletic officials plan to buy the well-worn municipal arena, apparently along with its debts, to satisfy the downtowners. The athletics director, facing mandatory retirement, picked his successor but has a contract as an advisor to insure that business as usual will continue. He left another insider to defend the mediocre basketball and football coaches. The ultimate good old boy sells his sports marketing business built on Kentucky athletics.

# In the Beginning

Kentucky sports, from the very beginning, have been filled with power, greed and corruption. Throw in the influence of alcohol, wagering and politics, and the result is nothing past and present managers of one of the nation's most powerful college athletic programs ever wanted to see in print. Managers had no control of how sports at the school began, and have since made improvements only when they had no choice.

Sports began in the rough and tumble western frontier life as pioneers searched for recreation in path racing, turkey shooting, bear baiting, wrestling, dice throwing and militia musters. These activities, along with pioneers' "jollifications," were interspliced with whiskey, wagering and politics. William Calk brought his distilling apparatus from Carolina to Fort Boonesborough in 1775, and made corn whiskey soon thereafter. On a frontier without specie, whiskey became a valuable commodity for more uses than medicinal and recreational. Soon after football began at Kentucky in 1881, the commonwealth had 171 registered distilleries with a daily mashing capacity of 36,265 bushels, the largest such operation in the nation. It was from these elemental distilling efforts that Kentucky's famous Bourbon whiskey emerged.[1]

Militias were required in the colonies, and later in the western county that became the commonwealth for defense from Indians and policing. All able-bodied men served in the militia, and their musters were sporting and political events that usually ended in drunken brawls. Despite attempts to reform the musters, they continued to dissolve into disputes

1

because of differences of political opinion, gambling and drinking. The musters had a profound influence on sporting activities that eventually overpowered the Protestant ethic that saw frivolity and idleness in the evils of recreation. The comradeship generated by the musters played a large part in establishing the "good old boy" network that later became such a significant part of college athletics.

Settlers brought their Thoroughbreds from Virginia, Maryland and the Carolinas, and raced them on dirt paths before their prodigy established some of the nation's premier tracks. With no Indians to be chased, Kentuckians looked for another avenue of action and a way to settle their arguments. Wagering on horse races satisfied that need for excitement, and many a farm and fortune changed hands as a result. Wagers were initially between the owners of the horses in the match race, and some of their friends. Later, bookmakers, with the agreement of the participants, sets the odds and conditions of the races. When bookmakers began changing the odds during and after races, betting pools were formed where the collected wagers were divided among the backers of the winning horses. Lexington's Standardbred track, The Red Mile, used betting pools until 1942. Pari-mutual betting, an earlier version of the system used today, was adopted by Churchill Downs, the home of the Kentucky Derby, for the 1878 racing season.[2]

That was the same year that Kentucky Agricultural and Mechanical College (later the University of Kentucky) separated from Kentucky University (Transylvania), and moved their campus to fifty acres of land donated by the city. Local governments and private citizens contributed $50,000 for the school's first three buildings. Those donations developed into an attitude that many Lexingtonians still have, the institution belonged to them, and it should be operated according to their wishes, especially where athletics were concerned.[3]

Baseball was the first of college sports played at the school. After the institutions separated, they became fierce rivals in sports. Each accused the other of using players who weren't students. A fight erupted after one game over KU keeping the baseball that belonged to A & M. The townspeople didn't take kindly to having their Sunday afternoons interrupted by baseball games, and several students were indicted on charges of nuisance.[4]

While the early baseball games were certainly a contact sport, they lacked the bloody excitement of football that appealed to a populace only a few generations removed from the frontier. Football, brought to Lexington in 1880 by C.L. Thurgood, a KU student who played on a rugby team in Australia, caught on immediately. The next year KU and A & M played one of the first games in the south, that saw the new school lose 1-7.2.[5]

Now, football was a game the good old boys could relate to in a big way. It was rough, bloody, and they could gamble on the outcome while enjoying their whiskey and tobacco. Newspapers carried notices of football games for days before the contests, and they listed the wagering odds daily. Local gamblers and bookmakers set the odds, and the games attracted big crowds. The good old boys, however, despised losing. After the December 19, 1881 game between A & M and Centre, in Danville, one fierce fan, hating the 0-10 loss, decided to do something about it. He organized a stock company of 200 people, each contributing five dollars, to hire a trainer to drill the team for a month.[6]

Just as Thoroughbred owners combined their funds to purchase shares in race horses, the good old boys saw nothing wrong in doing the same for college athletics, and then betting on the outcome. It was a move that was repeated over and over again through the years.

Although they needed instructions, the football team searched for a permanent place to play. The best location was president James K. Patterson's cow pasture. Patterson, a strict liberal arts disciplinarian who immigrated from Glasgow, Scotland, with his family in 1842, came to Lexington after receiving his bachelor and master degrees from Hanover College and teaching at the Presbyterian Academy in Greenville, Kentucky. He was often forced to yield, despite his aversion to athletics, to the town's strong sporting instinct during his twenty-two-year presidency. Once they had a field, the president's cow pasture, the next logical step was building a grandstand. Patterson allowed a stock company, composed of himself, his brother Walter Patterson, football coach A.M. Miller and others, to be formed to raise money, at five dollars a share, to build the grandstand. When the president realized two beautiful trees stood between the grandstand and the field, he halted all work. How he expected fans to see action on the field around the trees was a mystery, but he loved those trees. The matter was taken care of in the dead of night when the trees were chopped down. Patterson was so furious that he offered a reward for the name of the culprits, but it remained unclaimed.[7]

Patterson's efforts to get a handle on the growing popularity of football on the campus was no more successful than his efforts to save the trees. Students were in charge of their athletics program: they handled the scheduling and travel subject to Patterson's approval, and gate receipts. There were no codified rules for the game. Often regulations governing the game were agreed to by the teams just before the contest began. By December 1895, Patterson was at his wits end, and prohibited games off the campus. A short time later, and probably after some carefully exerted pressure, Patterson changed his mind, and A & M football was again alive and well.[8]

Patterson wasn't alone in his efforts to handle the problems football brought to his campus. College administrators throughout the south had the same problem. William Dudley, dean of Vanderbilt's medical school, began an effort to codify college athletic rules within an organization of regional colleges. Dudley wanted athletics under faculty guidance where they had charge of eligibility, scheduling, travel and, most importantly, a tight grasp of the purse strings. Dudley had another reason in mind. Such a regional organization, he thought, would eliminate fans' and boosters' involvement in the decision making of college athletics. It was already too late for that.[9]

The good old boys had their collective feet in college athletics' door to stay. Whether they were former jocks or not, they engaged in the annual autumn rituals of football that helped rejuvenate their aging male psyches. If Patterson and Dudley thought those fellows were going to give up their involvement in the sport, making book on the games and tipping their whiskey flasks as they watched the players they'd paid for perform, they were sadly mistaken.

In December 1894, Dudley held a meeting in Nashville to organize the Southern Intercollegiate Athletic Association, part of which eventually became the Southeastern Conference. Patterson neither attended the meeting nor sent a representative. Joining that year were Alabama Polytechnic Institute (Auburn), Georgia School of Technology, the University of the South, Vanderbilt and the universities of Alabama, Georgia and North Carolina. The next year A & M, and eleven other schools, Central, Clemson, Cumberland, Louisiana State, Mercer, Mississippi A & M, Nashville, Southern Presbyterian, Tulane, Tennessee and Texas, joined as invited charter members. The SIAA's big push was halting the importation of football players for pay. Their answer was the migratory rule that required students be enrolled at the school where they played.[10]

They hadn't counted on the way Kentuckians liked their games played.

A & M football was like a huge boulder rolling down a hill, picking up speed as it traveled, and along the way acquiring a certain style of playing the game. In 1898 the team, under first year coach A.M. Bass, out of the University of Cincinnati, posted a 7-0 record. What was even more impressive, "The Immortals," as the team was called, was not scored upon, and amassed 180 points when a touchdown counted only five points.[11]

How did a struggling football program, like A & M's, suddenly attain such an outstanding record? The Spanish-American War. A & M threw out the migratory rule, and allowed the best of the 20,000 soldiers, many of whom were former football players, stationed in Kentucky to play on their team. School officials were quick to accuse other teams of using the soldiers on their teams, but denied doing the same. Former Kentucky sports information director Russell Rice said the school was one of the worst offenders for using players not enrolled in school. Regardless, the school put an undefeated season in the record books less than a decade after they began playing the organized sport.[12]

The 1898 record illustrated that the good old boys, along with the school, were willing to do just about anything to win.

Regardless of their affiliation with the SIAA, the faculty athletics committee spent years searching for rules that fit their limited resources and talent. An almost rabid fan base developed at A & M, not only for football, but other sports. Administrators found it difficult to handle those expectations. A 1901 baseball game at nearby Georgetown College was an example. Umpire Joe Smith was attacked by spectators for calling an A & M player out. Smith's face and body were badly beaten before police could rescue him. The A & M coach and team demanded he reverse his call and, when he refused, they walked off the field calling him a thief and a coward. The president was forced to apologize for the team's unsportsmanlike conduct.[13]

The corps of cadets, reminiscence of the military musters of earlier days, were strong supporters of the school's athletic endeavors, and resented women using their armory for physical education. In April 1904, a group of cadets sneaked into the armory with a camera to photograph a women's physical education class. In the days when women wore long bloomers for exercise, it was doubtful if they expected to see any revealing sights. The cadets were caught and locked in the basement until the proper authorities arrived. All but three escaped by crawling out a window. Punishment for those three was an admonishment before the faculty. The incident wouldn't merit mention except that it set off a series of events that almost destroyed the delicate town and gown relationship Patterson had cultivated over the years, and illustrated what a trigger point Kentucky athletics were, even in the early days.[14]

When Commandant of Cadets Robert A. McKee was making his routine nightly inspection of the dorm the day of the incident, he was pelleted with rotten eggs, knocked down and students' threw the contents of their slop jars on his head. When Patterson heard about it, he temporarily suspended McKee, not offending the students but the commandant who was injured. The newspaper sent a reporter, D.B. Goode, to the campus to investigate. He was told Patterson was taking a nap and couldn't be disturbed. He went to the dorm to talk with some students he knew and water was dumped on him from the upper floors. Awake from his nap, Patterson had a brief meeting with Goode, who then went to the McKee residence to interview the commandant. Mrs. McKee feared for their lives as a mob of unruly students surrounded their home. When Goode came out of the house, he was beaten, and given two minutes to leave the campus. Watching the episode unfold was Walter Patterson, the president's brother.[15]

Walter Patterson claimed he witnessed no violence and said the students had a good reason for evicting Goode from the campus, he was a KU alumnus. Patterson wrote a letter, marked private, to the newspaper's editor protesting Goode being on the campus and writing the story. The newspaper printed his letter and, a few days later, in a stinging editorial suggested the school find new faculty members who had the respect of parents sending their children to the school.[16]

The message was clear, Lexington wanted the school run to their expectations and, for the most part, they were successful for over a century.

It must have pained Patterson very much to do the bowing and scraping that it took to placate downtown interest. He was still paying the price a year later. The athletics association opened a campus book store whose profits would benefit the sparsely-financed sports program. Downtown booksellers were up in arms at the thought of losing some of their business to the school they professed to support. A month later Patterson folded and closed the campus book store.[17]

Patterson abhorred gambling more than he did college sports, but he was in the wrong place to prohibit wagering on the college's games. Students, boosters and faculty members imported players from Columbia University and New York athletic clubs for the annual Thanksgiving Day game in 1903 with KU. Newspapers promoted the game by carrying the daily odds, and ran front page stories about the "ringers" the school imported. The game drew an estimated 3,500 spectators, and $12,000 was wagered on the outcome. The good old boys enjoyed their whiskey, but their spirits were deflated when the players they paid for lost the game 0-17.[18]

Patterson and trustees discussed the Thanksgiving game a few days later and attempted to find something positive about the ordeal. One trustee reasoned if ringers were actually used then "The question may not be a violation of the rule passed by the trustees, but one of propriety." His explanation was in the best Kentucky tradition, "On the race course, the man who enters a ringer is ostracized." Another trustee's most pressing concern was whether the wagers of students and faculty were settled in a gentlemanly fashion. The defense posed by the faculty athletic committee made absolutely no sense. "The only possible way to insure pure amateur athletics in the college and community was to import and use professionals." Trustees agreed with the illogical explanation.[19]

KU wanted to cancel the Thanksgiving series after the next season, and that put a substantial dent in the school's athletic revenues. The SIAA suspended the school over the game in what was the forerunner of today's "sudden death" penalty, no conference competition for the next season. KU supporters kept the scandal alive. Alfred Fairhurst, KU faculty chairman of athletics, jibed his A & M counterpart, St. Clair MacKenzie, "Whatever the composition of your team, KU will play you. You may bring your team as you did last year from the four corners of the earth and the fifth quarter, if you can find it. Bring Hottentots, Flat-Headed Indians, Patagonians, native Australians, Esquimaux, New Yorkers, Danvillians, Whatnots, Topknots, gather them from all the tribes and kindred of the earth, the more motley the conglomeration the merrier it will be and we will play you." Fairhurst spoke too soon for his team lost the 1904 game 4-21. The two schools played each other only periodically afterwards.[20]

The good old boys howled about the SIAA suspension just as they would over future penalties. Their claim of being unjustly black-balled by the conference fell on deaf ears. Nor was it the last time the school was suspended by the SIAA. A & M didn't play another conference school from November 1901 until the October 1906 game with Vanderbilt. It was possible there were other versions of the sudden death in that period. It was difficult to find records of the SIAA as the Southeastern Conference, the association's eventual successor, had none in their archives.[21]

Football had such a grasp on the school and boosters Patterson couldn't throw the sport off campus, but he didn't have the money to support it. He instituted a five-dollar gymnasium fee on students, with two-fifth going to athletics. Richard C. Stoll, chairman of the trustees' executive committee, former football player, Republican politician and judge, sued the school over the fee and won. Stoll was appointed a trustee, and served on the board from 1898 until 1948, with the exception of one term. His influence cropped up again and again in my research. A special allowance was made in 1895 for Stoll's brother, John G. Stoll, to play on the baseball team when his grades were below the level set by the faculty for athletic participation, and then rejected.[22]

Patterson always seemed at a loss in dealing with athletic problems. Herman Scholtz, who played with "The Immortals," dressed in feminine attire and accompanied the women's basketball team to a game in Georgetown. Only women were allowed to attend the games at that time. The president finally decided to send an apology to the college, and reprimanded Scholtz in chapel. The decision came only after much contemplation.[23]

The same year Scholtz was in drag, college football entered a watershed year. Formations such as the flying wedge, the hurdle and scrummage were killing and maiming football players at an alarming rate. The flying wedge, designed by Boston engineer Lorin F. Deland, consisted of five men protecting the ball carrier as they drove down field in that formation. The hurdle consisted of a small running back leaping into the arms of two larger teammates after receiving the ball, and being thrown feet-first over the defensive line. Scrummage was a pack of eight men surrounding the ball carrier as they advanced the ball. That year eighteen football players were killed, and 149 suffered serious injuries. President Theodore Roosevelt, a former athlete, called college football leaders to the White House and told them to reform the game or he would ban it from campuses. That resulted in the organization of the Intercollegiate Athletics Association of the United States, the forerunner of the NCAA.[24]

A & M continued to tinker with rules desperately searching for another undefeated season. The 1907 schedule contained only two powerful teams: Vanderbilt, which defeated them 40-0, and Tennessee who tied them 0-0. That season, 9-1-1, was the best since 1898. Basketball began in 1903 with little notice as teams played only in-state schools and athletic clubs. Baseball, the more established sport, played teams in Virginia, North Carolina, Ohio and Michigan. Neither of those sports, nor track and field, rivaled football in popularity.[25]

For playing teams outside the SIAA, the school adopted first one set of rules and then another. In 1905 they adopted the Pennsylvania Rules, and then proceeded to weaken the eligibility requirements. The actual Pennsylvania Rules called for an athlete to be a bonafide student in residence for an academic year. The school modified the eligibility rule to compute grades on a monthly basis, and the athlete couldn't fall below seventy-percent in academics. Where the Pennsylvania Rules prohibited participation in an intercollegiate game if the player received money, A & M decided the school would determine if a players' athletic skills were used as a means of a livelihood or if it was just an unintentional or youthful infraction. The school's news release boasted about the lofty aims of the Pennsylvania Rules to correct "The recognized abuses which have gradually crept into college athletics throughout the nation." They neglected to explain how the school watered down the new rules.[26]

There were just as many problems with keeping check on the finances. Patterson kept student athletic managers under closer supervision, auditing their financial reports. After all, there was a considerable amount of money involved. Baseball and football managers H.E. Read and J.C. Nesbit were admonished for their loose and irresponsible business methods.[27]

The older Patterson became, the more bewildered he was of dealing with the faculty, trustees and the good old boys on athletics. College presidents were caught between their faculties and governing boards on athletics, and Patterson appeared to be fighting both. He was especially resentful of the Lexington newspapers, and what he termed their intrusion into university affairs. It might be best, he reasoned, to let the trustees make some of the decisions concerning athletics.[28]

That's what happened, but it made little difference.

In 1907 trustees recommended the baseball, basketball and football teams play only seven games per sport against outside competition. Things didn't turn out that way. Football had an eleven game season, 9-1-1; the basketball team also played an eleven game schedule with a 5-6 record; the baseball team had fifteen games going 12-2-1.[29]

Finding the A & M handle cumbersome, the school's name was changed in 1908 to State University making it eligible for membership in the Association of American State Universities with standardized entrance requirements. The athletic teams, who had been called "Corn-Crackers," "Thoroughbreds," "Cadets" and "Colonels," now had an official name. In a 1909 chapel address, Commandant Phillip W. Corbusier told students the football team fought like wildcats the previous week against Illinois. The name, "Wildcats," lasted.[30]

The school also had a new football coach in 1909, E. R. Sweetland, who had coached at Cornell, Colgate, Syracuse and Ohio State. Initially the faculty senate lauded him for the high moral tone he set for athletics, but that didn't last. His first season of 9-1 didn't hurt, and the good old boys thought their savior had arrived.[31]

Two years later, another newcomer to the campus, John J. Tigert, would exert a profound influence on athletics for almost a decade. The son and grandson of bishops, Tigert was born on the Vanderbilt campus and, in 1900, won the entrance prize there for the highest marks in Greek and Latin. Tigert, who played football, baseball and basketball, delivered the Vanderbilt commencement address before studying at Oxford on a Rhodes Scholarship.[32]

Patterson decided to retire in 1910, but continued to berate athletics to the very end complaining about the activities disturbing him on Sundays. He yielded control of the school grudgingly and, unfortunately, trustees handled his retirement with such latitude it harmed the school for years to come. Patterson deserved some special consideration since, in the school's lean years, he pledged his savings as collateral for building and operating loans. What he got was beyond the pale. He received sixty percent of his $3,000 annual salary; was designated president emeritus; made a non-voting member of the board of trustees; allowed to represent the university at national meetings and he and his brother continued to live in the president's home for an annual rental of $240. In fact, his brother lived there ten years after Patterson's death.[33]

# A STACKED DECK

Patterson wasn't happy about his successor, Henry S. Barker, a Court of Appeals judge and trustee who lacked a college degree. Barker was a political appointee who had no notion about running a state university. He knew how to repay his debts to those good old boys who put him in office. One of his first acts was to remove the athletics program from faculty control, and put the athletics director, E.R. Sweetland, in charge of both the athletics committee and physical education department. Barker handled the faculty's resentment of their exclusion from the athletic loop by telling them they could appeal any decisions he made to the president.[34]

The faculty senate's committee on athletics was outraged, and collectively sent their resignations to Barker telling him he could handle athletic problems. SIAA regulations required each member institution to have a faculty athletic committee. Barker relented and did what all good politicians do in those situations, he appointed a new faculty committee on athletics, and stacked it in his favor. The committee was chaired by John J. Tigert, head of the physical education and philosophy departments, and the members were registrar Ezra Gillis, Barker's future biographer; professor Henry E. Curtis, who was involved in athletics up to his ears, and E.R. Sweetland, athletics director and football coach. Faculty members objected to Sweetland being on the committee saying he stormed on to the campus like a tornado in 1909 demanding, and getting spring football practice, a special training table and used intramural teams to select his varsity players.[35]

There was no doubt Tigert was in control, with Barker's approval. He attempted to appease the faculty's concern about what he termed "irregularities," the numerous SIAA suspensions. The state governing body for college athletics, the Kentucky Intercollegiate Athletic Association, suspended State in 1911 for a year for playing ineligible players in baseball and football. [36] If all the records were available, Kentucky would have an even more checkered past of athletic infractions and penalties.

At the same time Tigert was attempting to explain past "irregularities," he was creating new ones. It was one of the Rodes boys. William "Red Doc" Rodes demanded that his athletic eligibility be restored, and Tigert and Barker agreed. "Red Doc" was the first of two cousins named William Rodes to play for State. The names, "Red Doc" and "Black Doc," were used to distinguish between the two. "Black Doc" had two brothers who played football at the school. J.W. "Boots" Rodes was on the 1904 team that won nine of their ten games. Pete Rodes was a halfback on the 1907 team, and later entered the US Naval Academy, where he was captain of Navy's 1912 football team. [37]

In October the SIAA charged that the State football and baseball teams used five athletes who weren't eligible, and their information came from one of the school's own faculty members, engineering professor F. Paul Anderson, who had an intense interest in athletics and, I suspect, dealt a little graft on the side. Tigert and Barker knew those charges would eventually reach the SIAA. What better way to stem an investigation than to destroy the evidence in an era where record keeping was tenuous at best? Anderson's office, where athletes' grades were reportedly kept, was burglarized and burned on the night of October 30th. Fire marshal C.C. Bosworth ruled the fire an arson case and the investigation limped into November and December. [38]

The big Thanksgiving game with Central University, Richmond, was ahead, and athletic officials had no time for an arson investigation on the campus, especially under those circumstances. Days before Thanksgiving, William L. Dudley, SIAA president, telegraphed Central University,

State's opponent, and told athletic officials the game wasn't to be played because the association had suspended State for an indefinite period. The five violations included James Park, an amazing athlete who played baseball and football, being part of a semi-professional baseball team in Richmond, Kentucky, before entering college. "Red Doc" Rodes had played beyond his eligibility as had one other baseball player. One player lacked sufficient entrance credits, but he played anyway. A professional baseball player joined the team on a northern trip in the spring of 1911.[39]

When the allegations were made public, Tigert calmly denied everything, and advised the faithful not to worry. When South Atlantic Athletic Association agreed to honor the SIAA's suspension, Tigert headed north to find an opponent for the game. It was unthinkable to cancel the event, because the Thanksgiving game was the biggest gate of the year. He finally signed the Young Men's Institute, from Cincinnati, as State's holiday opponent.[40]

Despite the weak opposition, Tigert, Sweetland and Barker used chapel services for a pep rally to whip up enthusasium for the game, and they were successful. An estimated 2,500 watched "Red Doc" Rodes, one of the principals in the SIAA suspension, play his last game as State defeated the Young Men's Institute 56-0.[41]

The fire marshal's hearing on the Anderson's office fire was scheduled for December 7th, but was postponed for two hours while Bosworth conferred with the school's legal counsel, Richard Bush, one of Stoll's partners. After that meeting, twenty-five witnesses, with the exception of Sweetland, were questioned privately and fingerprinted. It was the first criminal case in Lexington where fingerprints were used. Much was made of former assistant coach and county probation officer Richard Webb's right hand being bandaged. Webb said his revolver fired accidentally injuring his hand. It was a moot point since the fire occurred six weeks earlier. Sweetland, afraid of Webb, went into seclusion during the questioning, and had to be coaxed out. Tigert confirmed Sweetland was afraid Webb would kill him, and indicated that such concern was justified since

Webb was so physically powerful he could jump flat-footed over an offensive line and scatter backs like straws.[42]

Webb objected to Sweetland's preferential treatment in getting his side of the story to the public. He swore out two warrants charging Sweetland and some football players with conspiracy in attempting to imprison him in the YMCA reading room. Barker, Gills and law school dean William T. Lafferty posted sureties for each man's $500 bond. Trustees suggested Barker conduct the school's own investigation, but the president was confident he could politically control the results.[43]

Barker, along with Tigert, was more concerned with the SIAA's meeting in New Orleans, and coordinating their efforts to snow the association about the charges. State was no exception among the SIAA schools for flaunting the rules of the loose confederation. They all operated on the good old boy assumption of "I'll scratch your back this time if you will scratch mine when I'm in trouble." That's why athletic officials weren't concerned about "Red Doc" Rodes playing in the Thanksgiving game. Barker and Tigert had a wonderful defense for all their "irregularities." All those allegations were the results of negligence by the faculty athletic committee. The academicians just weren't doing their job. Neither the school, the athletic director or the football coach would have ever violated the SIAA rules, they said. Executive committee members had their doubts, but it might be their school in the line of fire the next time. The committee sent State a message in the principle provision of their reinstatement. "Hereafter, no coach or athletics director shall be allowed on the faculty athletic committee or have anything to do with passing on the eligibility of any player."[44]

The ruling demonstrated the weakness of the SIAA. In his book on the SIAA in track and field, John W. Bailey said, "The association often failed to take proper action for rules violations such as athletes playing beyond their eligibility, using assumed names to play for more than one school, playing for pay and playing summer baseball."[45] Bailey argued it was impossible for the association to attain harmony of principles and actions among such diverse institutions.

While Barker and Tigert were pleading their case before the SIAA, three additional violations, alleging the athletes were being paid for jobs arranged by the school, made their way into the news. Sweetland, detained in Lexington by the arson investigation, saw his coaching future in jeopardy. He secured a direct telegraph line to New Orleans, and sent affidavits from himself, the three players and, most surprisingly, engineering professor Paul Anderson. Obtaining the direct telegraph wire to New Orleans was no problem as Lexington had one of the larger bookmaking operations in the nation. Sweetland boasted to the local media that State would be reinstated by the SIAA, and pointed to member schools proceeding with schedules for the next season.[46]

It wasn't a pleasant holiday season for anyone connected with State athletics. Five days after Webb filed a $5,000 civil suit against Sweetland and the players for false imprisonment, the former assistant coach was arrested and charged with arson in connection with the fire in Anderson's office. Sweetland was arrested on Christmas eve on two more warrants sworn out by Webb. Fire Marshal Bosworth finally announced the cause of the fire was crossed electrical wires, better known as a "friction fire."[47]

Sweetland was found not guilty on the breach of the peace and provoking an assault warrants, but was, along with the five football players, indicted for holding Webb in the YMCA reading room against his will. Court proceedings revealed Sweetland and Webb were partners in several houses and lots they purchased and re-sold to the school at a considerable profit. The two were then such close associates, that Sweetland recommended Webb succeed him in 1910 when he left to coach at Miami University. Instead the job went to P.P. Douglas from Michigan.[48]

Webb denied the arson charge and suggested Sweetland, angry over Park's disqualification, might have set the fire himself. Sweetland believed Anderson, instead of his players, might have burned his own office. The culprit came, literally, from out of the blue.[49]

Thomas Butler, a former student, was arrested in Youngstown, Ohio, and spirited back to Lexington without the benefit of extradition proceedings. Butler's confession, I've always felt, was too convenient, too timely and solved too many problems to be authentic. Butler implicated Webb in the arson charge. The jury, however, deliberated only two hours before finding Webb not guilty of the arson charge. Sweetland and his five co-defendants were also found not guilty. Sweetland resigned the next day. Webb continued to support athletics and paid for the annual football banquet for years until the school was able to assume the cost.[50]

After evading an elemental "sudden death," you might think the school learned a lesson. That wasn't the case. Tigert's "irregularities" went much further than just failing to meet the harmony of principles and actions Bailey spoke about. The entire fiasco of 1912-13 was symptomatic of a sports mentality that, in less than two decades, became totally ingrained in the school. The man responsible was Tigert, who was calling the shots although he wasn't the president.

Barker's presidency jumped from one athletic crises to another. In October 1913, State defeated Cincinnati 27-7, and students staged a wild fracas in downtown Lexington. Signs were destroyed, streetcars and beer wagons were overturned and policemen were injured attempting to restore order. When downtowners protested the students' actions to Barker, he told them it was one of the prices they had to pay if they wanted the university in their town. Barker previously wanted to move the school to his hometown of Louisville.[51]

There was little protest from Barker and Tigert when the faculty athletic committee again took control of the school's sports, and player eligibility. This time, an athlete had to be enrolled in school and in class attendance a full five days before he could participate in a game.[52]

Tigert replaced Sweetland as athletics director, basketball coach, track coach and assistant to football coach Alpha Brumage. Apparently, Tigert had little time to teach philosophy classes. It was no surprise that the star of the football team was none other than James Park, ruled ineligible in

1912. Park's football records, in the 1914 game against Earlham, stood until 1999 when Tim Couch eclipsed him for most pass attempts in a game, most pass completions in a game and most touchdowns thrown in a game.[53]

Tigert was spending money the school didn't have, and pressed Barker to ask trustees for more. The school began borrowing money from local banks to keep the football program afloat.[54]Barker was either oblivious to what was happening or just plain didn't care.

He did, however, participate in the discussion to award an engineering degree for a former football player who left school to go into business before he graduated. Professor Paul Anderson pushed hard, in faculty and trustees' meetings, for awarding a bachelor degree to George B. Carey, a former football player. Anderson pushed so hard that it gave rise to speculation he was being paid under the table by Carey. He proposed Carey fulfill degree requirements by submitting a thesis based on work experience since he left school, but neglected to disclose Carey hadn't taken such basic courses as English. Carey lost his bid for a degree by only one vote after a month-long battle with the faculty senate. At Carey's death in 1943, his obituary listed his 1893 graduation from A & M with an engineering degree.[55] Just one of the good old boys getting his due.

Another good old boy surfaced again in 1915, and with the same family problem. William "Black Doc" Rodes asked Barker and Tigert for permission to rejoin the football team after he was dismissed from school for not attending classes. What's more, he gave them a week to make up their minds, "I have a pretty good thing in view if you cant turn the trick here." Again Barker and Tigert decided it was left up to the SIAA to prove that "Black Doc" wasn't eligible although they knew he was ineligible. The president said that was the safest way to handle the matter. "Black Doc" played the 1916 season, and Tigert praised him to the sky. "He is so well known," the coach said, "that it is hardly worth while to dwell upon his ability and his spectacular feats of the past season are still fresh in the minds of the followers of the gridiron game."[56]

Tigert was adapt at working his way through the political forest, and that's why he and Barker were such a good team. They were both political animals. Tigert was concerned about the 1916 football schedule, and that nothing was forthcoming from Barker. A letter to the president from P.T. Atkins, a Lexington sportswriter, strongly suggested that influential backing awaited not only the football schedule but Tigert's status as coach. Atkins, who as a State student was secretary of the athletic association, wasn't disappointed. Tigert's 1916 season was 10-2-3.[57]

After the 1916 season Tigert began to fade from the athletic scene. His protege from Vanderbilt, S.A. "Daddy" Boles, succeeded him as athletics director and football coach. A smart man, Tigert probably saw the handwriting on the wall of the athletic mess he and Barker concocted, and went back to teaching. He left the school in 1921 to become US commissioner of education and, as president of the University of Florida, was SEC president in 1945-46. Sports author John D. McCallum claimed Tigert "Devised and implemented the athletic grant-in-aid program and led the fight for honest, aboveboard, realistic handling of financing of college athletes." If that's true, Tigert made a drastic change in his sports operations between Kentucky and Florida. Tigert tilted the wrong athletic windmill in 1947 when he clashed with Florida governor Millard F. Caldwell over selecting a football coach. He resigned the presidency of the university.[58]

Barker wasn't looking at the same circumstances as Tigert, or else he read the political tea leaves wrong. Desperate to increase enrollment to bring in more money, Barker lowered entrance requirements that unloaded tons of criticism. That and his general incompetence led Gov. A.O. Stanley to appoint a special team of national educators to investigate Barker's administration. Investigators filled three volumes, nearly 700 pages, with results of their inquiries. The only surviving document of that investigation is a two-page index.[59]

The overwhelming presence of Patterson was a problem for Barker, but it was his own inability to administer a university that, included increasing the school's debts by $20,000, led to his downfall. However, Barker's legacy of disreputable athletic management found a comfortable niche at the school. His successor couldn't have been more his opposite.

# But, We've Always Done It This Way

Frank L. McVey, a Ph.D. from Yale who taught at Columbia University, was president of the University of North Dakota and wrote for the New York Times' editorial page, was just the man to succeed Barker.[60] McVey arrived at a school that was under-funded by the legislature, lacked public support and the campus and athletic program were in shambles. The McVeys, she was the former Mable Sawyer, adapted much better to the Lexington social scene than the Barkers, who kept their close Louisville ties. McVey didn't share Barker's exuberance for athletics nor Patterson's distaste, but he had a rather simplistic view of athletics in the beginning.

He saw athletics as an academic steam valve. "If you were a shoe clerk," he told historian Thomas D. Clark, "who had to smell bad feet all week, and couldn't talk back to anybody; then Saturday afternoon gave you a chance to shout naughty things at somebody." McVey told Clark when the crowds were gnawing on the referees and opposing team, "They weren't gnawing on us."[61]

I suspect the new president, like the shoe clerk, wanted to avoid smelly things such as athletics. McVey, however, began by paying off $4,200 in athletic debts. He removed athletic bookkeeping from John J. Tigert and S.A. "Daddy" Boles, and placed it in the school's business office. McVey began discussions with the NCAA long before the school became an individual member, and agreed that control of athletics must be kept in the hands of faculty and trustees.[62]

The dynamic duo of Tigert and his old buddy, P.T. Atkins, gave McVey the wisdom of their advice in a complete, but unsolicited, plan for running the athletics program. Tigert lost his power base under McVey, but remained an athletics committee member. Atkins left the newspaper, opened his own brokerage firm in Louisville but kept his close Lexington ties. Atkins and Tigert moved first on the new president hoping to get there before Richard C. Stoll and his cronies.[63]

The plan was indeed grand and included setting up pre-season schedules; hosting a state-wide banquet for all high school football players; dropping Big Ten schools such as Indiana, Ohio State and Illinois and replacing them with Virginia, Washington and Lee and VMI because of the strong southern link between Kentucky and Virginia; building a new gymnasium and a stadium to include a dormitory for athletes, and restructuring the athletics committee to include only former lettermen and businessmen who would create jobs for needy players. Atkins's entire plan was, of course, built around Tigert returning as coach and athletics director.[64] There probably wasn't a school in the country that could have afforded the Tigert-Atkins plan for athletics.

McVey sought to stall Atkins by appointing a committee to study a reorganization of athletics under an athletic council. The committee was made up of Atkins, Boles and Enoc Grehan, head of the journalism department. That was his first mistake. Atkins and Boles drafted "A Proper System of Administration for Athletics" that was so outrageous Grehan refused to sign it and asked McVey to remove him from the committee.[65]

Once more the plan centered around Tigert, as football coach. His past associations with the school were described as "His splendid service on the field as a coach, his directing force in athletic administration and his experience in handling Kentucky boys." Of course, Atkins' plan was light on faculty, with only McVey and Grehan on the council. Suggested for alumni membership on the council were former football players George B. Carey, "Red Doc" and "Black Doc" Rodes, and White Guyn, who played for five year during Patterson's era and coached the team for three years.

The others were from the business and social community: Hogan Yancy, later mayor of Lexington; Louis Lee Haggin, a horseman whose father was a western mining magnate; businessman Frank Battile; Louis Hillenmeyer, whose brother Walter played football; Thomas B. Cromwell and Dr. J.A. Goodson. If those names weren't satisfactory, Atkins had others. McVey would appoint council members, but they would select their own chairman. Atkins pushed the president to act quickly so definite plans could be announced at the earliest possible time.[66]

McVey hadn't just fallen off the turnip truck. He said alumni influence was one of the worst features of college athletics, but no university dared tell them to butt out because their financial support was needed. He trashed much of Atkins' plan, and created an athletic council, heavy with faculty, that he thought he could control with a slim 6-5 margin and veto power.[67]

College athletics in the south were changing. A year earlier, the SIAA, too large to regulate, split into groups that became the Southern Atlantic Conference, later the ACC, and the Conference of Southern State Universities, that became the SEC. Since the Southern was primarily a football conference, Kentucky played basketball in the SIAA until 1924.[68]

By 1920 McVey had a handle on athletic expenses, and the deficit was only $1.15 compared to $4,321 three years earlier. He ignored Atkins' recommendation and hired William Juneau, from Wisconsin and Texas, as football coach. Juneau had the misfortune to be in Lexington when a small liberal arts college thirty-five-miles south was making football history. Centre not only defeated State by such lop-sided scores as 0-55 and 0-49, but Bo McMillin, "Red" Roberts, Hump Tanner and the "Praying Colonels" defeated mighty Harvard 6-0 in 1921.[69]

Tigert left a system firmly in place, and Stoll, Atkins and the good old boys gallantly carried the banner. McVey's ambitious building program, a girls' dorm, classrooms and an addition to the engineering complex, failed to halt their demands for a stadium and a new gymnasium. McVey sometimes appeared overwhelmed by their audacious attempts to dominate the school's athletics. They argued larger facilities would bring in additional, and needed revenue.[70]

Perhaps they caught him in a weak moment because McVey found himself building both the gymnasium and stadium. It was a decision that pushed the school to the brink of insolvency. McVey had faculty who had no problems with going over his head on athletic affairs. Biology professor W. D. Funkhouser and agricultural professor H.E. Curtis, not the president, approached trustees about building the football stadium. Trustees sent McVey the message to decide how to raise money for the stadium and to look at the possibility of using funds earmarked for other projects. In particular, they were referring to the Memorial Building Fund that showed a total of $175,692. The Fund had only $68,000 in cash; the remainder was in pledges from Lexingtonians and alumni.[71]

As the basketball teams' popularity grew, there was a push to build a gymnasium larger than Barker Hall that held only a handful of spectators. Two months later, Funkhouser, Boles, Curtis and Grehan asked trustees to borrow money to build a new gymnasium. Trustees refused to borrow the money, and suggested the gymnasium plans be placed on hold until a decision on the Memorial Building Fund was made.[72]

The president kept his counsel, but failed to halt the ambitious plans of his staff. At the July 20, 1923 board of trustees' meeting, an Alumni Association committee had the answer on the new gymnasium. They would pay for the new building if the school furnished the land. Trustees jumped at the offer for someone else to pay for the gymnasium since funds were so tight the school had to borrow $50,000 for operating money until the fall semester began.[73]

McVey was caught up in the excitement of at last having a new gymnasium. The president, Stoll and trustee H.M. Froman were authorized to sign the contract for the gymnasium.[74]

In October, McVey told trustees the foundation for the gymnasium would cost $20,000, and the total cost for the entire structure would be $65,000. He pressed for a decision about the use of the money in the

Memorial Building Fund because many Lexingtonians were declining to pay their pledges, saying they only promised the money for moral support in the first place. Obviously, they were holding back their pledges for the stadium.[75]

Two weeks later, former football player George B. Carey turned up at the trustees' meeting as chairman of the Greater Kentucky Fund, the Alumni Association's money raising vehicle. Carey knew all about wheeling and dealing. When he tried to force the school to give him an engineering degree, he held a "sweetheart" contract that the school gave to a favored few. His firm, Carey-Reed, had a verbal contract to do campus construction on a fifteen percent commission basis. Here Carey was asking trustees' approval to sign the contract for the gymnasium. The Alumni Association, he promised, would set aside $40,000 from their subscription campaign for the project. Here's how the good old boys did business. Carey pledged the net proceeds from the next basketball season, estimated to be $10,000, to the project. Carey, of course had no official connection with the university, but there he was using their money and credit. That still left the project $15,000 short of the estimated cost. McVey was too far in to back out, and his pledging basketball's net income until the debt was cleared opened the door for Carey.[76]

They really took McVey to the cleaners. Before it was over, he agreed to the Alumni Association raising money for the gymnasium, and the money from the Memorial Building Fund going to pay for the stadium, a statue of the school's first president, James K. Patterson, and student loans. It was all a loose package just waiting to explode.[77]

The gymnasium contract was negotiated between the Alumni Association and the Blanchard-Crocker Company for $86,137, an increase of $21,000 more than McVey expected to spend before the building began. Things went from bad to worse. Blanchard-Crocker agreed to a cash payment of up to $39,800, and the remainder in notes in denominations of $1,000. Half the notes were to be repaid in a year, and the remainder in the second year.[78]

By the end of 1923 the gymnasium cost climbed to $90,674. When Blanchard- Crocker tried to dispose of their notes in 1924, they weren't successful. Trustees were forced into a supplemental agreement with the company to stand good for $30,000 in notes. Liens were filed against the university that were very embarrassing to McVey. Carey's Greater Kentucky Fund paid $39,000 on the structure. Carey handled the money. McVey, unhappy with that arrangement, designated a business agent to oversee the process but Carey ignored him. Such elemental parts of the gymnasium as lighting, heating and plumbing were either not included in the contract or purposely taken out. The school had to ante up another $17,554 to pay for those elements left out of the construction cost. McVey was unable to hold Carey's costs down, and it was three years later before the school finished paying off the notes on the gymnasium.[79]

As Carey wheeled and dealed with the gymnasium project, McVey tried to get a handle on the stadium site selection Funkhouser was determined to have. The biology professor intended to build the stadium on the west end of Stoll Field, name for the trustee, regardless of that site costing an additional $18,000 for sewers and the grading was more expensive. William Townsend, from Stoll's law firm, agreed with Funkhouser on that site because it wouldn't interfere with on-going football practices. McVey objected to the increased cost, but Funkhouser and Townsend had enough votes in the trustees' executive committee to select their site over the one favored by the president, where the team presently played. When the matter came before the full board of trustees, McVey managed to get enough votes to have his site, on the east end, approved.[80]

Funkhouser, for whom the biological science building on campus is named, went into a huff and refused to turn in athletic council reports to McVey. After waiting for a month to get the reports, the mild-mannered McVey threatened to kick Funkhouser out of the athletics loop unless he turned over the reports. They were immediately forthcoming.[81]

There was no fiscal sanity in the construction of the gymnasium and stadium, but McVey was powerless to stop the momentum. Three companies bid on the six-section stadium. Turner Construction's bid was $204,000; Clark, Stewart and Wood's came in at $149,000, including an $1,800 surety bond; Louis des Cognets had the low bid of $148,000, but that included no surety bond. With the surety bond included in des Cognets' bid, Clark, Stewart and Wood were the low bidders.[82]

Louis des Cognets, a crony of Stoll's, had been the Lexington police and fire commissioner, was president of the Lexington gas and ice companies and served on the boards of three banks. His father Hippolyte des Cognets, a royal physician, belonged to one of the oldest families in Brittany, and his mother was the daughter of Kentucky's second governor, James Garrard.[83] He was firmly embedded in the Bluegrass.

The stadium committee, appointed by the trustees, was represented by D.V. Terrell, an engineering professor, and J. White Guyn, a former football coach and a five-year letterman. Terrell and Guyn changed the specifications on the stadium although they had already opened the legal bids. They were doing everything they could, at Stoll's urging, to see that des Cognets got the contract. Their new specs called for three stadium sections on the south side, two on the north side with a sixth to be built later. McVey's papers indicated des Cognets agreed to build the five sections for $100,000, plus an additional $16,500 for the sixth section, carry the school's notes for three years and contribute $1,000 to the project. On the amended specs, Clark, Stewart and Wood bid $98,400 on the five sections, plus $17,240 for the sixth and agreed to carry the school's notes for three years. When Terrell and Guyn again changed the specs to allow des Cognets to post a personal bond, that made his the low bid.[84]

Carey's Greater Kentucky Fund was again the fund raising vehicle for the stadium, and he promised to raise at least $140,000. In June 1924, Carey listed 5,863 pledges representing $221,549. As of that date, Carey had $69,000 in his bank account as treasurer of the Greater Kentucky Fund, but deposited only $1,700 in the school's account. Something happened on the way to the university's bank account since McVey had to borrow $50,000 from the Memorial Building Fund to begin work on the stadium. He expected to replace it with money from Carey's Greater Kentucky Fund.[85]

Carey, on the other hand, borrowed $30,000 from Louis des Cognets. The school's business manager, D.H. Peak, had ledgers showing that he, not Carey, collected $134,000 in pledges, and $105,300 was spent on the stadium. Things were in such a mess, McVey had to borrow on the notes of thirty-five Lexingtonians to pay for the sixth section of the stadium.[86]

How des Cognets was paid for that sixth stadium section, that he agreed to build for $16,500, gave new meaning to the phrase, "creative accounting." Terrell approved the bill for that sixth section in which the estimated cost, $9,837, and the actual cost, $13,900, were added together for a total of $23,838, "less fifteen percent equaling $20,176." It wasn't clear who got the fifteen percent, Terrell or des Cognets.[87]

Neither was there any mention that des Cognets wouldn't carry the school's notes for three years. Stoll demanded the school pay des Cognets, "Provided there is enough in the treasury to do so," two months before the job was completed. Peak suggested McVey talk with Stoll about the payment that "Would probably leave our funds short at the end of the month." Apparently, des Cognets didn't get all his money as the school still owed him $21,500 in November 1925. There was some problem with cast iron seat supports, and the school had to spend another $2,000 to fix them. [88]

The true nature of Louis des Cognets' bid for the stadium was finally revealed in a 1931 entry in McVey's diary. The stadium specs were changed for a third time, and des Cognets got the bid on a cost plus ten percent basis. McVey said he was quite embarrassed about how the school handled the contract but, by that time, he was firmly in the good old boys' pockets. "There must be a more adequate system for handling the business affairs of the athletic council," he told board members. The school's athletic debts were over $154,000, and McVey was concerned about what appeared to be $120,000 in uncollected pledges. If the school had to stand good for those pledges there would be no new construction in the near future.[89]

The stadium was named for football center Price McLean who was fatally injured in the 1923 game with Cincinnati. The field was named for Stoll.

Those good old boys were going to enjoy that stadium, but they also wanted winning teams. Coach Fred Murphy's 1925-26-27 seasons were collectively 15-10-1. After the 1927 season Murphy was gone, and Harry Gamage was elevated from freshman coach to head coach. Gamage endeared himself to the good old boys by beating Centre three times, and dropping them from the schedule. He replaced Centre with the University of Virginia, another point in his favor as the good old boys liked southern schools. Gamage used sideline theatrics such as propping 84-year-old Confederate veteran, Major Duke Redd, on a horse to ride the sidelines waving his saber shouting that the south was rising again. Alabama did just that, beating Kentucky 0-17.[90]

The south didn't rise again, and McVey's athletic fortunes experienced a similar fate.

The 1930s was a difficult decade for McVey. He was firmly in the clutches of the good old boys. Thirteen members of the Southern Conference, west and south of the Appalachian Mountains, left to form the SEC and McVey was elected their first president. He viewed his job as "Much ado about nothing." Kentucky was hard hit during the Depression, and McVey considered cutting staff, programs and departments. Stoll wanted to drop several departments, and that probably included social science professor William Sutherland in whose class Stoll's son was enrolled. The trustee charged Sutherland was emphasizing communism and socialism in his classes. The professor retaliated by drawing his money out of the bank where Stoll was an officer, and urged others to do the same. Stoll refused to allow his son to take any of Sutherland's classes. History professor Thomas D. Clark said it wouldn't have made any difference whose classes Stoll's son attended the results would have been the same.[91]

Journalism professor Enoc Grehan saw the SEC as an opportunity for colleges to make a fresh start athletically, and to eliminate the good old boys and their infernal meddling. Grehan, after being burned by Atkins and Boles earlier, thought the schools in the SEC were more evenly matched with similar educational ideals, and that would make them more compatible.[92] He was wrong on both counts.

McVey managed to snatch $2,000 from the Southern Conference to begin the SEC. He emphasized that scholarship and grants of aid must by handled by schools' faculties. McVey and Grehan hoped the new conference regulations would eliminate some of Tigerts' "irregularities" both at Kentucky and in the conference.[93]

Like death and taxes, those "irregularities" remained long after Tigert was gone. An example was the eligibility of football player Ralph Kercheval. Athletics director S.A. Boles wrote McVey that, after his junior year, Kercheval's academic record was a disaster. Boles said certain instructors were asked to allow the athlete to make up delinquent work. "It was later shown," Boles said, "that his delinquency was so great that all the efforts were dropped." Kercheval played his senior year, and his records of most punts in a season, 101, and most career punting yards, 9,749, still stands.[94]

The man who told the New York World that academic standards for athletes at his school were rigidly enforced, stood by helplessly as a talented but academic deficient player helped fill the stadium so the school's athletic debts could be paid.[95]

Although players like Kercheval and John "Shipwreck" Kelley, who was kept on a weekly retainer by the good old boys, were filling the stadium, McVey still had problems with athletic expenses exceeding receipts. Neither the athletic council nor Boles were helping him get a handle on finances. Boles was shuffled to the ticket manager's post in 1930, and McVey selected assistant football coach Bernie A. Shively as athletics director. Shively came to Kentucky in 1927 as part of the staff of Gamage with whom he played football at Illinois. An All-American guard in 1926, Shively opened holes in the defensive line for another All-American, Harold "Red" Grange. It was the beginning of a forty-year career for Shively who became a powerful figure in national college athletics.[96]

McVey, tired of all the creative accounting, told Shively to bring in a firm of outside auditors to prepare annual reports on athletic finances. McVey knew he had to control the fiscal side of athletics even if he was unable to keep academic ineligible and subsidized players off the teams.[97]

Another event occurred in 1930 that changed the complexion of Kentucky athletics. Trustees hired a brash young man from Kansas as the basketball coach. Adolph F. Rupp forever changed their beloved football school into a basketball institution whose teams would come to be known as "America's Team."

The Rupp saga encompassed the athletic administration of the remainder of McVey's presidency, and that of his three successors, Herman L. Donovan, Frank G. Dickey and John W. Oswald. That portion of the Kentucky athletic story is best told through Adolph Rupp because he was the central figure.

# THE COMBATIVE KANSAN

The nation's most successful college basketball coach backed into his profession. Adolph Rupp, a Midwesterner with a wicked sense of humor, a sarcastic tongue and a razor-sharp mind, had his eye set on a career in the banking industry. Armed with a Kansas University degree in economics and a strong belief that a man's limits were set by himself, Rupp looked beyond the family farm.

The fourth of six children, a sister and four brothers, Rupp was born in Halstead, Kansas, in 1901 to a German father and Austrian mother, first generation Kansas homesteaders, who instilled an intense work ethic in their children. He did janitorial chores during elementary school and worked in a grocery store while in high school. Elizabeth Rupp Lawson said her brother inherited his famed self-reliance from their parents.[98]

Rupp's mother encouraged his interest in the new sport by stuffing a sack with rags to make him a basketball. "Basketball was just beginning back then," Rupp said, "I threw it in the hoop (probably made from the top of a peach basket) all day long; it's fun, you throw the ball and it goes in." Rupp's high school team, one of the first in their area to have a real basketball, played their home games in the Halstead city hall, whose ceiling was only three feet above the basket. Their away games were played in general stores, garages and churches. "Adolph pretty much ran the team," his friend, Glenn Lehmann, recalled, "he was a natural leader that way."[99]

After graduation Rupp went to KU to play basketball for Forrest "Phog" Allen. He was a guard, scoring about two points a game, on

Kansas' championship teams of 1922 and 1923. One of his professor's was Dr. James Naismith, chairman of the physical education department and creator of the game of basketball.[100]

Armed with a degree in economics, Rupp left the family farm behind and set out to conquer the business world. He recalled the reception he received, "I went to the largest bank in Topeka, and one of the officers told me that only way you're going to get anywhere in the banking business is to marry into the family. I told him I wasn't sure I wanted to get into it that much."[101]

"Phog" Allen was an astute judge of his players, and recognized Rupp had potential for a coaching career. I found nothing in my research to indicate the two men didn't remain life long friends. Allen recommended Rupp for the coaching vacancy at Burr Oak High School in Kansas in 1924. The next year he moved to Marshalltown, Iowa, where school officials neglected to tell him he was expected to coach wrestling as well as basketball. "Well, I finally caught wise to the fact the boys were looking to me as the grapple professor," Rupp said, "the idea made me a little ill because I had never known a grunt about academic wrestling except for some boyhood street corner scrapes."[102]

He bought a book on wrestling, began to coach the sport like he knew something about it and took his team to the state championship. Rupp's rapid rise in wrestling and the championship had more to do with one of his athletes, Allie Morrison, than Rupp's wrestling coaching ability. Morrison became a two-time Olympic wrestling champion, and later coached the sport at Pennsylvania.[103]

In 1926 Rupp moved to Freeport, Illinois, where he met his wife Esther, and began working on a master degree in education from Columbia University. In four years at Freeport, Rupp's teams won seventy-five of their eighty games. He completed his degree while there, and began wearing his famous trademark brown suit. Explaining that a fellow was fortunate to have two suits in those days, Rupp said, "I wanted to look real nice in my second year of coaching, so I went out and bought a blue suit.

We went to that game and were shellacked. So, I said a blue suit isn't the kind to wear to a basketball game. I went back to brown suits and I've been wearing them ever since." He added that he had a closet full of nothing but brown suits.[104]

For many years sports columnists only casually mentioned the Freeport years. In the 1990s they became vitally important to the examination of the Rupp record. With the advent of that ridiculous, but popularly held, concept of political correctness, writers were quick to label Rupp a racist because it was 1967 before he signed his first black player at Kentucky. Few sports writers bother to mention that he coached a black player at Freeport.[105]

Another seldom mentioned point is Rupp's jump from high school to college coaching without serving an interim appointment as an assistant coach. When he came to Lexington in 1930 to interview for the vacancy, he was competing with seventy other coaches, many of them with experience in the college ranks. Rupp wasn't too impressed with Lexington during the Depression, but he saw the foundation of a program that had potential. Rupp persuaded athletic officials to hire him.[106]

Rupp's rise at Kentucky was meteoric, and for good reason. He hadn't taken over a program in the doldrums. John Mauer left a three year record of 50-14, two narrow losses in Southern Athletic Conference Tournaments, one current All-American and two players who were All-Americans two years later. Building on that, Rupp took a fledgling sport, learned from the creator, and stamped the game with such an impact that his winning percentage, .822, remains untouched seventy years later. Seldom has a college coach's influence extended beyond his conference to leave such an indelible mark on the national game.[107]

Rupp's official forty-one year (one year was lost to sudden death in 1952-53) won-loss record of 876-190 laid the foundation for four successors to push Kentucky's winning percentage to .764, the nation's best in 1999. His only competitor was UCLA's John Wooden. Wooden had ten NCAA championships to four for Rupp; 610 wins to 876; sixteen PAC

Ten titles to twenty-six SEC championships, and Rupp had an Olympic gold medal.[108]

Rupp's actual number of wins as well as his winning percentages were overlooked in 1996 by the media's fascination with North Carolina's Dean Smith breaking Rupp's number of wins. Smith was portrayed as a liberal coach much more willing to recruit black players. Actually, Smith signed his first black player only a year before Rupp signed his. Smith claimed he had no goal to break Rupp's record of wins. The NCAA said Smith exceeded Rupp's number of wins by three games. That failed to tally with my research. I called Gary Johnson, a NCAA statistician, to ask how they compiled coaches' won-loss stats. Johnson explained the NCAA counted only those games played against four-year American colleges with the exception of Simeon Frazer in Canada. In 1951 Rupp took his team on a six-game tour of Puerto Rico. His team won both games with Puerto Rico University, but the NCAA failed to credit Rupp's record with those wins. Johnson provided no explanation other than saying games played against Puerto Rico University were counted now. "I'm not sure when we began counting Puerto Rico University games," he added. Rupp's winning percentage, just based on NCAA recognized wins, was 82.8 compared to 77.7 for Smith. Rupp's overall won-loss record at Kentucky, including the Olympic Trial Games, the Puerto Rico tour and the 1966 International Universities Tournament in Tel Aviv, Israel, was 891-193.[109]

It's doubtful if any other college coach will ever win 891 games at one school. Rupp's flamboyant personality, competiveness and coaching skills elevated his renown above that of his institution. Something which may not happen again, either.

When Rupp came to Kentucky all attention was focused on football, the school's dominate sport was infused with students' spirits, and liquid spirits to keep them warm in the cold stadium. Football wasn't a winning program, but it provided an important social venue for the good old boys whose days of athletic glory, if they ever had any, was as faded as the autumn leaves. They liked to drink and gamble as they watched the games. If the coach was a hale and hearty fellow who joined them occasionally, that was fine. It was the perfect situation for Rupp, to slide into the vacuum, to exercise his coaching talents, to not only make basketball the school's consummate sport but to leave an impact on the game that remains visible today.

He wanted the job so bad that he agreed to take on the additional jobs of being an assistant coach in football and track for a two-year contract that paid him $5,800.[110]

Rupp used some of Mauer's fast paced offensive plays mixed with his own ideas and what he had learned from Allen and Naismith. The result was "race horse" basketball that was so exciting to watch it became a standard Kentucky coaching style. Not only was Rupp a great innovator, but he was far ahead of his time creating new rules of the game. In 1935 he advocated a double pivot that he said promised manslaughter under the basket. He proposed a thirty or forty-five second play clock in 1949. "That's plenty of time for a club to set up a play," he explained, "if it doesn't take a shot in that time; the ball should be surrendered to the opposition."[111]

His fast paced offensive system, that set the standards by which succeeding coaches would be measured, came from highly structured practices. Those practices were as precise as the starched khaki shirts and pants Rupp wore to the gym. They started at 3:30 and usually ended at 5:30 in the afternoon. There was thirty minutes of spot shooting before drills began, and fifteen minutes of shooting foul shots after they ended. "If the boys see there is a reason for them to repeat hundreds of times the fundamental details that are necessary in developing good basketball players, the work will not only be done well, but will be done with enthusiasm," he said.[112]

In 1998 All-American Ralph Beard, one the "The Fabulous Five," recalled those arduous practices as if they were yesterday. "Those scrimmages were twice as hard as games," Beard said, "I'm not exaggerating; those were blood lettings. And there would be coach Rupp, wringing his hands in glee. That's what made us so good, that competition in practice." [113]

Beard's team mate from "The Fabulous Five" and another All-American, Alex Groza, described Rupp's practices,"From the time you walked into that gym until you left, you were there to play basketball." Cotton Nash, another All-American who was drafted by the Los Angeles Lakers, agreed. "We knew what we had to do, and we did it; it was very efficient and wasted no motion. He gave his players a lot of freedom, and I think he was successful because of that wide open style."[114]

Rupp's coaching tactics were ageless. The great NBA All-Pro Clyde Drexler, before he left the Houston Rockets in 1998 to coach the University of Houston, talked about the need for such practices. "The key (to succeed) is to practice over and over again and staying ball ready."[115]

The practices were Rupp's stage, and he didn't share the spotlight unless it was to use his assistant coach, Harry Lancaster, as his straight man. "Simultaneously, he will stab with the stiletto comments of a caustic humorist while his mobile face and Kansas twang carry the tortured anguish of a Macbeth," was one sports writer's description of Rupp's demeanor at practices.[116]

Periodically, he delivered a soliloquy that sorority girls were more astute about the finer points of the game than his addled brain players. He was a master at playing mind games with his players. Watching a 5'9" guard warming up, Rupp turned to Lancaster and said, "That guy's too little to be playing basketball. It's a shame, Harry, that we have to waste a first class ticket on him." Lancaster suggested a half-fare ticket. All this was said, of course, within the player's hearing. In disgust over another players's ineptitude, Rupp barked, "Why don't you go over in that corner and take a crap so you can say you did something while you were here?" During a sloppy practice, Rupp bellowed the players were driving him to the town's insane asylum. When a guard lost the ball on a fast break, a red-faced Rupp blew his whistle and shouted, "You guards throw the ball away like Roosevelt did money." Bill Spivey, another of

Rupp's All-Americans, assumed somebody wrote the coach's practice remarks but later learned, the hard way, they were delivered ad lib.[117]

In order to garner publicity for his program, as opposed to football, Rupp utilized all his public relations skills. The glove couldn't have fit more perfectly, because the man had a mind like a steel trap. Sports writers sought him out because he was so quotable, and he made himself available to them. When a local reporter asked him about a supposed feud with John Mauer, then coaching at arch rival Tennessee, Rupp replied that civilians were being evacuated within a fourteen mile area of Lexington. In 1951 a New York writer asked Rupp how the game could be improved. With a straight face, he replied, "I'd put the center jump back in; take off the backboard, just leave the hoop, and raise it five feet." Astounded, the columnist asked if he was serious? "Hell no!" Rupp replied, "but it's something for your column."[118]

Rupp's total dedication to his sport brought him into conflict with football coaches whose programs were usually less successful. Rupp fought as furiously for administrative support for his program as he did on the court. Rupp and football coach Harry Gamage engaged in a shouting match in president McVey's office in 1933 over which program deserved the most money. Gamage's three-year record of 14-12-7 was hardly a match for Rupp's 50-8, and a Helms National Championship in the same period. Gamage was a smart man. He left for South Dakota where he became the school's winningest coach with an 82-67-7 record.[119]

When "the elite "boosters realized Rupp intended to make good his promise to turn Kentucky into a basketball powerhouse they could brag about, he was accepted. Attorney, power broker and trustee Richard D. Stoll's brother John published the Lexington newspaper where Rupp always received favorable coverage. Others included George R. Carey, a former football player turned contractor who had attempted to force the school to give him a degree without his completing graduation requirements. Carey's family made up four generations of power brokers. Horseman Louis Lee Haggin, II, whose father, a native Kentuckian, was a western mining magnate, spent most of his time clipping bond coupons. More actively involved were three attorneys in Stoll's office: William Townsend, who fancied himself a southern historian and represented the alumni association; Guy Huguelet, who later helped found the UKAA; Wallace Muir, who was accused of personally dipping into athletic funds, and resigned from the athletic counsel. A.B. "Happy" Chandler, of Versailles, was the ultimate power broker. A two-term Kentucky governor, US Senator, major league baseball commissioner and law school graduate, Chandler was deeply involved in the school's athletics for over half a century. His crony, Marcus Redwine, from Winchester, and Paris horseman Arthur "Bull" Hancock lived outside Lexington, but were very much a part of the inner circle that called the shots in athletics.[120]

Rupp maintained this group pressured McVey in 1934 to hire a big time football coach and they brought in C.A. "Chet" Wynne, who played at Notre Dame for Knute Rockne. They were so impressed with Wynne's "Fighting Irish" resume, he was made athletics director as well as football coach. He certainly had an impressive background as a player being part of the famous backfield of George Gipp, Frank Thomas and Johnny Marhardt. He was a former Nebraska attorney and legislator. He'd had championship teams at Creighton and Missouri College and took Auburn to an undefeated conference season in 1932. Nobody bothered to inquire why a coach with a resume like that would take a job that had Gamage cutting out paper dolls after seven years. Wynne, a handsome and dapper man, sported a big ego, and had an even bigger drinking problem.[121]

Wynne exercised little or no control or supervision over his players, and that drove McVey to distraction. In fact, he was so nonchalant the team could have gotten away with anything, and probably did. There was a story that an enterprising woman, who along with her lovely daughter and a stash of whiskey, visited the team before home games. The daughter's part was obvious, and the mother placed her bets the next day on the opposing team. Wynne charmed his way out of problems, and managed to stay for four years with a 20-19 record.[122]

As athletics director, Wynne was Rupp's superior, and the sparks flew between the two men. Wynne, during one of their confrontations, told Rupp the campus was too small for both of them. "Well," Rupp replied, "in that case when you go home tonight you ought to tell your wife to start packing because I don't plan to leave."[123]

Rupp didn't leave, instead he lasted forty-two years at Kentucky. During that time, seven football coaches arrived promising winning programs but, with one exception, left without fulfilling their commitments. Paul "Bear" Bryant who president Herman L. Donovan, successor to McVey in 1940, lured away from Maryland in 1946. Bryant, a native of Kingman, Arkansas, got his nickname, "Bear," from stories that he wrestled one. He played football at Alabama, and served in the US Navy before going to Maryland in his first head coaching job.

Since they contributed most of the $105,000 Donovan and Guy Huguelet raised to form the UKAA, the power brokers were in charge and the president, whose appointment resulted from politics, never contested their supremacy. The UKAA removed athletics from faculty control, and placed the school's president in total charge. It was clear that Donovan's athletic attitude was everything McVey's wasn't. Richard C. Stoll was fading from the scene, but his partner, William Townsend, took his place. George Carey's son, Burgess, carried his family's torch to such an extent that he berated a basketball player for missing a winning shot in a Sugar Bowl game in New Orleans. It seemed Burgess Carey had wagered $500 on the game. Liquor distributor Owen Campbell created a $50 a month job, much like the one John "Shipwreck" Kelley had earlier at Southeastern Greyhound, for basketball star, Alex Groza. Druggist Owen Williams always had cash to meet players' needs. Arthur "Bull" Hancock was there along with flamboyant liberal attorney John Y. Brown, Sr., several times a candidate for the Democratic nomination for governor. Brown's son finally succeeded in reaching his father's dream. Stoll's former partner, Guy Huguelet, was the glue that held them all together.

"Whatever I wanted, I could go to Mr. Huguelet," Bryant wrote, "if I'd asked for money he would have given me a sack full." Sacks full of money were there. I'm sure Bryant got his share. Donovan allotted 3,000 McLean Stadium seats to the STAC (Cats spelled backwards) Club run by Frank Sadler, a student manager Bryant brought with him from Maryland. STAC members paid a $15 annual fee, $2.50 each for their season tickets plus any donation they chose to make to the program. Members received game films, newsletters and socialized big time with players and coaches. Sadler, who later became a prominent Lexington real estate developer with firms that bear his name, turned the money over to Tom DeZonia, vice-president of Huguelet's Southeastern Greyhound Bus Lines, who distributed the funds.[124]

If all the STAC memberships were sold, not counting donations (and there were plenty), Sadler returned approximately $94,000 a year to DeZonia. If that arrangement continued during all of Bryant's eight seasons, and there's no reason to assume it didn't, an estimated $750,000 swelled some bank accounts in the late 1940s. There were no records on the distribution of the money.

Bryant admitted he was jealous of Rupp, but respected him as a worthy rival. He recalled how Rupp greeted a faculty committee investigating athletics. "By gad, come on in here," Rupp said, "I've been waiting for you bastards. I want to know what happened to my basketball player over there in your English class. By gad, you expect me to take these pine knots and make All-Americans out of them; I send you a 'B' student and he's making a Goddam 'D!'" Bryant apparently enjoyed the situation, "Rupp just ate their fannies (out), and they haven't opened their mouths. They're in there to investigate athletics and he's attacking academics. They got out of there in a hurry."[125]

Rupp acknowledged Bryant's coaching talents, but he was on a quest for a national championship. In 1946, with some of his best players returning from World War II, Rupp won the then prestigious National Invitational Tournament in Madison Square Garden, and also another

SEC title. His 1947-48 team, "The Fabulous Five," took him to his greatest heights professionally and worst depths. "The Fabulous Five," with Ralph Beard, Kenny Rollins, Cliff Barker, Wallace "Wah Wah" Jones and Alex Groza, were just that, fabulous. They worked so well together as interlocking parts that two All-Americans, Jim Jordan and Jack Parkinson, were left on the bench. They were the first Kentucky basketball team to bear a distinctive name.[126]

Beard, a native Kentuckian from Louisville, was recruited to play football. When he was injured, athletics director Bernie Shively switched his scholarship to basketball. Beard was the heart of the team. A prototype of later famous NBA guards such as Ervin "Magic" Johnson, Isiah Thomas and John Stockton, Beard could score from anywhere on the court as well as set up plays for his team mates. Rupp, always stingy with praise for his players, described the three-time All-American as being as near to the perfect basketball player as there had ever been.[127]

The other guard was Cliff Barker, who had been a gunner on a B-17 bomber that was shot down over Germany. He'd spent sixteen months in a prisoner-of-war camp, where he played volleyball whenever possible. A native of Yorktown, Indiana, Barker was a wizard with the basketball. He would put "English" on his bounce passes to Groza so they went to the center from different angles confusing defenders. One of the first guards to do a look-away pass, Barker was praised by Beard, "He could handle that dude (basketball) like a yo-yo."[128]

A star at Martin's Ferry (Ohio) High School, Groza was on campus only three months before he was drafted into the US Army. For two years he worked on his game at Fort Hood, Texas. He was voted the best armed forces player in the nation. Groza was Kentucky's leading scorer for three years averaging 20.5 points a game. Another three-time All-American, Groza was the most valuable player in the 1948 and 1949 NCAA tournaments.[129]

Captain of the team, a US Navy veteran and floor leader Kenny Rollins, initially doubted his ability to play with the rest of the team.

Those doubts were erased when Rollins held the great Bob Cousey to only one basket when they beat Holy Cross 60-52 in the 1948 NCAA semi-finals.[130]

Wallace Jones' nickname of "Wah Wah" came from his younger sister's inability to pronounce his first name. As a high school player in Harlan, Jones set a national basketball scoring record, starred in football and he was offered baseball contracts by the Chicago Cubs and Boston Braves upon graduation. An immensely talented athlete and three-letterman, Jones earned All-American honors in basketball and football, and he also played baseball.[131]

"The Fabulous Five" lost only two season games in 1948, to Temple by one point, and Notre Dame by nine. They beat Georgia Tech 54-43 for the SEC championship. After disposing of Columbia and Holy Cross, they clobbered Baylor 58-42 to win the school's first national championship. The team breezed by Louisville and Baylor in the Olympic Trials before losing to six-time AAU champions, the Phillips Oilers, 49-53. Rupp's starting five and the Phillips Oilers, a subsidized semi-pro team, made up America's entry in the 1948 Olympics, and he was named an assistant coach. Beard recalled him saying to the team, "I want to thank you turds for making me an assistant coach for the first time in my life."[132]

At the Olympics, in Wimbledon, England, the American team dispatched eight opponents by an average of 33.5 points. Their only close shave was the 59-57 win over Argentina. Rupp, despite being an assistant coach, was filled with pride as he stood on the platform with his players to receive their gold medals.[133]

With the graduation of Rollins and the addition of Dale Barnstable, Rupp's 1948-49 team had an equally impressive 32-2 record. They lost only one regular season game to St. Louis in the Sugar Bowl, and swept through the SEC undefeated. Attempting a grand slam in post season play, Rupp took his team to the NIT in New York. He didn't understand how Kentucky, seeded first in the tournament, managed to lose the final game to Loyola of Chicago, seeded sixteenth. They handled Villanova and Illinois with little trouble, and met Oklahoma A & M in the final game of the NCAA tournament. Coach Hank Iba's deliberative style of offense served the Aggies well until they met Kentucky. A & M was no match for Groza's twenty-five points, and a smothering defense that held the Aggies to only nine field goals. The 46-36 win gave Rupp his second NCAA championship.[134]

One of Rupp's favorite lecture stories came from that game. He prefaced it by saying the source was an airline pilot, who said, "I flew into Kentucky at Paducah and crossed the entire state to the Big Sandy (River), and about 1:00 in the morning I realized that almost every house in Kentucky had their lights on. I couldn't imagine what was going on to keep rural Kentucky up until 1:00 a.m. Finally, I turned on my radio, and there was a play-by-play account of a basketball game being played between Kentucky and the Oklahoma Aggies in Seattle."[135]

The story, true or not, accurately illustrated Rupp's achievement of making Kentucky basketball the commonwealth's unofficial religion. Rupp managed, in telling the tale, to insert the word, Kentucky, into the story four times. He probably repeated the yarn hundreds of times. It illustrated how he kept Kentucky, as well as himself, in the forefront of college basketball.

Jones, Groza, Beard and Barker left in 1949 to form the Indianapolis Olympians in the National Basketball League, now the NBA. Joe Holland, an All-SEC forward who warmed the bench his last two years, was the fifth Kentucky member of the team. Great as that loss was, Rupp bounced back the next season with a team made up of Jim Line, Walter Hirsch, Bobby Watson, Dale Barnstable and his first seven-footer, sophomore Bill Spivey, who led the team in scoring with 19.3 points. After losing four season games, the team slaughtered Tennessee 95-58 for the SEC tournament championship. As both the conference and defending national champion, Rupp waited for an invitation to the NCAA tournament that never came. He maintained the team could have won it all that year, and he was probably right. "We tried our best to get an invitation to that thing, and should have been invited," he said, "when you have won two consecutive NCAA championships and are not invited back to defend those championships then something is wrong with the committee." Two championships in as many years was probably the reason for no invitation. The next year the NCAA selection committee expanded the tournament field from eight to sixteen teams.[136]

In a huff at not being invited to the NCAA tournament, Rupp took his team back to the NIT in Madison Square Garden. It was a big mistake. City College of New York annihilated them 50-89.[137]

While not matching Rupp's NCAA championships, Bryant had built a thriving football program that took the school to their only major bowl games. In 1949, his team lost to Santa Clara in the Orange Bowl, but won the school's first SEC championship with a 9-3 season. More than 13,000 of the faithful followed the team to New Orleans for the 1950 Sugar Bowl, and reveled in the 13-7 win over Bud Wilkinson's Oklahoma team ending the Sooners' thirty-one game winning streak. Special trains took 10,000 Kentucky fans to Dallas for the 1951 Cotton Bowl where they beat Texas Christian 20-7. At a pre-game luncheon Donovan bragged about the athletic prowess of his institution.[138]

Donovan's bragging notwithstanding, Kentucky was in the middle of a national point shaving scandal involving six basketball players and a former football player. New York assistant district attorney, Vincent O'Connor, came to Frankfort in late summer of 1951 to meet with Gov. Lawrence Wetherby in his position as chairman of the university board of trustees. "He gave me the facts and figures about it (the point shaving scandal) and he said, 'your university boys are guilty of point shaving the same as this other crowd (players from eastern colleges), and I wanted you to know about it first,'" Wetherby recalled. The governor immediately informed Donovan of the bad news, and the president initially refused to believe him. After accepting the facts, Donovan did his best to "stonewall" the investigation in Kentucky.[139]

O'Connor's charges were based on Section 382 of the New York State Penal Code that made it a crime to offer bribes to athletes, or for players to accept them. The law, first passed in 1921 in reaction to the Black Sox baseball scandal, applied only to professional athletes. After an attempt to bribe five Brooklyn College basketball players was exposed in 1945, the law was amended to include amateur athletes.[140]

Donovan wanted his own sports bribery law. He instructed athletics director Bernie Shively to call state senator R.P. Moloney, and have the Lexington attorney rush a sports bribery bill through the state legislature. Moloney pushed Senate Bill 1 through the upper chamber, and the House, that made it a crime to attempt to bribe an amateur or professional athlete in the commonwealth. What impact a Kentucky sports bribery law had to do with offenses committed in New York was never clear. Donovan might have been scared that the large local gambling community might try to reach more of his players. In 1951, Lexington was wide open with a large, illegal handbook operations as well as small-time bookies with telephones in their office desk drawers. To give him the benefit of the doubt, Donovan may have just wanted something positive to say about his athletics program in the face of all the negative publicity.[141]

At the same time Donovan laid the blame for the scandal at everybody else's feet except his own. He ignored charges that the school was over emphasizing athletics, and made no moves before consulting his inner circle, especially Guy Huguelet. They all advised him to fight the charges. Thomas D. Clark, the history professor who was one of the original incorporators of the UKAA, said he walked by the president's home, Maxwell Place, that autumn and heard Donovan and his clique "Screaming in an emotional session over the point shaving charges. They wanted Donovan to fight them, which was the worst advice they could have given him."[142]

The Kentucky players became entangled in the point shaving scandals when Bradley players, arrested by New York authorities on similar charges, implicated them. Groza and Beard were arrested in Chicago at an exhibition game between the Rochester Royals and the College All-Stars coached by Rupp. Barnstable, coaching at Dupont Manuel in Louisville, was arrested at his home. Cliff Barker and Joe Holland, also with the Olympians, were questioned by authorities but released. The arrests were the lead story in the October 21, 1951 New York Times. The banner headline read, "3 Basketball Aces on Kentucky Team admit to '49 fix here, (district attorney Frank) Hogan Links Beard, Groza and Barnstable to $1,500 Bribes in the Garden."[143]

Rupp was devastated. A month earlier he bragged gamblers couldn't touch his players with a ten-foot pole. Donovan, deeply wounded by the scandal, attempted to portray the players as inexperienced victims of unscrupulous gamblers, and crowed about his Kentucky sports bribery law. Due to the attention and resources the school poured into their program, Kentucky received scathing negative national publicity.[144]

Hogan's investigation revealed that Nicholas "The Greek" Englisis, a former Kentucky football player, was the fixer for the Madison Square Garden games involving Groza, Beard and Barnstable. Despite ranking 219 in his Samuel J. Tilden (Brooklyn) High School class of 230 and being given a provisional diploma, Englisis was recruited by athletics director and football coach Bernie Shively, and given a scholarship. In Shively's defense, football players were scarce during the war years, and he was probably doing the best he could under the circumstances. While in Lexington, Englisis became familiar with the large handbook (betting and odds making) operation Edward Curd ran. Englisis played football for two years before heading back to New York.[145]

When Groza and Beard were confronted by Englisis in the New York district attorney's office, they confessed to fixing the Loyola of Chicago game, the NIT loss that Rupp found so puzzling. After Groza and Beard graduated and left the team, Barnstable became the conduit for gamblers during the 1949-50 season, and recruited Hirsch, Line and Spivey to continue the point shaving arrangement. O'Connor said he never forgot the emotional moment in Chicago when Groza, after he and Beard were arrested, spoke to Barnstable, "Barney, Ralph and I have told the men the truth, and I think you should do the same; you'll feel all the better for it." In return for their cooperation, the three Kentucky players were charged with a misdemeanor instead of a felony.[146]

Even after the players admitted to the point shaving charges, Donovan and his cronies attempted to lay all the blame on the gamblers. If they admitted culpability, then questions about "over emphasis of athletics" arose. Everybody had a cover story, but none were as creative as Harry Lancaster's. According to the assistant coach, he and Rupp met the morning after the story broke involving the Kentucky players, and initially agreed the charges weren't true. Then, Lancaster recalled, they talked about the Loyola of Chicago game and some of the one point losses in the Sugar Bowl, and began to see a pattern. Lancaster remembered players on the bench shouting to Groza to get open for passes in the Loyola game. Groza, the team's top scorer, was 0-3 in the first half of the game, and backed away from the hook shot of Loyola center Jack Kerris.[147]

Lancaster, I suspect had an agenda, since he was deeply involved in the illegal subsidization of Kentucky athletes, and he knew where a lot of bodies were buried. His time line was fatally flawed. O'Connor visited Wetherby in the summer of 1951, and his investigation had advanced far enough for him to tell the governor of the Kentucky players' involvement. Donovan was told immediately, and certainly informed his cronies. He and Huguelet had many meetings in the president's office on the matter. It was impossible that Donovan hid those facts from Rupp and Lancaster. Donovan, where athletics were concerned, was the "Mouth of the South" long before anyone ever head of Jerry Clower, the late country comedian from Mississippi who identified himself with that title.[148]

While Donovan and some state officials attempted to stonewall New York officials' investigation of Kentucky athletics, O'Connor strongly suspected Spivey was involved in the point shaving despite the player's repeated denials. Finally, Donovan had to ask O'Connor for assistance. In December 1951, Donovan, Dean A.D. Kirwan and Spivey's attorney,

John Y. Brown, Sr., convinced the player to voluntarily surrender his athletic eligibility until his name was cleared. There's always been some doubt about just how voluntary their request was. Spivey, at the time, was unsophisticated in academic politics, and he was forced to trust men who certainly put the institution's interests above his. As the basketball season and the investigation progressed, there was no effort made to reinstate his eligibility. Spivey complained he was being victimized. Sports writers took up his cause. Caught in the embarrassing position of being unable to publicly explain why Spivey's eligibility hadn't been restored when he hadn't been charged with any crime, Donovan swallowed his pride and asked O'Connor for help.[149]

The prosecutor arranged for Kirwan to read secret New York grand jury testimony of Walter Hirsch that implicated both Spivey and Jim Line. Donovan, as part of the bargain, was suppose to keep quiet about the arrangement. Kirwan was prohibited from making any notes or copies while reading the grand jury testimony. He rushed back to his hotel and made copious notes about Hirsch's testimony. His notes revealed that Barnstable went to Hirsch in late 1949, and outlined the point shaving scheme as a way for both of them to make money; that Line and Hirsch each received $700 for going under the point spread in the 1949 DePaul game that Kentucky won 49-47; that Line and Hirsch each received $1,000 for again going under the point spread in the January 1950 game with Arkansas. Fixing that game, Kirwan's notes revealed, was difficult since the Razorbacks were such a poor team, and Kentucky looked foolish winning 57-53. Gamblers Eli Kaye or Jack West, Hirsch failed to remember which, wanted them to go under the spread in the game with St. Johns, but Spivey refused, the notes indicated, because he and the Redmen's center, Bob Zawoluk, were rivals for national scorers and All-American honors. Kentucky won the game 43-37.[150]

Hirsch and Line agreed, according to Kirwan's notes, to get Spivey to help fix the 1950 Sugar Bowl game with St. Louis for $5,000 each. That plan failed when St. Louis won 43-42. The dean's information showed the three settled for $800 each to fix the consolation game with Syracuse that Kentucky won 69-59.[151]

Donovan ignored his agreement with O'Connor to keep the source of Kirwan's information confidential. When faced with criticism of his athletics program in general and handling of the Spivey situation in particular, the president had no problem in identifying the source he used to invalidate the player's eligibility. Spivey's eligibility was never restored, but he vowed to make Donovan hand him his diploma. That was some picture with the seven-foot Spivey hovering over the rotund, short president at graduation ceremonies in Memorial Coliseum. Spivey, after repeated refusals, finally testified before a New York grand jury, and denied accepting money to fix games. He was indicted for perjury, and the case resulted in a hung jury. The case was never retried. The biggest mystery of the Spivey case was his attorney's apparent refusal to respond to O'Connor's offer of immunity for the player in exchange for his testimony.[152]

Was Spivey's attorney, John Y. Brown, Sr., afraid the player's testimony would further damage the athletics program and draw more of Lexington's rich and powerful into the sinister web they had woven around Kentucky sports? Was Spivey even told of the offer of immunity? There were no answers then and now as both Spivey and Brown, Sr., are dead.

Five years after Spivey died, his college roommate, athletic director C.M. Newton, directed that the athlete's jersey be retired in a Rupp Arena ceremony. Newton spoke of the potential Spivey had to play in the NBA.[153] Not only was Spivey banned for life by the NBA, but Groza, Beard, Barnstable and the other Indianapolis Olympians were forced, at a terrific financial loss, to sell their interests in the team. The Olympians were also excluded from any association with professional basketball.

Donovan probably wished for an island exile in April 1952 when New York court of general sessions judge Saul Streit unleashed a brutal tirade against the university's over emphasis of athletics and subsidization of players at Groza, Beard and Barnstable's sentencing. For their cooperation, the players received the suspended sentences recommended by O'Connor.

Kentucky, the judge said, was guilty of spending more money on their football and basketball teams than many professional teams. He detailed the illegal subsidization of players, much of it with Rupp and Lancaster's knowledge. Streit had the figures to back up his statements, but he missed Shively's secret petty cash fund that had as much as $3,500 in it at times. The judge blamed Donovan for allowing the program to run amuck in efforts to please over zealous fans, and condemned athletic officials for associating with a known gambler.[154]

The gambler Streit referred to was Edward Curd, whose illegal handbook operation Englisis frequented. In court documents, Rupp admitted knowing Curd, asking him for betting odds on games, requesting contributions for his favorite charity, the Shriners' Cripple Children's Hospital and speaking to him twice at the Copacabana night club in New York. At the first meeting, Curd came by the tables occupied by Rupp, Shively and the team. The program paid the tab for that outing. The second meeting occurred when Curd had dinner with Rupp, Shively, Donovan and others including commissioner of major league baseball, A.B."Happy" Chandler. When asked if Curd picked up that check, Rupp, who was notorious for avoiding tabs, replied, "I don't know, I didn't pick it up."[155]

Chandler's association with Curd illustrated how casually the Lexington power brokers treated gambling. Curd was an important part of the national setting of point spreads on games. Sen. Estes Kefauver, a Tennessee Democrat who chaired a 1951 Organized Crime Investigating Committee, found Curd was a principal odds-maker in the gambling operation of "mob boss" Frank Costello. Major league baseball frowned upon players and managers associating with gamblers. Chandler, as baseball commissioner, suspended Brooklyn Dodger general manager Leo Droucher for, among other things, associating with known gamblers. Rupp's teams played at Madison Square Garden from 1947 to 1951, which included Chandler's term as commissioner, and the former governor was usually at the games. Sometimes he traveled on the train with the team. Rupp recalled that Curd was on the train with the team for one of those trips. Chandler was forced out of the commissioner's job by baseball owners in 1951.[156]

Chandler was eager to help his good friend, Donovan, who was consumed with bitterness over Streit's remarks about his beloved athletics program. The president sought every avenue of redress against the judge. Chandler embraced Donovan's efforts to mire Streit in scandal and bragged, "If you will give us some more ammunition we will finish the job. We are outraged at the judge's (Streit's) attempts to smear the university, its officials and the coaches." Chandler's attitude spoke volumes about the Kentucky mind-set. When there were problems in athletics, the blame always lay elsewhere. Donovan did his best to supply Chandler with incriminating information. He asked one of Kentucky's United States Senators, Thomas Underwood, to get Federal Bureau of Information files on Streit. When that failed, Donovan pressed University of Maryland president Harry C. Byrd for any derogatory material he had on the judge. Byrd told him to leave the matter alone, but Donovan couldn't. As a last resort, he insisted his law school dean, William L. Matthews, make a case of judicial misconduct against Streit. It was a ridiculous request, but illustrated just how desperate Donovan was. If they couldn't make a legal case against Streit, they'd certainly talked him to death. Clark said he overheard anti-Semitic remarks Donovan and his cronies made about Streit that were too vile to repeat.[157]

Streit's tirade and the resulting publicity caught the attention of the SEC and the NCAA. Donovan and Huguelet knew that serious penalties awaited, and hastily instituted cosmetic reforms that reduced the size of the coaching staffs and traveling squads, required Kentucky to play only in campus arenas or stadiums and limited each sport to scholarships for just five out-of-state players per year. Donovan threw himself prostrate before the SEC executive committee claiming protection for the school's infractions under the Eighth Amendment prohibiting cruel and unusual punishment. He was remarkably unsuccessful.[158]

The committee found Groza, because of his $50 monthly payments from liquor distributor Owen Campbell, was ineligible for his entire career. Beard was ruled ineligible from 1947 to 1949 due to money he received from druggist Owen Williams. "WahWah" Jones, the committee said, was ineligible for the same period of time due to money he received from his home town of Harlan. Jim Line and Dale Barnstable, the committee found, were ineligible for the same time frame for money they received from Williams. Walter Hirsch, Bobby Watson, Frank Ramsey, Shelby Linville and Lucian "Skippy" Whitaker, the committee ruled, were ineligible for part of the 1950-51 season because of the $50 they received from Rupp, Lancaster or Stoner Creek Stud owner Charles Kenny after the Kansas game.[159]

The SEC prohibited Kentucky from playing any conference basketball schedule during the 1952-53 season. Two months later Donovan received twelve pages of NCAA allegations of illegal subsidization of athletes from 1947 through 1951. The NCAA said, with the exception of Jones, Rupp was aware of the payments. Donovan wrote denials in the margin of the allegations, and suggested Rupp be blamed for others. Publicly, Donovan orchestrated the official denials and stubbornly insisted the problems came from the point shaving scandals, not from his cronies' subsidizing practices.[160]

Donovan almost collapsed under the intense publicity. William Townsend, the Stoll partner who was also alumni association president, was the designated attack dog for the president. "We contend that no man or set of men, reeking with athletic halitosis, has any right to point an accusing finger to a speck on Kentucky's vest," Townsend railed in the Lexington newspaper. His denials were without specifics because there were none. "The harsh and unexpected actions of the NCAA doesn't surprise the alumni," Townsend continued, "since the SEC's recent attack of virtue, the alumni have become inured to the hard-faced hypocrisy of 'so-called' athletic conferences and associations."[161]

The NCAA was so overwhelmed by the number of Kentucky violations, they slapped their first "sudden death" penalty on the school, no intercollegiate basketball for the entire 1952-53 season. It was by no means the school's first such penalty. Rupp refused some coaching clinics and speaking engagements until the point shaving scandals and "sudden death" publicity blew over. During the sanction year, he filled Memorial Coliseum with intra-squad games. He also concentrated on his business interests. By 1953, Rupp owned 653-acres of prime Bluegrass farmland with a thirty-five-acre tobacco allotment and a herd of 160 registered Hereford. He was an original investor in an immense tobacco warehousing complex. Crediting his business success to the free enterprise system, Rupp said, "It means that a man has a right to go as far as his ability and industry will take him. This is true in sports as well as business.[162]

The Louisville newspaper, whose sports editor was once a good friend of Donovan's, put distance between their publication and Kentucky athletics. "Those who complain that the university was unfairly treated," the editorial read, "that the penalty was 'unduly severe,' as president Donovan put it, surely must see that something has been grievously wrong for years." The newspaper blamed Donovan for refusing to look at the truth, and found Rupp less liable for the program's failures than the president and his cronies.[163]

If there was any luck in the whole mess, it was Bryant's. Executive director Walter Byers admitted that the NCAA was so staggered by the number of infractions in the basketball program that most of the football violations simply fell through the cracks. Bryant was relieved that his program escaped "sudden death," but let Donovan know of his anger over what the point shaving scandal did to the school, and the president's reneging on a promise to fire Rupp. That didn't mean Bryant's program was clean, but he never let the small details bother him. Chester Lukawaski was ruled ineligible his entire career because of the $500 given him by assistant coach Frank Mosely. Gene Donaldson was ruled ineligible in 1950-51 because of his questionable employment by architect

Hugh Merriwether. The entire 1949 traveling squad was ineligible because of the $100 each they'd received from the power brokers. Bryant's big problem was the cap on out-of-state recruiting. He made a living recruiting players like All-Americans Steve Melinger and Vito "Babe" Parilli from Pennsylvania. Being limited to only five out-of-state players a year put a serious dent in his program.[164]

The coach had another problem that few outside Lexington knew about. There was open gossip about an alleged affair between the football coach and "Happy" Chandler's daughter, Mimi, who was an aspiring movie starlet and radio commentator. Both Chandlers, father and daughter, and Bryant denied the rumors, but those closely associated with the program said otherwise.[165]

Bryant decided to resign, but Donovan refused to release him from his contract. The coach asked his good friend, Gov. Wetherby, to intervene. It took a face-to-face meeting between the three men in the governor's office before Donovan acquiesced. Bryant's eight-year record of 60-23-5, and three major bowl games was one future coaches aimed for but failed to reach.[166]

Bryant later said leaving Kentucky was the dumbest thing he ever did. "If I had it to do over," he said, "I would have gone in there and asked Rupp to do something for me. He'd have liked that, and he'd have done it and been my friend." Although he benefitted from the money Donovan and his cronies spread around, Bryant said he hated the way they handled the point shaving scandal. He held them more accountable for the basketball problems than Rupp. After Bryant's first year at Texas A & M, his only losing season, the two coaches met at a coaching clinic in Utah. Rupp stood up for him. "I want to tell you gentlemen something," Rupp said, "Paul Bryant over there was at Kentucky, and he left us for more money. You think he's down a little now, but I'll tell you, he will win; five, ten years from now he will be the top man. Make no mistake about that, and don't forget Uncle Adolph told you." When Rupp's name was taken off the football team's traveling list, after his retirement in 1972, Bryant offered to send a plane to Lexington to bring Rupp to Birmingham for the Kentucky-Alabama game. "I know we respected each other," Bryant recalled, "I think he was the best there was in basketball."[167]

In August 1953 the NCAA restored Kentucky's membership, and Rupp expected to win another national championship. His team, with All-Americans Frank Ramsey and Cliff Hagan and the returning Lou Tsioropoulos, was 25-0, and nationally ranked number one. There was a small hitch that everyone overlooked. Ramsey, Hagan and Tsioropoulos graduated during the sanction's year, and were playing as graduate students. Athletics director Bernie Shively erroneously assumed since SEC rules allowed graduated athletes to play in post season games the same also applied to the NCAA. At that time, the NCAA not only barred graduate students from post season play, but they had no appeals process for the rule. Donovan and Huguelet launched a highly publicized appeal that Byers buried in the bureaucracy. Rupp refused to take his team, minus those players, to the NCAA tournament.[168]

There's a story that the other players on the team asked Rupp to accept the tournament bid. He bluntly told them it was unlikely that he would take a bunch of turds like them into NCAA tournament play.

After a three-year rebuilding process, Rupp was unsure his 1957-58 team could win him another championship. "I didn't expect to go anywhere with that team," Rupp said. "I think the boys were the only ones that expected to, and they weren't too sure." Vernon Hatton, Johnny Cox, John Crigler, Adam Smith and Ed Beck were starters on the team that Rupp said, "Just fiddled around and fiddled around, and finally with two or three minutes to go; they'd get busy and win a ball game. Just about killed me. I'll tell you that was a bone crushing season for me." Temple, in the season's third game, took "The Fiddling Five" into three overtimes before Hatton launched a desperate last minute shot to win 85-83. They faced Temple again in the NCAA semi-finals in Louisville barely winning 61-60 before going into the finals with Seattle and the great Elgin Baylor.[169]

Rupp was surprised that Baylor came out guarding John Crigler, who failed to score in the Temple game, instead of center Ed Beck. Rupp told Crigler to drive on Baylor and get him in foul trouble. "With Baylor in foul trouble," Rupp recalled, "we made them go into a zone in the second half, and we tore that zone apart." The 84-72 win gave Rupp his fourth national championship.[170]

Rupp won those championships by attracting outstanding players through a network of former players, alumni and coaches he developed over the years. If that failed to work, he took matters into his own hands. In the late 1950s, Rupp had difficulties recruiting the highly sought after Jerry Lucas who led his Middletown (Ohio) High School to two state championships and a seventy-six game winning streak. Lucas, a 4.0 student, wanted to keep college coaches at bay. A knock on the door of Lucas' English class revealed Rupp standing in the hall waiting to talk with him. In a polite manner, Lucas told Rupp he wasn't interested in coming to Kentucky.[171]

Usually Rupp had no problem recruiting players. Some even came to the campus on their own hoping to be accepted. One such player was Forrest Tucker, who later became a popular movie and television actor. "By gad," Rupp greeted him, "you just walked through the pearly gates of basketball." The coach decided Tucker was too short to play basketball for him, gave him a dollar to get something to eat and told him to go home.[172]

At times Rupp had too much help recruiting. Three years after the "sudden death" sanction, Chandler, once again governor, helped the university into another NCAA investigation. At issue was the recruiting of Ned Jennings, the 6'9" star of Nicholas County High School who scored fifty points in one game. The player's signing with Kentucky appeared predicated on his father getting a job in state government. After some behind the scenes maneuvering, Lancaster just happened to be in the office of Harry Davis, Chandler's executive assistant, with Robert Jennings in tow, when state senator Stanley Blake just happened to be there to recommend the player's father for a state job.[173]

Davis blew the whole thing by telling the Associated Press Jennings was given a job so his son could play at Kentucky. He claimed out-of-state schools offered the same deal. "Why should we let our Kentucky boys go elsewhere when we can keep them here honestly and justifiably," Davis asked?[174]

Chandler, as he often did when his skin was on the line, hung Davis out to dry. "To my knowledge," he said, "no one in my administration has ever given a job or other inducements for a student to go to a state college." His meddling caused a real problem for Frank G. Dickey, who had succeeded Donovan as university president two years earlier. In line for the SEC presidency, Dickey and other SEC representatives had earlier found Auburn guilty of overt subsidization of football player Donald Fuell. They levied an unusual penalty on Auburn, the football program was placed on probation with no termination date. After the Jennings affair hit the media, Auburn protested long and loudly. The NCAA came calling about the recruiting violations, but their infractions committee found the school violated no rules in the Jennings case. There were some extenuating circumstances. Kentucky's A.D. Kirwan was a member of the infractions committee, but recused himself from the case. While not sitting in judgement of the Jennings affair, I always felt that Kirwan exerted some influence. Auburn continued their protest, and Dickey and the SEC terminated their probation just in time for their football season to begin.[175]

Chandler's meddling wasn't over. After the point shaving scandal, Rupp decided to pass up the Sugar Bowl tournaments and stage his own University of Kentucky Invitational Tournament during the Christmas holidays. When "The Fiddling Five" came along, Rupp changed his mind and decided to take them to the Sugar Bowl, although there were some rumors the tournament might be canceled. Upon learning that, Chandler decided to stage his own Blue Grass Invitational Holiday Festival

Tournament in Louisville. He told Kentucky and Louisville they would participate and invited St. Louis and Dayton. Chandler's idea had little to do with college athletics. The new Kentucky Fair and Exposition Center's costs far exceeded construction estimates, and it was in deep financial trouble. Chandler planned to use the tournament's profits to reduce the center's deficit. The Sugar Bowl Tournament came off as planned, and Kentucky beat Houston 111-76 in the finals.[176]

After his second gubernatorial term ended in 1959, Chandler continued interfering in athletic affairs for the next thirty years. At times, he became a real embarrassment for the university he claimed to love so much.

The 1960s was a difficult decade for Rupp. He went into a snit when he discovered the football coach's basic salary was higher than his. Eventually he would have to recruit black players, and he worried about the dangers that awaited in the deep south where segregated eating and lodging facilities still existed. Despite declining health, he expected to win another championship.

Blanton Collier, hired to replace Bryant, had a base salary $3,000 higher than Rupp's, who had an unaudited expense account of $3,000 and received five percent of the net earnings from post season games. Rupp's protest over his salary probably had more to do with the honor and respect he wanted from the school he put on the map. In a successful year, Rupp's basketball income could exceed $20,000. That was far more than Collier made. To placate Rupp, Dickey and Shively gave him a new contract, with the same terms, and left blank the number of years for the coach himself to determine. Rupp, who had plenty of money, prolonged the matter for six months by refusing to pick up his salary check.[177]

Dickey was so concerned about Rupp's refusal to pick up his salary check that he called an athletics board meeting to help him decide a course of action. "Well, that just flew all over me," board member Thomas D. Clark recalled, "and I asked Dickey if he would fire me if I refused to pick up my salary check, and he said he would." Clark then made a motion that the board fire Rupp for not picking up his salary checks, and Dickey was stunned. "If I had turned a fox loose in the hen house, I couldn't have created more pandemonium," Clark said. After stewing for a few minutes, Dickey adjourned the meeting without taking any action on Clark's motion. Rupp signed a seven year contract that included a tenured professorship with unspecified annual increments decided by the board.[178]

Unhappy with Collier's 41-36-3 record, Dickey arranged to buy out the remaining three years on his contract for $51,000 in January 1962. [179] Compared to Bryant's .710 winning percentage, Collier's .531 failed to measure up. Firing him, to appease the power brokers who wanted another Bryant, was a mistake. Bryant wasn't available, so Dickey took what seemed like the next best thing, one of his former assistants. Charlie Bradshaw, a former US Marine Corps drill instructor, had two notable accomplishments: his scrimmages sent players to hospitals in droves, and he successfully recruited the first black football player, Nat Northington, in the SEC in 1965.

The football program was hurting for money. The situation was so bad that Shively convinced twenty-seven players to sign documents, that were unclear, refusing their grants-in-aid in order to save money. Some sued and forced the school to reinstate their scholarships. Shively's actions caught the attention of the NCAA, but nothing happened. The school had more pressing problems.[180]

The violent reaction Rupp's basketball team experienced in the deep south was only a portion of what he could expected when he traveled there with black players. The 1961 game with Mississippi State, in Starkville, demonstrated what happened when Kentucky played there with all-white players. The cracker-box gym was never a friendly place since State had won only two of their games there against Kentucky since 1921. Students screamed obscenities at Rupp and his team, and showered the bench with a constant volley of peanuts. Signs in the gym read, "See You In Hell, Rupp" and "Rupp Sucks." Returning to the floor from the half-time break, Rupp found a dead skunk in a burlap bag under his chair.

Kentucky won the game 69-62, and made a hasty exit. Shively protested State's conduct to SEC commissioner Bernie Moore who passed it on to the conference president, Dickey. Rupp fanned the flames among the partisans, and Dickey was once again in a real muddle. Paris horseman Charles Kenny protested State's conduct to Dickey and demanded the school apologize for besmirching Rupp and the entire commonwealth. Dickey finally told Moore to handle the protest since his telephones had been tied up for two days with calls from angry fans. Mississippi State athletics director Wade Walker sent Shively a letter of apology a week later.[181]

Dickey's concerns about integration were economic, and he knew Lexington's racial climate. Blacks on the campus were nothing new as they had been admitted to the undergraduate colleges since 1952, two years before the Supreme Court's decision in *Brown v Board of Education of Topeka* that integrated the nation's public schools. It would be another decade before athletics were integrated.[182]

Dickey wasn't the firmest of decision-maker and, whenever possible, avoided conflicts in athletics board meetings. Integrating athletics was on the agenda for the April 1963 board meeting. Student athletics board member Raleigh Lane, unable to attend the meeting, gave fellow board member, Thomas D. Clark, his proxy vote. When the secret ballots on integrating athletics were counted there was a tie. It appeared that Dickey, as president, would cast the final vote. Clark enjoyed prolonging the president's agony. "I sat there for a little while," he recalled, "and watched him squirm; then I took the envelope (containing Lane's vote) and laid it on the pile, and that broke the tie."[183]

Two months later Dickey resigned. Clark described Dickey's management style. "He was a veritable rabbit in a greyhound race," he said, "with "Happy" Chandler on one side; Huguelet and Townsend on the other, and Rupp stirring them all up."[184]

Rupp and the rest of the university braced for a change when John W. Oswald replaced Dickey in 1963. An All-American football player at DePaul, Oswald was the choice of Gov. Bert T. Combs, a Democrat Party adversary of Chandler's. Oswald's selection by Combs made him a natural political enemy for the former governor. Coming to Kentucky from the position of vice-chancellor of California's state-wide university system, Oswald had no fear of instituting reforms, both academic and athletic. He broke up departmental kingdoms by installing a system of rotating chairmen, something that angered Clark to such an extent that he left for Indiana University. Oswald improved the curricula, built up graduate and research facilities, searched for outstanding faculty, laid the foundation for a model community college system and named a vice-president to supervise athletics.[185]

Robert L. Johnson's job was to institute athletic reforms wherever needed and to supervise integration. His appointment, in essence, relegated Bernie Shively to athletics director in name only.[186] I've wondered if that demotion didn't lead to Shively's demise; if he didn't see it as a loss of his national influence.

Lexington at that time, and vestiges remain even now, was more attuned to the racist attitudes of the old south than a border state that remained in the Union during the Civil War. There were strong sympathizers on both sides. After the war, the city became increasingly more southern due to post-war occupation by federal troops and Lexingtonians revered their Confederate ancestors with such fervor that it was difficult to determine if they realized their cause was lost a 100 years earlier. Many of the old families, while demanding involvement in Kentucky athletics, sent their sons to southern schools such as Washington and Lee, Duke or Virginia. It was a mind set Oswald, perhaps, underestimated.

Despite the board's approval of integrating athletic teams, it wasn't going to be easy. Oswald was elated over Bradshaw's signing of Northington, an All-State defensive back from Louisville's Thomas Jefferson High School. He wrote his friend, Clark Kerr, then president of the University of California at Berkeley, "Through my efforts we have now awarded a football scholarship to a Negro, the first in the history of the SEC, and I expect other schools in the conference to follow suit shortly." Oswald didn't do it by himself. He had the assistance of Gov. Edward Breathitt, Comb's hand-picked successor, in persuading Northington to come to Kentucky.[187]

The player's parents were irritated they weren't invited to the historic signing. Mrs. William E. Northington accused Gov. Breathitt of pushing her son into signing with Kentucky. "If I find that his life is in danger by playing football in the southern states," she told the governor, "I will be forced to take action to haul him somewhere else where he won't be abused."[188]

After an outstanding freshman season, the first black football player in the SEC played part of his sophomore year and suddenly left school. Oswald pressed for a reason, but the only explanation anyone could provide was that he withdrew due to grades. His freshman grades were adequate for him to move up to the varsity level. Something happened in the second home game of the season that may have made him decide to leave the team. Northington suffered a dislocated shoulder in the 1967 game with Mississippi in Lexington. Or, it could have had to do with the crippling injury of Greg Page, the second black player Bradshaw signed. Page, a Middlesboro high school star, suffered a paralyzing neck injury in one of Bradshaw's brutal practices and died a month later.[189]

Oswald was never forgiven for his active role in pushing integration in athletics. Indicative of that was the chapter on his years in former sports information director Russell Rice's book on Kentucky football. Rice entitled the six-page chapter on Oswald, "The Black Cloud." He accused Oswald of being more interested in integrating the football team than participating in bowl games.[190]

Rupp had less success than Bradshaw in recruiting blacks, but there were reasons. He had long since turned the football school into one of the capitals of college basketball. It was the university's showcase sport, and many wanted to keep it white. Some went so far at to sabotage Rupp's efforts in recruiting blacks. An example was Louisville star Wes Unseld.

Unseld led his Seneca High School to two state championships, but was loudly booed when he played in Lexington. "I wanted him and wanted him badly here at the university," Rupp said. Not everybody agreed with the coach and they let Unseld know of their feelings. One unsigned letter, sent to Unseld at his school, advised, "The majority of the city of Lexington, Kentucky, do not want you to attend UK. We would suggest you play ball for Kansas or some other out of state school of your choosing. We feel you will attain greater success elsewhere."[191]

That was one of several similar letters the player received. Shively, who hired experts to determine the signatures were false, advised him to forget the letter and make his planned campus visit. Shively told Oswald the letters were something the program was unable to combat. The damage was done. Unseld went to Louisville where he was twice an All-American. Drafted in 1968 by the Washington Bullets, Unseld was the NBA's "Rookie of the Year," and played out his career there until 1981 when he retired and moved into the front office as general manager. In 1988, Unseld was elected to the Naismith Basketball Hall of Fame in Springfield, Massachusetts.[192]

Unseld learned about the racial climate in Lexington, and his image would haunt the recruiting of black basketball players from Louisville and elsewhere for decades. In 1961, the Boston Celtics, with former Kentucky All-American Frank Ramsey and five black players, and the St. Louis Hawks, with former All-American Cliff Hagan and two black players were in Lexington to play a benefit game. The Phoenix Hotel, after promising to treat the black players fairly, refused to serve them in their dining room. The teams caught the next plane out of town. The hotel later hired thugs to physically carry Congress Of Racial Equality members from their coffee shop and dump them on the sidewalk. Games between Temple and Kentucky, begun two decades earlier, where canceled in 1962 when another hotel refused to serve the Owl's players. Rupp knew any black college players he recruited could expect the same treatment.[193] It's easy to see why Rupp hesitated to subject anyone to such violent abuse.

Harry Lancaster spread the story that Oswald was constantly pushing Rupp to sign black basketball players. It wasn't true. Oswald knew in 1966 that Rupp would sign no black players that year, and accepted the fact. He also knew that Rupp had no trouble attracting top high school players who were academically eligible and white.[194]

Rupp continued to search for black players, but few were brave enough to not only take on the hostile crowds in the south but to play in Lexington. Toke Coleman, from Cythianna, one of the finest players in the state, was academically ineligible. Players from Louisville and Nashville turned Rupp down and went elsewhere. In 1967 Rupp signed his first black player, Felix Thurston, from Owensboro, who had all the needed credentials: he was personable, an All-State player and made excellent grades. His parents asked Rupp to make no announcement of his signing until he arrived on the Lexington campus. Thurston never made it to Lexington, but signed with a college in Texas. In May 1969 Rupp signed his second black player, Thomas Payne, a 7'1" Shawnee (Louisville) High School athlete. In his sophomore year, Payne was the third highest scorer on a team that was 23-6 and SEC champions. Payne later served time for rape convictions.[195]

In the 1960s there were no accusations that Rupp was a racist because he failed to sign a black player before 1967. That came three decades later when sports pundits, infected with a revisionist virus called "political correctness," resurrected the 1966 Kentucky-Texas Western Final Four game as college basketball's pivotal event. It was an all-white team that Rupp took to that final game in College Park, Maryland, to meet Texas Western's predominately black team. "Rupp's Runts" were so named because the tallest players at 6'5" were Tommy Kron and Thad Jaracz on the starting five that included Larry Conley and All-Americans Louie Dampier and Pat Riley. Rupp's coaching peers said "The Runts" were the best ball handling team they'd ever seen. "It was a small team," Rupp said, "but certainly a courageous team; a wonderful ball club, and it will be a long, long time I believe before we're about to put together a bunch of ball handlers like we had in '66." Had the Runts won it all, he was prepared to say they were college basketball's greatest team.[196]

It wasn't to be. Texas Western beat Kentucky 72-65 in what became the most discussed college basketball game of the century. From the beginning writers had problems getting their facts straight. Popular novelist James A. Michener called the story of Texas Western's win "The most wretched in the history of American sports." He claimed their players were imported from New York, poorly paid and none graduated. They were totally unlike the Kentucky players, Michener pointed out, who had a chance at a real education and were winners in every respect except for the final game.[197]

That came as quite a shock to the Texans. Michener's errors, according to Derek Smolick, assistant sports information director at the University of Texas at El Paso, as the school is now called, caused the institution many problems. Smolick was sure Harry Flournoy, Willis Cager and Orstin Aries graduated, and thought Bobby Joe Hill, David Lattin and Willie Worsely might have their degrees. He was unable to locate the proper records. All were apparently quite successful in their chosen careers.[198]

The only starter among "Rupp's Runts" who didn't graduate was Academic All-American Louie Dampier. Dampier played for the Kentucky Colonels in the ABA, and joined Dan Issel on the coaching staff of the Denver Nuggets. Jaracz retired from the military with the rank of lieutenant colonel. Conley was a businessman and a national television sports commentator. Kron worked at the Mellon Bank Center in Pittsburgh. Riley, the most famous of "The Runts," was a successful NBA coach, author and lecturer.[199]

Branding Rupp a racist, without all the facts of why he was unable to successfully sign a black player before 1969, became cool. The line of scribes formed to the left and it was long. In 1991 the Washington Post's George Will, the paper's token conservative, referred to Rupp as "A great coach, but a bad man." Will apparently based his assumption on what he read about the 1966 Kentucky-Texas Western game. It was evident from his column that he hadn't a clue about the racial climate of Lexington in the 1960s, or the threatening letters Wes Unseld received, or how other teams with black players were treated. Five years later, the Rupp bashing continued. The Louisville Courier-Journal's Pat Forde insisted the coach would have been more comfortable with a sheet over his bust in Memorial Coliseum to avoid looking at the all-black Kentucky team that won the national championship that year. Forde's reference to a sheet, the symbol of the Ku Klux Klan, was another example of political correctness gone awry. Forde also failed to mention the bigoted letters received by Unseld, a Louisville native.[200]

A comparison of southern coaches indicated Rupp wasn't that far behind in signing black players. He signed Thurston in 1967, just a year after Dean Smith signed Charles Scott as UNC's first black player. Maryland had the first black players in the ACC with Billy Jones and Pete Johnson in 1966. The first black basketball player in the SEC was Perry Wallace at Vanderbilt in 1966.[201]

The media wasn't the only revisionist. Former North Carolina coach Dean Smith, in his autobiography, claimed when he signed Charles Scott in 1966 there wasn't a black basketball or football player in the SEC. He was wrong. Perhaps coach Smith didn't bother to notice that Kentucky signed the first black football player in the SEC in 1965, a year earlier.[202]

The political correctness of the 1990s, no matter what their proponents argue, can't be juxtaposed on events that occurred three decades earlier. A man must be looked at in context with his times. Was Rupp a racist? I don't believe he was. It was possible that he experienced a certain amount of discrimination in Kansas with parents of German and Austrian extraction, but they certainly drilled a strict work ethic into his soul. Rupp socialized with the movers and shakers and, business-wise, probably gained financially from the association but I found no evidence of him adopting their racial attitudes. Every bone in that man's body was competitive, and I don't believe he would have let the color of a great player's skin keep the athlete off his team. Rupp had to deal with a social, political and economic climate in Lexington where racism wasn't concealed but openly embraced, and that's something that few were willing to discuss.

Adolph "Herky" Rupp made a forceful argument against those who were quick to label his father a racist. He said his father was addicted to winning, and he didn't give scholarships for political purposes. Rupp spoke of his father's reluctance to take black players into the south in the early sixties when he couldn't protect them. His statement was backed up by comments from former sports information director Russell Rice.[203]

The decade ended with Rupp losing Bernie Shively to a sudden heart attack in 1968. Shively had come to Kentucky as an assistant football coach two years before Rupp, and they were close associates. Shively, who had been athletics director since 1938, was hardly buried before Lancaster applied for his job. Oswald had other ideas, and launched a national search for a new athletics director. In the middle of all this, "Happy" Chandler roared back into prominence again with seats on the athletics board and the board of trustees courtesy of a new governor. Chandler, a life-long Democrat, deserted his party's weak candidate, Henry Ward, backed by the Combs-Breathitt factions of the party, to support Republican Louie B. Nunn. Both appeared to have Oswald in their sights.[204]

Before the search for a new athletics director concluded, Oswald resigned. He committed the unpardonable sin of placing academics before athletics. Gov. Nunn denied he called for Oswald's resignation, but said, "I didn't encourage him to stay." Chandler, restored to the element of power he felt he deserved, claimed the governor asked him "To clean up that mess over at the university." Oswald's "mess" of accomplishments were considerable: enrollment grown from 9,000 to 16,000; a community college system expanded from five to fourteen campuses; a medical center complex that was becoming one of the best clinical research institutions in the nation, and an intellectual excitement the university had never known.[205]

While all the political in-fighting was going on, Oswald's search committee recommended William McCubbin, a Virginia Tech physical education professor, for athletics director, and he was an outstanding choice. He was an experienced athletics manager, had written several journal articles on the biomechanics of athletes and he was familiar with the athletics program from his days as a UK professor. Oswald made the mistake of telling McCubbin the search committee's recommendation was tantamount to final approval. Meanwhile, Lancaster's backers hatched a plot to make sure he got the job. Chandler and four other board members, including Jim Host, a former member of Nunn's administration, intended that Lancaster get the job. A number of board members were absent from the summer meeting, but sent their proxy votes. When the first vote went against Lancaster, the Chandler clique protested, successfully, the count of members' proxies. That was a perfectly acceptable procedure under UKAA by-laws. After barely defeating Chandler's motion to submit both McCubbin's and Lancaster's names for trustees' approval, the athletics board voted 8-5 to hire McCubbin. The vote had to be confirmed by the board of trustees.[206]

When McCubbin's name came before the board of trustees for approval, Chandler simply suggested the selection of Shively's successor be postponed, and members agreed. Since the athletics board vote wasn't unanimous, he said, the procedure should start all over. Nobody disputed that convoluted reasoning either. There was some "horse trading" to be done. Kirwan, who was adamantly opposed to what Chandler and other boards members did to McCubbin, became interim president after Oswald's resignation. It appeared he and Chandler made a deal. Lancaster was appointed interim athletics director after vice-president Robert Johnson left. In January 1969, Kirwan quietly made Lancaster's selection permanent. Chandler recommended, and trustees approved, Kirwan's designation be changed from interim president to the school's seventh president.[207]

Rupp's health declined. An ulcerated foot, that he insisted on treating at home, never healed properly. A year later it landed him in the hospital. The question remained whether or not he could fight both advancing age and a new president determined to retire him in order to become a major player in national college athletics.

# DR. JOCK

Campus unrest over Vietnam and the anti-war movement and racial tensions over civil rights, spread rapidly across the nation in the late 1960s. Oswald kept much of it in check by allowing students to invite radical speakers, such as attorney William Kunstler, to appear on campus; protecting the student newspaper's right to criticize the administration and state officials; refusing to evict the chapter of Students for a Democratic Society from campus; lobbying legislators against passing a bill limiting students' free speech; establishing a free speech area on the campus, and integrating athletics.

Oswald's departure changed the campus climate. With the installation of Kirwan, the good old boys were once again in charge. They became a permanent fixture when they discovered the new president was as enamored of athletics as they were. After all, Kirwan coached the football team in 1942 and 1944. Due to World War II, there was no football team in 1943. Kirwan was little more than a care-taker president, while officials searched for, and found a younger man.

Otis A. Singletary quickly recognized the center of power was in downtown Lexington, and he knew how to cultivate it. Or, so it appeared. A native of Gulfport, Mississippi, he attended Perkinson Junior College and Millsaps College in his home state. After receiving his Ph.D. from LSU in 1954, he began teaching history at the University of Texas in Austin. Leaving the classroom, he became the chancellor of the University of North Carolina at Greensboro, before agreeing to head up the Job Corps for president Lyndon B. Johnson. After a year as vice-president of the American Council on Education, the Washington lobby representing university presidents, Singletary returned to Texas as vice-chancellor of academic affairs for the university system. It was obvious that he enjoyed decision-making positions.[208]

His return to Texas wasn't a happy one. Singletary locked horns with Frank Irwin, the university system's powerful board chairman, who considered himself the decision-maker. Apparently, Irwin tolerated no interference from his vice-chairman. "I never believed the proper function of the board was to operate the place," Singletary said. At the same time he was looking for a campus to command, Kentucky was in the market for a new president.[209]

A suave personality with an uncanny talent for politics, Singletary was hired in May 1969 by Nunn and his trustees. The campus he inherited was described by sociologist John B. Stevenson, later president of Berea College, "If you think of it in terms of a pendulum swinging, it was still swinging hard from the old undergraduate country club school to the aspiring state land grant university with ambitions for really solid programs in research and graduate training."[210]

Stevenson accurately described Oswald's legacy, but that wasn't what the establishment wanted. In April 1968, a Fayette County grand jury rebuked university officials for allowing a national meeting of SDS on the campus. The grand jury report urged trustees, "To take a close look at the persons in authority at the university and try to encourage and develop in the institution an attitude more compatible with the desires of the alumni and general public."[211]

The establishment wanted to go back to "We've always done it this way." The grand jury's report prevailed and Oswald was history despite protests from faculty and students. Like Donovan, Singletary was a president who understood just how important winning football and basketball teams were to keeping his job. Before he could comply with their wishes, he had to deal with dissatisfaction over Oswald's departure and campus unrest.

While at ACE, Singletary wrote a tract on campus unrest that basically said, regardless of the cause, all parties bore responsibility in such conflicts. In his first few months on campus, he had ample opportunities to implement his theories. In April 1960, president Richard Nixon sent American and South Vietnamese forces into Cambodia to attack North Vietnamese sanctuaries. In opposition to the policy, campus riots occurred at Ohio's Kent State University where four students were killed and nine wounded in a confrontation with the National Guard. Two students were killed and twelve wounded at Jackson State in Mississippi. At Brandeis, in Waltham, Massachusetts, students set up a national strike center.[212]

The new president found his theories on campus unrest failed, and his school was in anarchy. Federal court documents described the situation: mass demonstrations extended far into the night; fires damaged several buildings and destroyed a wooden Reserve Officers Training Corps structure; adjoining women's dormitories were evacuated in the middle of the night; breaking and entering occurred with considerable damage to school property, and university police and staff were hit by rocks thrown by demonstrators. Singletary lost control of his campus. Nunn called in the National Guard, and slapped a curfew on all campus movements from 7:00 p.m. to 6:30 a.m. for three days.[213]

There were outside agitators on campus with guns, dynamite and Molotov cocktails. Twenty-one had been active in campus disorders elsewhere, four were identified as convicted felons and one was a convicted arsonist. Student government president Steve Bright filed suit in Federal District Court claiming Nunn and Singletary's actions, taken for political reasons, interfered with students' First Amendment rights of speech and assembly. Bright was denied a temporary restraining order, and later lost his case in both district and appeals courts.[214]

Singletary's first graduation exercises were canceled, and the unrest gradually subsided. With that chapter of his presidency behind him, he could concentrate on the total management of athletics. Singletary appointed former president, A.D. Kirwan, to chair a committee to study a new make-up of the athletics board. Kirwan, who evidently mis-read his successor's intentions, recommended keeping the present board of eighteen members. That wasn't what Singletary had in mind. He accepted the resignations of the entire board, and created a larger body, nineteen, padded with his own administrators, himself and faculty members willing to do his bidding. There was no doubt who was in charge.[215]

That concept was reinforced in a NCAA questionnaire Singletary filled out on who should control college athletics programs. Faculty input into athletics was tolerated only in an advisory, not regulatory, capacity. Alumni involvement, however, was a positive force for athletics. He found nothing wrong with his program being invaded by the power brokers as long as he was in control.[216]

He was the right man in the right place at the right time to cater to those who demanded a successful athletics program. Robert F. Sexton, executive director of the Pritchard Committee for Academic Excellence, described that aspect of the president. "I think he quickly picked up," Sexton said, "that Kentuckians wanted UK to have a strong athletics program, and that he honestly believed if you did that, you would strengthen the university in ways that were really important and money and support would follow from the athletics program." The committee, created by the legislature, was named for Edward F. Pritchard, Jr., legal counsel and advisor to president Franklin D. Roosevelt before he was sent to prison for two years for stuffing a ballot box in his home town of Paris.[217]

Singletary followed the path Sexton outlined, but he had another problem. There was an obstruction on campus to his over-riding ambition to be a major power in college athletics. The nation's most successful college basketball coach was across the street. Singletary began laying the ground work to make sure Rupp retired at the mandatory age of seventy in 1972, or preferably before. He told athletics board members Rupp came to see him in October 1970 to discuss his retirement, and that he would probably coach that season and maybe the next. My research revealed that it was Singletary who approached Rupp about his retirement months earlier. The athletics board had no way of knowing that.[218]

If Rupp failed to retire at or before the mandatory age, Singletary had a problem. When Kentucky athletics were mentioned, people automatically thought of Rupp and his basketball program. With Rupp and his almost larger-than-life reputation out of the picture, Singletary could cultivate the media, stroke the right political contacts and achieve his ambitions. There was another reason to make sure Rupp retired on time. He planned to move basketball games off campus into a municipal arena. That might be difficult if Rupp was still coaching and holding court in Memorial Coliseum. The president set his pegs carefully.

When Rupp's former assistant coach, Harry Lancaster, was appointed athletics director, Rupp made a former player, Joe B. Hall, his chief assistant. Hall, who wanted Rupp's job in the worst way, began creating a cadre of deep-pocketed coal barons from the eastern Kentucky mountain. Most of those coal barons wanted to move to the Bluegrass for social prestige and so they could join the power brokers in running the athletics program. Their manners may have been a little rough, but the power brokers loved the color of their money. The coal barons influence was so great and their money so over-powering the power brokers gradually faded, many of the old guard had already died, as the dominate factor in athletics, and they all became the good old boys.

Hall pushed for a commitment that he would succeed Rupp. At the 1969 basketball banquet, three years before Rupp's mandatory retirement date, Hall audaciously proclaimed, "Right now (it) is critical to my position at Kentucky. I think for the sake of the basketball program at UK and myself, coach Rupp's successor should be named now." Unable to get a commitment from athletic officials, Hall left in a huff for an alleged job at St. Louis University. He neglected, however, to resign his position as Rupp's assistant. A week later, Hall was back armed with assurances from well-known Lexington attorney Harry Miller, trustee

Albert Clay and, presumably, Singletary that he would be Kentucky's next basketball coach.[219]

Singletary needed an intermediary to deal with Rupp so he could be thought above the fray and, apparently, he wasn't quite ready to test the coach's clout. He found a kindred athletic soul he could trust in law professor William Matthews, an athletics board member, the NCAA faculty representative and a refugee from the Donovan days. Matthews came away from his verbal encounters with Rupp bruised and battered, but those were about the only wins the coach got out of the situation. Matthews recommended that no exception be made for Rupp, and that he be made to retire at the mandatory age of seventy in 1972. The board unanimously accepted that recommendation.[220]

Wanting to carefully document his version of the road to Rupp's retirement, Singletary began writing memorandum to the files. He described a February 1971 meeting with Rupp and the pressure he exerted to get him to agree to retire the next year. The president told Rupp he could choose the time of his retirement announcement. "He assured me," Singletary wrote, "of his acceptance of this fact (retirement) and of his willingness to accede to this position without bitterness and rancor."[221]

Rupp came from an era where a man's word was his bond, and Singletary must have vexed him to no end. The following October, the president reneged on his agreement to let Rupp determine the timing of his retirement announcement. He used media speculation of the expected event, as an excuse to go to Rupp's office and, "Discuss the situation for this year." Rupp again asked that no retirement announcement be made until the season was over. Singletary, however, said he told the coach, "I agreed to put his preference before the athletics board, but told Rupp that I could not guarantee they would accept my recommendation."[222]

There was never an athletics board that Singletary didn't control. If a member here or there happened to stray, the president quickly brought them back in line. As for media speculation about Rupp's retirement, that had been going on for twenty years.

In 1951, before the point shaving scandal broke, Ed Ashford suggested Rupp might retire if he won another championship, and devote his time to farming and business interests. Twenty years later, Dave Kindred surmised that the coach might retire after winning another championship just to prove he could in basketball's larger world. Kindred saw Rupp's life and Kentucky basketball as so entwined that the coach was unable to see one without the other.[223]

"Happy" Chandler, who considered himself Rupp's best friend, advocated the coach's retirement. "I've tried to talk him into retiring," Chandler said, "but he won't do it. I've said to him,'quit Adolph before they kill you.' Maybe that's what he wants, to die on the bench, to die stomping his foot at a referee." Chandler assured everybody that Rupp's retirement situation had been worked out with the athletics board, and that he would retire after the 1971-72 season. "I'm glad to see them work something out," Chandler boasted. "I didn't want it to come down to a bitter thing. I didn't want Adolph to go out that way, all bitter, and I didn't want the university to mistreat him. If it ever came down to a vote on whether or not to retire Adolph , I'd have to vote the way he wanted me to (vote)."[224]

Chandler was present and voting at the October 1971 athletics board meeting when Matthews' recommendation to retire Rupp received unanimous passage. Chandler had prized his seats on the athletics boards and board of trustees since the late 1930s. He would do anything to keep them. If going along with Singletary on Rupp's retirement was necessary to keep his position, Chandler was duplicitous enough to betray his best friend.[225]

Aside from being cursed with friends like Chandler, Rupp had to deal with Singletary telling him one thing and doing another. There was also Lancaster who seldom missed a chance to aggravate him as athletics director. Knowing Rupp had to retire after the 1971-72 season, Lancaster chastised him for exceeding his recruiting budget and demanded he immediately produce a budget for the next fiscal year. Both Lancaster and

Singletary salivated at the prospects of getting control of Rupp's forty-nine season basketball tickets after he retired.[226]

As head coach, Rupp was allotted eight complimentary season tickets, had twenty more to sell and had accumulated an additional twenty-nine. Lancaster claimed the extra tickets came from Rupp reading obituaries and intimidating the ticket manager. People actually left Rupp tickets in their wills. When Lancaster and Singletary were finished, Rupp was allowed to keep his eight season tickets in his retirement. Hall, ever hungry for tickets, had an allotment of twenty season tickets, twelve more than Rupp, before he ever coached a game. The remaining twenty-one were left for the athletics director and president to divvy up to good old boys such as paving contractor H.C. Adams, attorney Don Sturgill and developer J.W. Davis, who was later disassociated from the program. In their generosity, Lancaster and Singletary gave Rupp the option of purchasing four season football tickets.[227]

Singletary's promise to keep Rupp's retirement plans confidential was the worst kept secret in the commonwealth. The legislature attempted to honor him with a resolution that was a poor facsimile of the Gettysburg Address. There was no mention in the resolution of Rupp continuing to coach. The most eloquent plea against his retirement came from the Tennessee house of representatives. Their resolution said, although his retirement was in the best interests of the University of Tennessee, Vanderbilt and the SEC, it would be travesty of justice to prohibit him from sharing his wizardry and talents as long as he was physically able. They pointed out that a similar rule was relaxed for UT legendary football coach, Gen. Robert Neyland, to continue beyond retirement age.[228]

In February of his last season, four of Rupp's former players, Dan Issel, Mike Pratt, Louie Dampier and Gerry Calvert, circulated a petition urging the university to allow him to continue coaching beyond the mandatory retirement age. "I think a rule that says a man has to retire because he reached a certain age is, to put it quite frankly, ridiculous," Issel said.[229]

Nothing was going to move Singletary from his position on the legendary coach's retirement.

A month earlier, the Commonwealth Athletic Club was organized in Louisville. Their annual selection of the nation's best basketball player would receive the Rupp Award. They envisioned the Rupp Award becoming the equivalent of the Heisman Trophy given each year to the nation's best football player by New York's Downtown Athletic Club. Singletary and Chandler jumped at the chance to sit on the club's board of directors.[230]

The absence of any legislative support for Rupp's continued coaching was puzzling considering the icon he was. Since the athletics board and university refused to bend the rules for him, the legislature could have repealed their actions. Singletary covered that base quite well. A university administrator explained the school really had no reason not to keep Rupp if he wanted to stay, but added if the coach was allowed to remain beyond retirement age some senile professor would demand the same treatment.[231]

It was ironic that the same thing happened to Rupp's college coach. "Phogg" Allen, who reached mandatory retirement age in 1965, wanted to remain at Kansas to coach his prize recruit, Wilt Chamberlain, through his varsity career. The university refused to bend their retirement rules. The Kansas legislature over rode their decision, but the university refused to budge.[232]

Kansas honored Rupp with a doctoral degree in 1970, and he was moved by the ceremony. There was no indication of Kentucky ever doing that, then or later. Rupp, who had done so much to bring the university into the national spotlight, was not going to be so honored while Singletary was running things. Rupp was inducted into the Naismith Basketball Hall of Fame in 1969, and it was an honor he prized.[233]

Somebody forget to tell the Browns that Rupp's retirement was a done deal. "Kentucky Fried Chicken" magnate and future governor, John Y. Brown, Jr., his father John Y. Brown, Sr., a prominent attorney and political figure, KFC founder Harlan Sanders and former player, Gerry Calvert, asked Singletary to address the March 27, 1972 athletics board meeting in an eleventh hour effort to keep the coach. Sanders was a most effective example for working beyond the retirement age. He was over sixty-five and drawing Social Security when he began marketing his famous fried chicken. Before his death in 1980, Col. Sanders was one of the most recognized people in the world.[234]

After the Brown delegation left the board meeting, Singletary gave members his version of events leading to Rupp's retirement. He was so delighted with what he had accomplished that he told Rupp of the board's decision hours before the meeting. The final vote to retire Rupp was, of course, unanimous. Singletary set up a sham committee to select a new basketball coach.[235]

The annual basketball banquet was held the next evening. A newspaper photograph of Singletary, Rupp and banquet speaker, William L. Wall, president of the National Association of College Basketball Coaches, spoke volumes. Singletary, basking in his victory, called Rupp the greatest coach the game had ever known. Wall obviously wished he was elsewhere. Rupp, pain etched in his face, looked away from Singletary. His last words as the Kentucky coach were as concise and eloquent as one of his patented fast breaks, "To those who went down the glory road with me, my eternal thanks." His voice broke with emotion as he said, "Good night," and walked away from forty-two years of his life.[236]

Singletary conducted the swiftest search in the annals of sports history for Rupp's successor. Two days later he announced that Joe B. Hall was the new Kentucky basketball coach. Hall eagerly accepted, and Singletary rushed a news release to the media. A slight hitch developed, the new coach was unhappy with his salary.[237]

When Hall demanded more money than Rupp was making, he received a cold shoulder from Singletary and the board. So, he tried another avenue by asking Lancaster to increase his public relations budget $3,000. Lancaster informed him that, until 1969, Rupp's top salary, after four national championships, was $19,000. "Your demand," Lancaster told him, "would backfire for it would be regarded as an attempt at a salary increase before you've even coached one varsity game." By the end of the year, Hall's salary was increased to $23,000.[238]

In negotiating with Rupp to retire, Singletary promised him a part-time job associated with the university. Six weeks passed with no contact from Singletary, and Rupp wrote him about the job. The president finally arranged a personal service contract where Rupp would spend no more than one-third of his time in public relations, recruiting or doing special assignments for Singletary and Lancaster for $10,000 a year.[239]

It was doubtful if Singletary ever intended to use Rupp's talents after he had so carefully planned his retirement. The president complained often and loudly about the university's need for additional funds. Rupp, with his fame and wit, could have been a prodigious fund raiser for the school because people responded so easily to the coaching legend. An example of that was an incident related by former Gov. Louie B. Nunn. The governor said he asked Rupp, near the end of his coaching days, to appear at an event with him. Rupp was so popular with the audience and so well received that he upstaged the governor. "I never asked him to share a speaking event with me again," Nunn recalled.[240]

A month after he signed the personal service contract, Rupp accepted the presidency of the Memphis Tams of the ABA. He immediately wrote Singletary asking that his contract with the school be canceled, and offered to scout the Memphis area for high school players. Singletary ignored the scouting offer in his reply, and sent Rupp his check for July.[241] From that point on, it appeared Singletary and Lancaster jumped at every chance to batter the old coach.

Rupp, who still maintained an office in Memorial Coliseum, asked Lancaster about scheduling a game between the Memphis Tams and the Kentucky Colonels in the facility. He pointed out that all the season tickets were sold, and the game wouldn't interfere with the college program. Taking his cue from Singletary, Lancaster told Rupp it was doubtful if the athletics board would meet before the requested date and, if they did, approval of the game wouldn't be forthcoming. "I'm interested in knowing just how much your thinking has changed since you joined the pros," Lancaster jabbed, "you know you were the one who was absolutely opposed to professional use of our facilities." Lancaster ignored the fact that the Colonels played part of their season games in the Coliseum.[242]

Rupp's comments to a Memphis newspaper sent the thin-skinned Hall into orbit complaining to Singletary. Memphis Press-Scimitar sports editor George Lapides interviewed Rupp about the team's difficulty with SEC play. Lapides made it clear that Rupp, forced into retirement, lived up to his word not to say anything critical about the team's performance under Hall. He said Rupp, like other Kentucky fans, was concerned. Rupp told Lapides the team hadn't jelled yet. "I don't understand it either," he said, "because on that team is (Jim) Andrews, an All-Conference center; (Ronnie) Lyons, a second team All-Conference guard; (Larry) Stamper, whom I consider the best defensive man in the league. I would have thought from that super freshman team, he could put two sophomores in there and it wouldn't be a sophomore team." Rupp pointed out that coaching college basketball was the process of building a new team each year.[243]

Hall went ballistic. "I surely think it would be a good idea if someone other than myself approach coach Rupp concerning this type of criticism," Hall told Singletary. "He has every right to criticize, if he so chooses, but I see no reason for me to have him in the same building with me and my players if he is to criticize publicly."[244]

In the spring of 1973, the Tams were sold to New Jersey interests, and Rupp chose to return to Lexington rather than follow the team. Seeking a continued involvement with the sport that had been his life, he asked Singletary about reinstating his personal service contract. The president curtly informed him the purpose of that contract was to ease him into retirement, and any decision to reinstate it required an official action by the athletics board. "I did tell him," Singletary wrote, "if he severed all connections with the professional club, and did so state in writing, that I would at that time place the situation before the athletics association."[245]

Later that year Rupp spoke of his retirement in a meandering article in Inside Kentucky Sports, a short-lived publication of former athletics board member Jim Host. "I have to stay active," he wrote, "and I have to stay active in basketball. It's my first love." He rambled on about the personal service contract, the Memphis Tams and his recent association with the Kentucky Colonels. John Y. Brown, Jr., bought the ball club and made his wife, Ellie, the major stockholder and asked Rupp to sit on the board of directors after he discussed it with the president. Singletary told him the coach was officially retired and had no connection with the university. Rupp's column continued, "They (the Browns) asked me to take leave from my job as a consultant which I have done although I will still continue to have an office in Memorial Coliseum. I'm sure if someone at UK wants some advice from me, I can still consult with them."[246]

This time it was Singletary who went ballistic. He verbally tore the old coach apart informing him that he had no official connection with the university "Other than the office you are occupying as a result of an earlier decision by me." Singletary was being generous in allowing Rupp to keep an office in the building he was responsible for creating, and that spoke a lot about the president. He told Rupp he failed to understand his position, and proceeded to enlighten him. "When you accepted a position with the Memphis Tams the personal service contract was voided because of my expressed unwillingness to have an employee of a professional team on the university payroll." Singletary allowed his venom to spew to a point where his facts were in error, and it wasn't the first time. It was Rupp, not Singletary, who requested the personal service contract be canceled when he took the job with the Tams.[247]

Singletary and his minions' treatment of Rupp in his post-retirement days made the breach between the school and the coach's family irreversible. They even went so far as to take away his parking place at the Coliseum. Lexington fire chief Earl McDaniels painted a parking space for Rupp on the Euclid Avenue pavement by a fire hydrant in front of the Coliseum.

Rupp's papers were given to the Commonwealth Athletic Club in Louisville, not the university archives. Finally, two years after his retirement, Singletary appointed a committee to create a memorial to the coach. The result was Rupp's life-size bust that sits in the conference room in Memorial Coliseum.[248]

There were other insults. Singletary's ticket committee just happened to forget about Rupp when distributing tickets for the 1975 NCAA regionals and the Final Four in San Diego. Rupp told the media he begged for tickets, but the committee failed to allot him any. There was hell to pay. A firestorm of letters rained down on Singletary. He put out a lame news release denying any blame for the slight and saying Rupp wasn't given tickets, and claiming the old coach hadn't requested them. After having been informed he no longer had any connection with the university he served for forty-two years, Rupp certainly wasn't going to press for tickets. As a past president of the National Association of College Basketball Coaches, Rupp had two lifetime tickets to the Final Four. Singletary, probably out of embarrassment, asked Rupp to fly with the team to San Diego where they lost the finals to UCLA 85-92. Rupp wrote him a gracious note after they returned.[249]

When Kentucky played their first game in the municipal arena named for the coach, they forgot about him again. Incidentally, the name, Rupp Arena, was first used by a local committee that urged Singletary to build a campus arena on the site selected for the new football stadium. With three surgeries in as many years, it was impossible for Rupp to climb seventeen rows of steps to sit with his family. Last minute seats were found for him and his grandson Chip behind the visitor's bench. In contrast when Western Kentucky's great coach, Ed Diddle, retired the school designated an entire section of the Diddle Arena, for him and his family.[250]

Rupp said nobody told him he would be introduced. When he stood up, the applause was thunderous, and the crowd refused to stop. Rupp stood up again and the roar was even louder. It must have been sustenance for his soul. At half-time, he was presented with a blue reclining chair, a basketball and a portrait. Rupp was mobbed with requests for autographs, and had to refuse countless requests for photographs. Seems the university considered the $2,000 in photographic expenses to produce the pictures prohibitive.[251]

On December 10, 1977, Rupp, in a coma at the University Hospital, died as Kentucky was beating his alma mater, Kansas, 73-66. None of Singletary's crew of athletic administrators were among the pallbearers at his funeral. Nor were they among the honorary pallbearers that included Rupp's former lettermen, directors of his tobacco warehousing complex, the board of governors of the Shriners' Cripple Children's Hospital, representative of the National Association of College Basketball Coaches and directors of the Naismith Basketball Hall of Fame.[252]

Protocol demanded that Singletary send flowers to Rupp's funeral, but he certainly wasn't going to pay for them with his own money. The florist's bill for the flowers was paid for with money from a charitable and educational trust the president tapped into often.[253]

When he retired as LSU coach, Dale Brown recalled his friendship with Rupp. He said the coach, although appearing gruff and opinionated, had an inner softness, and he found Rupp to be sensitive, loving and caring. "I hated to see the bitterness he carried around in his final days at Kentucky when he felt he was run off the job."[254]

Rupp was a man of his time, but he had dignity, integrity and a humanity that his tormentors would probably never attain.

# STRONG ARM POLITICS

With Adolph Rupp out of the way, Singletary devoted his attention to building a new stadium that showcased his political skills. He deftly worked through road blocks, toadied to the right politicians, cannibalized ideas of an opponent and cleverly used a deficit, when it no longer existed, to separate the good old boys from even more of their money.

The need for a new stadium came not from Kentucky being a perennial football power, but from conference opponents' objections to their share of the 37,000 McLean Stadium gate. In 1971, Kentucky was 90-191-23 against SEC opponents. Hardly a stellar record, but football made up the majority of the athletics' income and had to be protected.

A new stadium was approved by the state before Oswald resigned, but the process bogged down over the politics of site selection. The athletics board, to Oswald's consternation, selected a site on a college farm six miles from the campus. Chandler purchased Coldstream Farm for the school in his second gubernatorial term. It was a ridiculous selection for a number of reasons: it was too far removed from the campus, there were no utilities and it would have required a reconfiguration of a major Interstate-75 interchange.

Students objected to locating the stadium on Coldstream, and Oswald let them hold a student referendum on the matter. The vote was 2,133-268 against the Coldstream site. Oswald resigned and nothing happened until Singletary took office. Early in his presidency, Singletary discussed building the new stadium in downtown Lexington, but there wasn't enough available land. His refusal to fill the vacancies on the stadium site selection committee was an indication he would make that decision.[255]

While Singletary considered his options for the new stadium site, Lexington dentist Roy Holsclaw organized the Citizens' Rupp Arena Committee, Inc., to push for the construction of not only a 50,000-seat stadium but a 25,000-seat arena on another college farm adjoining the campus. The president was stunned at both Holsclaw's bold plan and his audacity to intrude into his athletic affairs. Holsclaw's plan made a lot of sense: it was on the campus, the two structures could share utilities and parking facilities and, when finished, they would belong to the university. His architectural and engineering data placed the cost of the stadium at $10.1 million and $12.8 for the arena.[256]

Holsclaw conducted public opinion surveys in the newspaper about his proposal. Ninety-seven percent of those responding favored building the two structures on the Cooper Drive location. Eighty-six percent said they would join in a priority ticket plan to provide $4 million for debt payment on the construction bonds. In addition to football and basketball revenue, the facilities were projected to bring the university additional income from livestock shows and sales, concerts and other events.[257]

It was impossible to disregard public support for Holsclaw's plan, and that presented a problem for Singletary. The president's main concern appeared not to be the soundness of the plan, but that the public might think the committee had some official connection with the university and athletics. Athletics board members brushed aside Holsclaw's priority ticket plan idea, but Singletary didn't. He told Lancaster to meet with them and pick their brains.[258]

Nobody was going to trod on Singletary's athletic turf. Four days after Holsclaw's committee made their announcement, the newspaper ran a story, quoting an unusually reliable source, saying there were plans to enlarge Memorial Coliseum from 11,500 to 18,000-seats. It was the old political two-step Singletary was so adept at executing, and aimed at defusing the popularity of Holsclaw's idea. I don't think he had any intentions of enlarging the Coliseum. A month earlier, he approved an expenditure of $125,000 to replace the structure's ceiling. He would never have spent that much money on the Coliseum if he intended to enlarge it immediately.[259]

By April of 1971, Singletary was negotiating a lease to move basketball games into a proposed municipal arena. The good old boys' reasoning for the move was to revitalize a dead and decaying downtown. They miscalculated by counting on sports fans' and visitors' money for the answer. Singletary told the board the stadium was the first priority, and shuffled plans for the basketball facility to the back burner. There was a good reason. He transferred athletic funds, earmarked for a new arena, to the stadium project.[260]

Aside from Singletary's considerable opposition to the Holsclaw plan, there was other evidence it would never work. There were some influential names on Holsclaw's committee, but most of the good old boys were absent. The committee included IBM president Morris Beebe, team physician E.C. Ray and presidents of the Wildcat Club and the Committee of 101. The Committee of 101 began in 1966 when 101 IBM employees contributed twenty-five-cents each to send telegrams of support to Rupp and the team on their away trips. The booster group grew to 300 members with a waiting list of 200, and had a six-figure operating budget.[261] The usual names of Carey, Graves, Hancock, Huguelet, Clay, Young, Parrish, Haggin, Stoll, Chandler and others were absent from Holsclaw's group.

Gov. Louie B. Nunn arranged for Singletary to present his stadium plans to the State Property and Buildings Commission for their approval to use state revenue bonds for the stadium construction instead of those backed by the university. To demonstrate the need for the new stadium, Singletary contrasted Kentucky's share of the Georgia gate in Athens, $110,000, to the Bulldog's share in Lexington, $40,000. With such a wide disparity, conference schools suggested Kentucky keep all of the gate in Lexington, and they would do the same in their stadiums. That would have destroyed the revenue base for Kentucky athletics. He told the committee that he didn't want to be responsible for the downfall of Kentucky football, and he was sure they didn't either. The president pressed the board for an immediate answer since it was impossible to postpone negotiating SEC football contracts beyond 1975.[262]

"Candor requires," he told the committee, "that I point out to you that this facility will require approximately $200,000 more per year in debt service in the next biennium." That amount figured prominently in stadium affairs for the next thirty years. The commission approved the issuance of $9 million in state revenue bonds to build the stadium with the university providing the remaining $1.8 million.[263]

The source of that $1.8 million changed depending on who was talking with school officials. Singletary was so sketchy with his presentation that some committee members thought the university's part was coming from private sources. Initially Singletary's vice-president for business affairs, Larry Forgy who yearned to be governor, said the amount came from an unallocated surplus, the fire fund, a budget restoration, athletic surpluses and $600,000 in anticipated athletic funds over the next two years. When the media asked Forgy about the source of the university's $1.8 million contribution, the vice-president simply said the money came from surplus construction and athletic funds. There was no mention of the $600,000 they didn't have.[264]

Spending money they didn't have for their contribution to the stadium fund made the $200,000 Singletary mentioned for debt service on the bonds more critical. Not to worry, the president told board members, that money would come from direct legislative appropriations. They swallowed it hook, line and sinker. The legislature only met every two years, and wouldn't convene again until following January after the state-wide elections in November. Apparently Singletary had a commitment from somebody in state government for the additional money, but the board failed to ask any questions. Members were, however, deeply concerned that athletic funds might somehow find their way into academics. Singletary assured them that wouldn't happen.[265]

Chandler held out for the Coldstream Farm site despite the additional expense. "There is a lack of wisdom," he whined, "in locating the facility on campus." Evidently, the former governor hoped the new stadium, if located on Coldstream, would be named for him. Singletary located the stadium on Cooper Drive.[266]

Somewhere between June and September 1971, a fly landed in Singletary's stadium ointment. On September 15th, only five days before the revenue bonds were to be sold, he suddenly placed everything on hold. The $200,000 to complete debt payments wasn't quite secured. It was a beautiful example of Singletary's political expertise. State wide campaigns were in full swing for the general election two months later, and nobody wanted to be blamed for the decline of Kentucky football. His point man, Lancaster, gave it all away. "We really can't do anything now until the November election. It was great to have Gov. Nunn back the proposal a few months ago but, let's face it, we're getting a new governor and legislature in a few months and we gotta see how things work out."[267]

Things worked out just fine.

A confidential memo from controller Henry Clay Owen said the state agreed to provide an additional $150,000 a year for the bond debt deficit. On Singletary's initialed copy of Owen's memo that amount was marked out and the figure, $3 million, inserted. Days after the general election, the stadium lease was revised with $3 million, in state funds, in an escrow account. At seven percent interest, the escrow account would produce the needed $200,000 and change. Just how good a deal Singletary's worked out with the state wasn't revealed for a quarter of a century.[268]

With the stadium financing in place, Singletary began damage control with those opposing the project. His modus operandi was to forge ahead at full steam, ignoring opinions other than his own. Invariably he had to retrench and solve public relations problems he either created or aggravated.

Maisie McMichael, a Lexington horse farm secretary, was opposed to spending $10 or $11 million on a structure used only a few times a year. She spoke for a number of people in her letter to Singletary asking why not build an arena were conventions, horse and cattle shows and sales could be staged? Sheila Maybanks, also of Lexington, thought the stadium was a stupid use of school resources. "The university needs counseling services, scholarships, more and better paid faculty, books, services, etc., and what does it get," she asked? "A stadium to be used about six times a year primarily by a bunch of our more prosperous and provincial alumnus."[269]

Neighborhood associations in the vicinity of the stadium were concerned about the impact of added traffic in their area, parking on game days and the possibility of street extensions. Singletary brushed their concerns aside saying the local government, not the university, was responsible for street planning. He had more important things to do than address such mundane questions.[270]

With the $3 million escrow account in place, stadium financing was complete. The president, however, smelled more money out there waiting to be plucked. He incorporated Holsclaw's idea of a priority ticket plan, added some innovations of his own and came up with the Blue White Fund. Wealthy boosters, paying the fund's top price, got the best seats in the stadium. They flocked to the Blue White Fund just as Holsclaw's survey predicted. The appeal was based on the athletics program's need for additional money without revealing the bond debt deficit problem had been solved. Singletary selected a newcomer to college athletic management, former All-American Cliff Hagan, to handle the Blue White Fund.[271]

With Lancaster's health declining, Singletary began grooming the former All-American for the athletics director's position. A member of Rupp's 1951-52 championship team, Hagan's playing days encompassed the school's involvement in the point shaving scandal, overt subsidization and "sudden death" sanction. Former NCAA executive director Walter Byers named Hagan as one of the basketball players involved in the overt subsidization. "Three players were named," Byers said, "as having received illegal aid; the report indicated Hagan was probably ineligible in 1951-52 because of a $125 gift certificate he received, but no specific finding was made regarding him." It was just another Kentucky violation that slipped through the crack.[272]

Had Byers and the NCAA looked deeper into Donovan's athletic quagmire of the early 1950s they would have found additional information about Hagan, who came from a western Kentucky family of modest means. In November 1951, Courier-Journal sports editor Earl Ruby wrote his old friend Donovan of some things about the Kentucky program that bothered him. He sent Donovan a copy of a note he received from a friend about her conversation with Hagan's younger brother, Bobby, who caddied for her at an Owensboro golf tournament. "Bobby proudly told me about the silver Cliff was giving their mother every Christmas, Easter, etc.," she told Ruby. Maybe Hagan used his gift certificate money to buy silver for his mother or, perhaps, the silver was just part of rewards he received from the "deep pockets."[273]

Drafted into the NBA by the Boston Celtics, Hagan played most of his career with the St. Louis Hawks. He earned a master degree in education from St. Louis University. He returned to Lexington in 1971 to manage a shopping mall and start a chain of Cliff Hagan's Ribeye restaurants.[274]

Hagan, who wore embalmed hair long before Jimmy Johnson made it famous, picked up the stadium priority ticket plan with relish. More money guaranteed better seats. The Blue White Fund was structured on four levels from $25 to $250 plus the cost of tickets. The 7,422 stadium seats reserved for the Blue White Fund were expected to produce $601,850 the first year. Purchasers could pay for membership and tickets in installments, but Hagan preferred the entire amount in one check.[275]

The Internal Revenue Service gave the Blue White Fund tax exempt status, but placed specific guideline on how and by whom the money was handled. Blue White monies were placed in a restricted fund account to be used only for athletics. The IRS gave trustees the option of accepting or rejecting athletic officials' recommendations for the use of the money, but their approval was mandatory. No mention of the Blue White Funds was found in trustees' meeting minutes despite an extensive search in the university's archives, where an index of subjects discussed and actions taken by trustees, is kept. Archivist Frank Stanger could find no mention of Blue White Funds in those indices.[276]

With the $3 million in escrow and the Blue White Funds rolling in, Singletary began adding extras to what he called a "bare bones" stadium. Those extras included an elevator for his guests, 5,760 chair-backed seats, another scoreboard and a VIP area. Maysville banker J.M. Fitch, Jr., advised him about the elevator. "I truly believe," Fitch said, "the president of the university and the governor of the commonwealth should have a private elevator at their nearby convenience for their personal use. I do not think you people should be climbed over and be pushed around by other people in the stadium."[277]

Singletary didn't need much encouragement to spice up his new stadium. Soon there was a lounge where he could wine and dine the commonwealth's political and social leaders, Fitch included. There must have been a measure of apprehension about how this largess would appear. Folders in Singletary's papers, containing the invitation lists to his pregame luncheons and elevator passes issued to his guests, were marked "restricted."[278]

The president lounge wasn't included in the original stadium bid, and wasn't completed in time for the 1973 opening. Documents found in his papers indicated the president's lounge and offices for the football coaching staff were bid under separate contracts to avoid seeking permission of the Council on Higher Education to exceed their $100,000 construction cap. The CHE controlled all aspects of universities' spending as well as curricula. Singletary appeared to enjoy by-passing the CHE whenever possible. A 1985 incident was a good example. He wanted the state to buy a $10 million super computer for the university, and the CHE told him to use the school's money for the purchase. He figured out something else. Singletary invited state senator Mike Moloney to accompany the football team to Baton Rouge to play LSU. Not only was Moloney a law school graduate and chairman of the senate's powerful appropriation and revenue committee, he was the son of the legislator who rushed Donovan's sports bribery bill through the legislature in 1951. It was a good investment. The university got a $5 million appropriation from the state for the super computer.[279]

Moloney's name was also on Singletary's guest list for pre-game luncheons in the president's lounge. The exclusive area was designated only by a blue and white canopy over the entrance. The gathering room was decorated in the team colors of blue and white with comfortable sofas and chairs, tables with large lamps and thick pile carpeting. The other room was used for the buffet luncheons served to 150-200 guests before home games. Student Center Catering prepared the meals, whose price ranged from twenty to thirty-five dollars each for prime rib or country ham with all the trimmings. The catering costs were paid by the same charitable and educational trust used to pay for flowers Singletary sent to Rupp's funeral.[280]

Singletary's guests, in addition to the invitations, special parking and elevator permits, had their photographs taken with the president. The pictures were later mailed to the guest with a presidential note. Photographic costs were paid by the same trust.[281] The school earlier had no funds to pay for pictures of Rupp that fans wanted.

Elitism didn't stop there. To make sure the proletariat were kept out, Lancaster suggested stationing a doorman to collect invitations as guests entered the lounge. Hagan advised against allowing anyone else to use the lounge since it "Had a number of fine prints, decorations, carpets, furniture and equipment that could be easily damaged, destroyed or certainly abused." Such contamination, Hagan maintained, would destroy the special purpose of the suite.[282]

Everything went very well for Singletary's new stadium. Only a small problem remained. It was unthinkable that coach John Ray, despite his having worked as hard as anyone to get the new stadium, should take his 10-31 record into the facility. An attractive and affable man, Ray was popular despite his losing record. In November 1973 Singletary appointed an athletics board committee to discuss contract negotiations with Ray. Somebody missed the signal, and the committee recommended Ray's contract be renewed. The president had hired a new coach, but depending on the board to get rid of Ray hadn't worked. He suggested that, because the committee's decision wasn't unanimous, they should reconsider. The message came through loud and clear. It was Singletary's way or the highway. The board voted 12-8 not to renew Ray's contract. It wasn't a unanimous vote either, but it was the one Singletary wanted.[283] It was amazing how often that old ploy of a vote not being unanimous cropped up again and again in athletic affairs.

His handling of Ray's dismissal brought the president much criticism. Paul F. Maddox, a Campton physician, suggested that a guillotine was badly needed on the campus, but the football coach wasn't the person whose head should roll. Ronald Forester, a Montgomery, Alabama, alumnus questioned whether Kentucky really wanted a winning football program since they never sought the advice of outstanding former players and assistant coaches. He mentioned former assistant coach Howard Schellenberger, who had a national championship at Miami; Bill Arnsbarger, who coached at LSU; Ermal Allen, who played for both Bryant and Rupp and had an outstanding career under Tom Landry in Dallas.[284]

Singletary told the December 1972 athletics board meeting they were there to hire Fran Curci as the new football coach. That was the way it was going to be. KFC magnate John Y. Brown, Jr., had successfully lobbied Singletary on Curci's behalf. An All-American at Miami, Curci played one season with the Dallas Texans, now the Kansas City Chiefs, before returning to Miami as an assistant. He won thirty games in three seasons at Tampa before going back to Miami. Curci opened the 1973 season in

Commonwealth Stadium with a 31-26 win over Virginia Tech, but ended with a 5-6 season.[285]

With the new stadium under his belt, Singletary appeared ready to handle the basketball arena situation. Everything, so far, was going according to plan.

# SEE WHAT THE BOYS DOWNTOWN WILL HAVE

What the good old boys downtown wanted and got was a sizable slice of the university's basketball revenue when Singletary moved the games into a new municipal arena, twice the size of Memorial Coliseum, for the same basic revenue. Decades later, the school's continued excuse for moving the games off campus was to rescue a decaying downtown. Not even Kentucky basketball could stop the erosion left by merchants moving to suburban shopping malls. Twenty-five years later, empty storefronts lined Main Street. Large municipal complexes with specialty shops, without the elemental service outlets, were seldom the cures for urban blight. Lexington's was no exception.

The downtown establishment had talked about a municipal arena for forty years, ever since Rupp, tired of playing in tiny Alumni Gymnasium, broached the subject. In the 1930s, Rupp's fame and that of the basketball program was yet to come, and the downtowners saw little benefit for themselves. When Memorial Coliseum opened in 1950, it was only four blocks away, near enough to be a financial asset to Main Street businesses.

Forty years should be adequate time to plan a project to some degree of refinement. The downtowners honed considering to a fine art and, if their conclusions were flawed, arrogance seldom allowed them to reconsider. It was finally pointed out in a June 2000 study, commissioned by the economic development group Lexington United, which criticized the city for their elitist attitude in efforts to attract businesses.[286]

Finally a plan evolved to anchor downtown Lexington with a new newspaper plant on one end, and a sprawling complex of a tri-level retail mall, hotel, arena and convention center on the other. The restoration of a crumbling, 1,200-seat Opera House, with no parking facilities, was thrown in the mix. After all, the downtowners had to have some place to meet and greet. The big question was the size of the arena. It made no difference that 11,500-seat Memorial Coliseum was just blocks away. If Kentucky basketball moved downtown, a 25,000-seat arena was feasible. Otherwise, a 8,000-10,000-seat arena, basically the size of the Coliseum, would suffice. Regardless, they were going to have a downtown arena.[287]

It was doubtful if the smaller arena was every seriously considered. It was just a given that the university would fall in line, as they always had, with downtown's wishes. In 1902, the student athletic association, desperate for money, had opened a used book store on campus to earn the needed funds. Downtown bookstore owners raised such a hue and cry about the damages to their businesses, from the students' operation, that president James K. Patterson closed the little campus store.[288]

The practice of protecting downtown Lexington at the university's expense is so ingrained and incestuous that it continues today. Few people ever give it a thought and, if they do, surely ask no questions.

No evidence was found that Singletary ever seriously considered building a new arena on campus. He claimed the school was unable to use education building revenue bonds as they did with the Coliseum, a multi-use facility. A larger arena wouldn't have been a multi-use building? What about state revenue bonds, such as those used to build Commonwealth Stadium, to build a campus arena? Singletary's excuse was a shortage of state funds since two additional institutions, Northern Kentucky University and the University of Louisville, were brought into the state-wide system. To some extent that was true in the early 1970s. Singletary did create a bachelors degree in general studies, known as a "Bluegrass Special," to increase enrollment and bring in more tuition money.[289]

While Singletary planned to move basketball games off campus, another event occurred that enriched state government coffers. In 1972 Kentucky enacted a severance tax on coal, a commodity that experienced booming sales when mid-Eastern nationals created a crude oil marketing cartel. For the next fourteen years, Kentucky led the nation in coal production, and every ton was taxed by the commonwealth. A portion of the severance tax was returned to the coal-producing counties, but there was plenty of money left over for political favors. Roads were paved that never saw asphalt before or after.[290]

There was tax money available for political favors, for bailing out downtown Lexington's building debacle but it appeared little thought was given to education in the commonwealth. There was always Arkansas and Mississippi to keep Kentucky from the bottom of the education barrel.

Gov. Wendell Ford, who succeeded Nunn in 1971, had $4 million in state money to bail out downtown Lexington's Civic Center project. It was rumored that Singletary was so taken with Ford, a fellow Democrat, that he wanted to name the new football stadium for him rather than the Republican governor, Louis B. Nunn, who hired him and arranged the stadium financing. The compromise was Commonwealth Stadium. Julian Carroll, who followed Ford as governor in 1974, spread money across the Bluegrass like the dew. He built a special football dormitory at the University of Louisville, and offered Singletary $1 million for a similar structure at UK. The argument, that state funds weren't available for a campus arena, failed to hold water.[291]

Why did Singletary not look closer at the state as a source of financing for a new campus arena? That's difficult to answer since he refused requests for interviews. The only real answers came from documents in his presidential papers, and his actions. They point to a man who, for whatever reason, put the special interests of downtown Lexington above those of his institution. The cost was astounding.

When calculating the university's projected revenue from the downtown arena, Singletary used Memorial Coliseum's 1971 net revenue as the basis. It was apples and oranges. The municipal arena, if Kentucky played there, would be twice the size of the Coliseum. Logically, such an arrangement should produce nearly twice as much income. Singletary's explanation to the athletics board was "The university already has 11,463 very desirable seats for basketball, free of debt; it could not risk assured revenues without reasonable assurance it would be equally well off in any new arrangements." The board, of course, didn't question his actions.[292] It wasn't as if tickets would languish unsold in the box office. This was Kentucky basketball, where people prized their tickets to such an extent they were bequeathed in wills and contested in divorce settlements.

Singletary did more than move basketball games off campus. For decades, community concerts, lectures and other special events were held in the Coliseum. The structure was a pivotal part of campus life. During the arena negotiations with the Lexington Civic Center board, he agreed to move all ticketed events, once held in the Coliseum, to the new arena complex. The president offered no resistance that I could find, and did a good job of shielding his actions from the public and, to some extent, the athletics board.[293]

In September 1971, the athletics board, with little real information on which to base their decision, voted for Singletary to join forces with the Lexington Center Corporation for Kentucky to play basketball in the new arena. Board member Charles Roland said Singletary told them he must be assured that as many tickets would be sold for the new facility as were for the Coliseum. Apparently nobody questioned that reasoning since they were moving into a facility twice as large as the Coliseum. "We are safe as we can always fall back on the Coliseum," Roland recalled him saying.[294] This wasn't the bold move of the shrewd politician who pulled off the stadium deal.

Singletary sent the LCC a letter outlining an interim agreement for playing in the new arena. Gross revenue from Memorial Coliseum tickets in 1971 was $775,194. He agreed to a base, for playing in the new arena, of $430,228, the Coliseum's net ticket revenue in 1971, and gave the LCC a base of $63,620. The remaining ticket revenue was split with 82.5 percent going to the school, and 17.5 going to the LCC, whose total take would be $112,856. In addition the LCC received a fifty-cent bond debt fee from all non-student and non-complimentary tickets sold.[295]

Notice anything wrong, from the school's perspective, with the agreement Singletary crafted? The only revenue discussed was from tickets. There was no mention of other income the games would generate such as concessions, parking, inside arena and scoreboard advertising, souvenirs and game programs. As events unfolded the answer became apparent.

After the interim agreement was signed, the LCC asked the school to contribute more money to the project. The state department of finance discovered the LCC planned to use a projected cash flow from the center's hotel to complete revenue bonds' debt payments, and vetoed the idea. The school got away with using money they didn't have for their part in the financing of the new stadium, but officials were keeping a closer check on state's money. The logical place to find the needed money was to soak the school the way downtowners always have. LCC chairman Jake Graves, a banker from an old Lexington family, asked Singletary to pay the needed $56,000 a year to complete the bonds' debt payments. When the hotel made a profit, Graves said, the money would be paid back to the school.[296]

The president was furious, but he capitulated. "This must be the final increase in the university's participating in the center's financing," he told Graves. Any control Singletary had over the project was gone when Gov. Ford used the university to channel $4 million in state funds into the floundering project. Ford couldn't give the state money directly to the LCC since it was a quasi-public, not a state owned, project. Ford arranged for the fiscal transfer through the school apparently without alerting university officials.[297]

After being forced to cough up more money and being out maneuvered, Singletary suddenly found problems with the interim agreement he had so willingly signed. When faced with perplexing problems, the president often resorted to "talking papers," where he wrote down the pros and cons of an issue to help him reach a decision. His presidential documents contained several "talking papers." The president claimed the LCC abrogated four points after the agreement was signed: an option to renew the pact before the end of the year, architectural input into the building, control of tickets and the number of games professional basketball teams played in the arena.[298]

It was only necessary to read the interim agreement to learn Singletary had agreed to give the LCC the option of extending the proposal before the end of December 1972. As for architectural input, the school was just one of many temporary tenants using the facility. If control of tickets was in jeopardy, Singletary had only himself to blame. The number of professional, as well as high school basketball games, played in the new arena was clearly spelled out in the interim agreement.[299]

Singletary appeared to have a blind spot about professional sports but, in this case, his position was exceedingly weak. At the same time he was objecting to the number of professional basketball games scheduled for the new arena, the Kentucky Colonels were playing part of their ABA schedule in Memorial Coliseum, his own campus arena. In 1973 and 1974, the Colonels, owned by KFC mogul John Y. Brown, Jr., averaged 9,000 for their Coliseum games attendances. That dropped off to 6,098 in 1975, when the Colonels won the ABA championship. The ABA, not as well established or financed as the NBA, folded in 1976. The four strongest teams, the New York Nets, Indiana Pacers, Denver Nuggets and San Antonio Spurs, joined the NBA. The Colonels and the St. Louis Spirits were purchased by the NBA for $3.3 million each.[300]

Nobody mentioned the duplicity of Singletary's position on the professional basketball games.

To protect himself, Singletary declared any criticism over the interim agreement should fall on LCC officials who agreed to his terms in the first place. It was doubtful the president admitted in public the interim agreement was his idea. Such an admission would have required an explanation of the large amount of Kentucky basketball revenue going into the LCC. Whether it was sheer frustration, his ego being bruised or an effort to shore up his position, Singletary made an untimely, and, for him an uncharacteristic, move. He released a copy of the interim agreement with the LCC to the media. An accompanying statement said the university had no obligation to play in the new arena.[301]

All hell broke loose as everybody involved rushed to fortify their positions.

The media launched an immediate attack on Singletary. The Lexington newspaper criticized him for his opposition to professional basketball games and the income they would bring the center. The Louisville publication accused him of failing to act in the public interest, and called groundless his contention that professional games in the new arena would reduce his athletic revenue. On a copy of their editorial, in his presidential papers, was the notation, "An opinion we don't share."[302]

Then, the Urban-County council went after him. The local merged government not only put $300,000 into the project, but they were responsible for any deficits.[303]

Singletary was no longer dealing with locals such as Graves, automobile dealer Bruce Glenn or Jim Host, the former athletics board member who, as the LCC consultant, negotiated with Singletary on the lease. Host, who attached himself to Kentucky athletics after an unsuccessful bid for lieutenant governor in 1971, had an interest in the games moving into the new arena. The LCC hired Marshall graduate Tom Minter as the center's general manager, and he took over negotiations with an iron hand. He informed Singletary he had no business conducting their disputes in public. Minter pointed out that an additional $8 million was spent for the larger arena to accommodate Kentucky basketball. Coach Joe B. Hall, who protested moving the games off campus, said things changed when Minter came into the picture and the school became more lenient in its demands.[304]

Attempting to blunt the criticism, Singletary defended his actions by saying the LCC was acting in the best interests of central Kentuckians by bringing them more events, cultural opportunities and more seats for UK basketball games. Plans to enlarge Memorial Coliseum, he said, were abandoned when the interim agreement with the LCC was signed.[305] He sure got a lot of mileage out of expanding the Coliseum scheme.

Singletary put himself in a position where any decision he made alienated one segment or another. He complained the UKAA was carrying the largest financial burden of any group using the center, but that was the result of his own actions. Another talking paper didn't help him decide how much to tell the athletics board about his negotiations with the LCC. As a last resort he appointed an ad hoc committee. If anything else went wrong, he could blame them. The committee was such a jumble of personalities and politics it was difficult to follow his thinking in selecting them. With one exception, they all had one thing in common: none had an official connection with the university.[306]

The committee was composed of Jim Host, holder of game broadcast rights who had his own agenda. Jack Guthrie, director of the Kentucky Derby Festival and Joe Diess, public relations director of Phillip Morris, were both from Louisville. Clyde Mauldin, a Lexington banker and president of the Wildcat Club, was one of the good old boys. Corbin newspaper publisher Jim Crawford, later arrested on drug charges, was another good old boy. Jay Spurrier, a utilities executive and racing commission chairman, was there because of his political contacts. Called a "supper lobbyist" by many, Spurrier later turned informant in the Federal Bureau of Investigation's probe of corruption in state government called, "Bop-Trot," that sent several legislators, including the speaker of the house, to prison. Vice-president Alvin Morris warned Singletary not to give the committee any real power, and to only use them in an advisory capacity.[307]

It wasn't possible to determine if Singletary used the committee at all in his decision about what to tell the athletics board. He finally decided to give the athletics board an artfully abbreviated version of his negotiations with the LCC. The board gave their unanimous consent for him to sign the lease to play Kentucky basketball games in the downtown arena. Had the board acted otherwise, there would have been problems considering the date of the lease. The board approved Singletary's signing the lease with the LCC at their meeting on April 2, 1976. The lease, signed by Singletary and LCC officials was dated April 1, 1976. When I mentioned the conflict in dates to the legal counsel's office they blamed the notary for making a mistake about the dates.[308]

The lease was just about everything the LCC wanted; for the school it was a constant financial drain. The document was a "Roll Over" lease that either side could change or cancel, within a specific time frame, every two years. Rental payments to the LCC were capped at 21.75 percent of earned ticket revenue, and the center received a fifty-cent bond debt fee on each non-student and non-complimentary ticket sold. The LCC received twenty-eight choice, lower arena tickets free. The school was responsible for printing the tickets, and collecting them from students, faculty and staff. Administrators at the director and dean levels collected the students' tickets.[309]

Advance cash payments of $1,000 before each game was standard procedure, but here's the biggie. All income from concessions, souvenirs, tapes and record albums, parking and scoreboard and inside advertising went to the LCC. Singletary even gave the LCC the basketball game program, but where it ended up was even more interesting. The school was required to furnish photographs and editorial material, but received none of the programs' advertising or sales revenue.[310]

From the beginning it was evident the good old boys took Singletary and the school to the cleaners. LCC officials even confirmed that Kentucky basketball was the center's fiscal bread and butter. The first season's figures showed the UKAA paid the LCC $320,506 for the season's use of Rupp Arena. That was considerably more than the $168,865 called for in the lease. There were so many extra items charged to the school, the LCC must have billed them for the toilet paper used in the restrooms.[311]

Twenty years later the school was paying even more to use the leased facilities. Expenses for the 1996-97 season climbed to more than $700,000. The LCC did only routine maintenance on the arena, but it had millions of dollars to expand their convention facilities in the center in an effort to draw more people downtown.[312]

Moving basketball games downtown cost the university even more in lost revenue which they would have received from a new campus arena. The LCC, in 1989-90, netted more than $500,000 from concessions, food sales, novelties, parking and scoreboard advertising from the games. Multiply that by the twenty-four years they played in the arena, and it represented, without taking into consideration outside factors, over $12 million in lost revenue.[313]

There would, of course, have been operating expenses from a campus arena, but the profits would have belonged to the school, not downtown Lexington. There was already an infra-structure in place on campus to handle tickets, parking, maintenance and a police force for security. Campus food facilities would probably have charged less than $7.57 per person for soft drinks and chips served to the media. The school paid the LCC $75 per game for each of the twelve rooms they used on game days for players, athletics directors, coaches, the media, officials, cheerleaders and security. The university had its own printing plant and, if their equipment was insufficient for printing the game program, they could have bid the job out just as they did for other work beyond their capacity. The school could also have improved their facilities by purchasing the equipment to do the work.[314]

Why would a municipal arena want to own a college basketball team's game program? Money. Jim Host, the consultant who pushed to move the games off campus and one of the ultimate good old boys, ended up controlling the game program rights. How did he do that? The LCC conducted no competitive bidding , and Host paid the center an agreed upon price for the program rights.[315]

The only record for the basketball game programs available was for the 1986-87 season. Host claimed he was losing money on his contracts with the school and he wanted athletics director Cliff Hagan to give him a break. Hagan, of course, did. Host's statement showed he grossed $222,129 on the basketball game programs that year, and it wasn't an especially successful season with a record of 18-11. A conservative estimate of the school's losses on the game programs over the last twenty-four years was more than $5 million in gross revenue.[316]

The university's generosity continued in regard to the extra $56,000 a year Singletary had to cough up to play in the downtown arena. The lease called for the LCC to repay the athletics association when they began collecting revenue from the hotel operation. Vice-president Jack C. Blanton tangled with Minter when he asked for the first two payments in 1979. Blanton was a bulldog when it came to money due the school. Minter refused to pay the $112,000 because the lease required them to pay only $56,000 per year. Legal counsel John Darsie got into the dispute, and finally capitulated by saying the school never really expected to get the money back in the first place; that it was a matter of judgement on how far to push the LCC to live up to the terms of the lease.[317] It was the perfect example of how the town and gown relationship worked.

LCC controller Larry Stebleton confirmed the center made the two payments in question, but no more. Nobody seemed to know why no further payments were made or they wouldn't say. Over the twenty-four years the school used Rupp Arena, under the terms of the lease that called for the repayments, the LCC saved $1.3 million and the athletics association ate the loss.[318]

With the records and documents I had access to, it's safe to say Singletary's moving basketball games into the downtown arena cost his athletics program an estimated $34 million in lost revenue. That's not counting what they paid to play in Rupp Arena for twenty-four years.

It was understandable the downtowners went after every cent they could get. They needed it. Early in the process, the LCC fell into deep financial trouble, even with the $4 million Gov. Ford pumped into the project. Whether it was a question of mismanagement or the dilapidated Opera House soaking up money like a sponge, I don't know. By July 1979, the total cost of the project, that began at $28 million, reached $53.4 million.[319]

Singletary endured six seasons in Rupp Arena with only his special reserve seating and holding court in the locker room after games. It just wasn't enough; something was missing in his basketball life. In 1983 he amended the Rupp Arena lease, not to get more money for his athletics program, but to have his own reception area. The locker rooms must have been too crowded. The UKAA paid the LCC $35,000 for 2,500 square feet of the High Street Lobby to create the president's Blue Room. How much the school paid the architectural firm of Chrisman, Miller and Wallace to reconfigure the space wasn't available.[320]

The Blue Room, marked with a door of that color, could comfortably seat seventy-five to 100 guests. It was furnished with sofas, chairs and sectional seating covered with a fabric that felt like silk damask. Three round tables, costing $800 each, seated twenty-four. A large portrait of Rupp hung in the foyer above a console table. Rupp's portrait hanging in a room created by Singletary for his after basketball games' entertainment was something of an paradox.[321]

# WHOSE TRUST IS IT, ANYWAY?

Singletary wasn't a happy camper. He was unable to control campus unrest arising from anti-war and civil rights protests, and he was burned on the downtown arena deal. His stadium project went well, and he efficiently shuffled Rupp into retirement. Athletic coffers were filling nicely, but he wanted more money in his own pocket.

In May 1975, Singletary told trustees he was going back to Texas to meet with Southern Methodist University officials who were searching for a new president. Trustees went into an absolute dither. Athletic life as they knew it could be ending! They passed a resolution of adoration that was just barely short of canonization. The adoration appealed to his ego, but he was after something more substantial.[322]

Singletary wanted more money, and he knew just the person to help him. Strip-mining mogul William B. Sturgill was a close friend of the president but, more importantly, he was chairman of the board of trustees. It doesn't take a mind reader to determine what happened next.[323]

In the trustees' executive committee meeting, Singletary introduced a resolution calling for the chairman of the board to execute the employment contracts of the president and his vice-presidents. With the chairman of the board handling those contracts, the compensation packages were concealed from public knowledge because they were never mentioned in any of the trustees' meeting minutes.[324]

It was exceedingly clever. The resolution was found in trustees' board meeting minutes where the entire body approved the move, but I was unable to locate any further mention of the compensation packages. I explored every possible avenue, and searched documents without success. Even university archivists were at a loss of where else to look. A dead end loomed ahead in my research.

Persistence and diligence, however, have their own reward. While examining some routine files in a box of Singletary's papers, I found a 1986 voucher, drawn on the Margaret Voorhies Haggin Charitable and Educational Trust, calling for a $60,000 payment, "To the trust agreement, June 20, 1975, between the University of Kentucky and Citizens Fidelity Bank and Trust Company for the Benefit of Otis A. Singletary."[325] It was truly the smoking gun I needed, The voucher provided the basis for an Open Records Act request of the legal counsel's office for production of all related records.

Despite the law requiring a reply to an Open Records Act request within three days, the university produced no documents. Accounting department officials stonewalled claiming those particular records were stored in an old warehouse and were difficult to retrieve. It was not even a good evasion. Earlier, I had located a 1991 year-end statement containing the assets of the $20 million James Ben Ali Haggin Trust, of which the university was one of many beneficiaries. I questioned the university's handling of the important trust documents saying, "That's really an irresponsible method of handling records from the school's portion of a $20 million trust, isn't it? Public disclosure of such sloppy record-keeping might effect your donations and development program." Almost overnight the requested documents were made available to me.

Singletary's 1975 employment contract called for a salary of $50,000, an $8,000 increase, plus the usual presidential perks of living in Maxwell Place, two cars, insurance, funded retirement, etc. Documents the school produced, revealed that a special trust was created for Singletary by the trustees' chairman in 1975 that called for *at least* (emphasis mine) $20,00 each year from the Margaret Voorhies Haggin Educational and Charitable Trust to be deposited into Singletary's personal trust at the Louisville bank. Using a Louisville bank instead of one in Lexington lessened the chances of the trust being discovered. The trust document said the university intended "To provide the said salary supplement from private funds available to the institution."[326]

If Singletary's personal trust arrangement was only a salary supplement, then why go to the trouble of changing the contractual procedure of employing a president? Why keep it out of records of trustees' actions? If it was all above board, why hide the trust in a Louisville bank? A copy of the original Haggin Trust answered some of those questions while, at the same time, raising others.

Mrs. Haggin established the trust in 1938 with the university receiving half the income from 150 shares of the estate of her late husband James Ben Ali Haggin. A Harrodsburg native and Centre College graduate, Haggin went to California to practice law in 1851. In the aftermath of the 1849 gold rush, he accumulated a vast fortune. Along with partners Marcus Daly and George Hearst, Haggin owned the home stake in Anaconda Copper. He also owned more than 100 gold, silver and copper mines in the western states, Mexico and South America, including the Cerrode Pasco in Peru. His California ranch was stocked with 2,000 Thoroughbred horses.[327]

After the death of his first wife, Eliza Jane Sanders, Haggin married her young niece, Margaret Voorhies, also from Versailles, in 1889. He purchased Elmendorf Farm on the Paris Pike, and built a palatial twenty-room marble and stone mansion, Green Hills, for his young bride. Bluegrass socialites who frequented the Haggins' lavish parties referred to the mansion as "The Biltmore of Kentucky." In 1905 Haggin sold his California ranch to concentrate on Elmendorf's 8,544 acres that boasted, along with its well-appointed stables, its own power plant, green houses and a dairy that became a model used by the United States government. A system of tunnels allowed employees to reach isolated farm buildings without being exposed to the weather. Haggin could board his private railroad coach in New York, and be deposited at the gates of Green Hills without ever leaving the car. After his death in 1914 at his Newport, Rhode Island, mansion, the settling Haggin's vast estate took ten years. Principal heirs were his second wife, and his five children, some of whom lived in Lexington.[328]

Mrs. Haggin established the trust to honor her husband, but it carried her name. The James Ben Ali Haggin Trust, Inc., was administered by the Bank of New York. Mrs. Haggin's trust was also handled by the same bank and one other trustee. Other recipients of the income from the 150 shares were the Woodford County Hospital, in Versailles, and an educational institution or charity yet to be named. Trustees could change the trust's recipients as they chose.[329]

What does the Haggin Trust have to do with athletics? Not only did Singletary dip into the Haggin Trust for his own gain, but he used their funds for athletically-related purposes which appeared to violate the HagginTrust's 1938 authorizing document.

The Margaret Voorhies Haggin Educational and Charitable Trust was a broadly drawn document that contained two clear provisions: no part of the trust was to be used to benefit an individual, and none of the funds were to be used to lobby or influence legislation. Documents in Singletary's papers showed that he used Haggin Trust funds to pay for personal items, food, furnishings for his stadium lounge, game programs for guests in his stadium box, basketball tickets, membership in exclusive clubs, magazine subscriptions, license plates for the car the university furnished him and even the gasoline he used in it. This was the same trust that paid $64 for flowers for Adolph Rupp's funeral. The lavish pre-game football luncheons were also paid for with Haggin Trust money, and the invitation list for those events read like a lobbyist's dream.[330]

Like earlier presidents, Singletary sought clarification of the exact nature of the Haggin Trust funds. Haggin trustee William Haup told McVey in 1938, the indenture contained no restriction upon the use of the income by the university. Apparently Haup didn't read the trust carefully. Legal counsel Henry Durham told Dickey in 1964, the indenture was "So general in nature that it would be difficult to argue that any legitimate expense paid for with Haggin Trust funds were not for the general welfare of the university."[331]

In 1970 Singletary had his legal counsel, John Darsie, make discreet inquiries of his contact at the Bank of New York to determine if there were trustees other than the bank and Miss Laura Christianson. When assured they were the only trustees, Singletary plied the lady with books, gifts and letters of flowery prose while sending her carefully edited reports of Haggin Trust expenditures. Miss Christianson asked few questions other than why the annual reports were sometimes late.[332]

Singletary's use of Haggin Trust funds were too numerous to detail, but there were some interesting expenditures. Trust funds paid $53,000 for china, crystal and fine prints for his lounge at the stadium. In 1983, trust monies paid $2,300 for a television set for Maxwell Place, and $8,000 for football and basketball tickets and game programs for his stadium box. Before the 1984 Vanderbilt game, the Singletarys hosted 200 for a pre-game luncheon, and the Haggin Trust picked up the $3,500 bill plus the tab from a Cincinnati florist for $183.[333]

In 1985, the president's office spent $47,000 in Haggin Trust funds for pre-game luncheons; a basketball dinner; legislative, alumni and faculty receptions; membership in Lexington's exclusive Idle Hour Country Club, that had no black or Jewish members; the Keeneland (Race Course) Association box; publication subscriptions and other items.[334]

The legislative receptions, basketball dinners and pre-game luncheons were filled with elected and appointed state and federal officials who held positions where their authority could, and probably did, benefit Singletary and/or the university. It would be naive to think Singletary failed to lobby those officials at events paid for with Haggin Trust funds. When asked about his method of lobbying, Singletary was evasive, saying, "If you mean, 'do I like pounding the corridors?' No, I've never liked that. Different people will do it different ways."[335]

Haggin Trust year-end statements were carefully prepared. Even the statements' preliminary work, found in Singletary's papers, were edited until it was difficult to determine just where the money went. A comparison of the year-end statements for the 1975 and 1976 fiscal years revealed where the first $20,000 payment into Singletary's trust was apparently closeted. The 1975 statement listed $6,117 in Haggin Trust funds spent on special insurance for the president. The next year's statement listed an expenditure of $26,622 for special insurance for him. During the next twelve years, Haggin Trust funds deposited into Singletary's personal trust grew from $20,000 to $40,000 to $60,000 for each of his last two years in office.[336]

Singletary wasn't the only president to use Haggin Trust funds, but he probably spent the most. Donovan and some of his top administrators used trust funds to supplement salaries during the WW II state employee salary freeze. Donovan's retirement was modestly supplemented with $3,500 a year from the trust. Dickey and Oswald were both careful in handling the trust monies. Before Singletary took office, Haggin Trust funds had ten accounts handled by various administrators. During his term, the president's office alone had seven funded Haggin Trust accounts with forty-seven others in various departments.[337]

For years the Haggin Trust funded graduate fellowships, as they did under Singletary. Trust funds also built a men's dormitory, paid for Memorial Hall's organ, purchased property adjoining the campus and provided seed money for the University Press. Much of the money served the purpose Mrs. Haggin intended.[338]

The Lexington Haggins were among the social elite of the Bluegrass, and had connections with Kentucky athletics. Louis L. Haggin served on McVey's athletic council in the 1930s. A staffer on one of the Thoroughbred magazines, who wished to remain anonymous, described him as being more occupied with his dogs and clipping bond coupons than with athletics. Doug Parrish, married to Louis L. Haggin's sister,

Emily, was appointed to the athletics board by Dickey for his matrimonial connections alone.[339]

Haggin's Green Hills mansion was sold and torn down in the 1930s, so the story goes, because the owners wanted to avoid paying property taxes on the mansion. All that remains of the Biltmore of Kentucky are the mansion's four graceful columns and two statues of lions. For years, the columns and lions were the elegant background for the Lexington Ball, a charitable dinner and dance held the night before the running of the Blue Grass Stakes Race at Keeneland. Two generations of Haggins, Louis Lee II and Louis Lee III, and their wives served on the ball's committees.[340]

With his personal trust established and other perks, some paid for with Haggin Trust funds, Singletary decided to remain at Kentucky. He remembered the man who helped him out in 1975, William B. Sturgill, and honored him by naming the Outstanding Faculty of the Year Award for the strip-mining mogul. The $2,000 stipend professors received came not from Sturgill's deep pockets but from the Haggin Trust.[341]

In 1975 president Jimmy Carter asked Singletary to chair the National Endowment for the Humanities. By then his base salary had grown to $70,000 a year plus all the perks afforded by the Haggin Trust. Again, he decided to remain at Kentucky where, in the next ten years, he padded his retirement assets, achieved his athletic ambitions and brought the university its most embarrassing athletics scandal since the point shaving debacle and the "sudden death" penalty in 1952.[342]

# THE GREAT INDIANA CAPER
# & OTHER FOLLIES

Sitting on national athletic committees studying the problems of college football, chairing the College Football Association and negotiating multi-million-dollar television contracts left Singletary little time to keep watch on his own campus where there were major problems with rape, drugs and murder. His own football and basketball programs were rife with violations.

Initially it appeared Curci would be the exception to Kentucky being the "Graveyard of SEC football coaches." His first team was 5-6, and he was SEC Coach of the Year. In 1974, the team was 6-5, and a game short of an invitation to the Liberty Bowl. The next year his record declined to 2-8-1, and gave the faithful a scare. Curci, bounced back in 1975 with a 9-3 record and the school's second SEC championship. Thousands braved an ice storm to glide down I-75 to the Peach Bowl in Atlanta where Kentucky defeated North Carolina 21-0.[343]

Recruiting problems coincided with Curci's arrival, and one of the examples was James "Dinkey" McKay. A student at Mississippi's Gulf Coast Junior College, McKay accepted financial aid from Kentucky and practiced with the team before he graduated. The NCAA came calling again. Athletics director Harry Lancaster admitted there was a tiny violation, but denied any intentional wrong doing. Investigators said otherwise, and McKay was lost to the team. Lancaster appealed to the committee on infractions and the full NCAA council, but nothing changed.[344]

In 1974 athletic officials knew it was only a matter of time until the NCAA would return again, and they began damage control. In October, law school dean William Matthews, Singletary and Donovan's well-used operative, Lancaster and his assistant Cliff Hagan, vice-president Alvin Morris and Curci began discussing a possible investigation. Singletary presumably was taking care of national athletic business. Notes from their weekly meetings indicated they suspected the NCAA was looking for the football team's slush fund. Matthews fingered a former recruit, Elvis Peacock, who he thought might have told the NCAA about the fund.[345]

Their meeting notes indicated they wanted posterity to know they weren't really investigating, but just checking rumors. Their actions said otherwise. They decided to halt all activity; presumably, the slush fund. What had happened in the past they would defend as much as possible, but would take no responsibility for what happened in the immediate future. Their major concern appeared to be money from outside sources going directly to football players.[346]

That certainly wasn't a new problem at the school. It was what brought the NCAA's first "sudden death" sanction down on them in 1952. From all indications, the school previously received several similar penalties from the SIAA in the early years.

Instead of correcting the problem, they did what Kentucky had always done; found another way to channel illegal money to the players. In the future, they decided to route money and other items through the K-Men, an organization of former athletes who earned varsity letters. Since the K-Men was one of the booster clubs attached to athletics, they thought it would be safe. When Singletary reorganized the athletics board, he made the K-Men's president a voting member.[347]

Without a doubt Singletary knew what was happening as Morris would have kept him informed. His athletic administrators were too well versed in his on-hands management procedures to do otherwise. Had nothing else occurred, their ruse might have worked.

In November 1975 the first of many problems surfaced in Curci's program. Former All-American Elmore Stephens was implicated in a homicide investigation, and later went to prison on the charge. The team's star running back, Alford, "Sonny" Collins, Jr., was questioned several times during the investigation. The investigation revealed what many had known for months, Sonny Collins lived a lifestyle that was far beyond the means of an athlete on a grant-in-aid. Collins lived in an off-campus apartment complex where the least expensive unit rented for $195 a month. Collins' father, a Madisonville fork-lift operator, said he paid the apartment's rent. There were no explanations for the sources of revenue that provided the late model luxury car Collins drove, his expensive clothes or the extended trip he took to Las Vegas with a man said to be a heavy bettor on college football games.[348]

Rumors of athletes' drug use surfaced. After the January 1976 investigation was completed, Singletary announced that twenty-three students, including sixteen football players, were disciplined by the school for violating the drug section of the student code. The drug problems, he said, "Left an implication that was basically unhealthy and many fine young men were not involved." Keeping the investigation on campus lessened the negative publicity. Singletary's solution was to instruct Hagan, by then athletics director, to review the athletes' drug education program, to move the team into a campus housing facility and to improve his supervision of the program.[349]

Hagan dragged his feet for seven years before implementing a comprehensive drug testing program for all athletes. He appeared more concerned that the media might learn about the testing procedures than the drug problem itself. Hagan did move the team into student housing, and quipped, "I'll jokingly say we might need to get them (the team) back in a dorm to keep the average student from contaminating them." Hagan's supervision of the athletics program was learned from his mentor, Singletary.[350]

Curci built a reasonably successful football program, and that appeared not to sit well for Hall, who had his own problems. Eager to make a name for himself as Rupp's successor, Hall was only .688 his first four years although his teams won two SEC titles. The 1974-75 team lost the final game in the NCAA tournament to UCLA 92-85. The next year Hall's team had a 20-10 season, but won the NIT over UNC Charlotte 71-67. By 1977, his team improved to 26-4, won the SEC, but lost to North Carolina 79-72 in the NCAA east regional tournament. Hall's best season was 1977-78 when his team, with All-Americans Jack "Goose" Givens and Rick Robey, Kyle Macy (an All-American the next year), Mike Phillips and Truman Clator ended a 30-2 season by beating Duke 92-88 for the national championship, Kentucky's fifth.[351]

For some reason Hall's teams never had official nicknames. His national championship team, with the twin towers of Robey and Phillips, could have certainly been called the "Intimidators." All season, the media remarked about how serious and business-like they were, and how they appeared to have little fun playing Hall's constrained-style of offense. Race horse basketball was a staple offense at Kentucky, but Hall wanted to put is own imprint on the game. After he retired, and went to work for a Lexington bank, one of the local jokes was that during a bank robbery he yelled, "Don't shoot," at the guards thinking he was back on the basketball court.

The real story of Hall's program was how he approached recruiting with such frenzy. "The Great Indiana Caper" in December 1974 was a case in point. One of the finest high school basketball players in the nation that season was Kent Benson, of New Castle, Indiana, who averaged twenty-eight points and thirty rebounds a game. He appeared headed for Indiana to play for Hall's arch rival, Bobby Knight. Hall, determined to change Benson's mind, led a delegation to visit the player and his family in New Castle. Accompanying him were Singletary; Seth Hancock, scion of Paris' famous Claiborne Farm; multi-millionaire businessman and trustee Albert Clay, and the Rev. Larry Hehman, a priest from the Newman Center that adjoined the campus.[352]

Benson's father owned a farm implement business and, during the visit, happened to mention to Clay that his allotment of Allis Chamlers diesel tractors fell short of customer demands. Clay sprung into action calling David Scott, chairman of Allis Chamlers and a Kentucky alumnus. Scott invited Benson to dinner and a tour of the factory. Clay, however, couldn't leave well enough alone. Two brand new Allis Chamlers diesel tractors suddenly showed up at Benson's dealership. "I probably cut him off pretty short," Benson said, "but no way was I going to take the tractors that way."[353]

Clay didn't give up, and relentlessly doubled his efforts to bring the player to Kentucky. After the Bensons flew to Lexington, in a private plane, for the athlete's campus visit, Clay wrote Robert Benson that his son would never regret signing with Kentucky. His letter, between the lines, was rich with promised favors. "I'll always be available to counsel with him for you on any problem he might have," Clay told Benson, "and will take a personal interest in him throughout his career." Leaving nothing to chance, Clay asked Scott to call Robert Benson and tell him "That the personal attention I will give Kent, as expressed in my letter, could have great bearing on his future, and I intend to live up to that statement." Singletary's initials were on copies of Clay's letters to Benson and Scott.[354]

When the Benson recruiting story broke, all but the Rev. Hehman ran for cover. Robert Benson pulled no punches as he recounted the recruiting visit and its aftermath. Clay, through his secretary, issued a statement saying he was unavailable and would have no comment. Scott's office said he was traveling and unable to return telephone calls. Hancock had the best excuse. He was the man who executed multi-million-dollar syndications of Thoroughbred stallions, such as the great Secretariat, but remembered absolutely nothing about the Indiana trip to recruit the nation's best basketball player for Kentucky.[355]

Singletary got himself into a real bind even discussing the trip with the media. Apparently, he admitted he was aware of improper offers made to the Bensons, but quickly declared, "I was not present; I did not hear that conversation; that was not said in my presence." When the reporter called back for clarification, Singletary refused to take the call.356

The Rev. Hehman said Hall asked him to go on the trip because the Bensons were Catholic. "If that were true, what Clay did, I would think the Bensons would be upset because I don't think they would have done anything (accept the tractors) like that," the priest said.357 Benson signed with Indiana.

Kentucky's soft underbelly of athletic improprieties smelled loud enough in June 1976 for the NCAA to notify Singletary their committee on infractions was conducting an investigation. Three months later, the school sent their response to the committee's allegations. None of those documents were found in Singletary's papers. Along with ten university athletic officials, Singletarys flew to Kansas City on a state-owned plane in October to defend his program.358 He might as well have saved the commonwealth's money.

The NCAA, two months later, found Kentucky guilty of fifty-one violations. Seventeen were in improper recruiting, twenty-one concerned illegal benefits given athletes and three were improper inducements. Others included two out-of-season football practices, a hold over from coach Charlie Bradshaw's days when such practices were called physical conditioning, and three false certifications of compliance with NCAA regulations and rules. The violations revealed how far Singletary had let his athletics program slide. Evidently, he practically begged the committee for mercy.359

NCAA president Arthur Reynolds confirmed that saying the penalties would have been more severe if the university had failed to self-disclose many violations his investigators missed relating to the football program. Kentucky's standard operation, in those circumstances, was to reveal violations they were likely to get minor penalties for, but rest assured they didn't bare their athletic soul. Reynolds complimented the school for severing relations with numerous representatives of the school's athletic interests who were significantly involved in the violations.[360]

After receiving notification of the penalties, Singletary called a rare 9:00 a.m. board meeting to lightly touch on the response prepared by law professor Robert Lawson, legal counsels Joe Burch and John Darsie and himself. He had no intentions of going into the fifty-one violations. He informed the board there would be no discussion of personalities, penalties or actions taken against coaches or representatives of the school's athletic interests. Singletary said he regretted the findings of the violations and wished they hadn't occurred but he felt the committee on infractions had been fair.[361]

His willingness to cooperate with the NCAA, he told the board, was part of the membership relationship and the decent thing to do. Decency had little to do with anything. Saving Singletary's national athletic reputation was at the top of his agenda. The real purpose of the meeting was to inform the board of his disagreement with the NCAA's definition of representatives of the school's athletic interests. That term, he said, "Covers both those whom you have asked for help, and those who become persons the university is responsible for without your knowledge." The problem, he emphasized, was maintaining control over people you didn't know.[362]

Singletary had to be one of the most astute politicians around. He sold that explanation to the board, and they gobbled it up like it was gospel. Lexington was a small city, and the circle of movers and shakers was even smaller. Just about everybody knew everybody else.

Eighteen of the violations Singletary chose not to contest or discuss with the board concerned actions taken by representatives of the university's athletic interests. They weren't strangers; Singletary knew most of them. The school, at the NCAA's strong urging, disassociated eleven of those representatives from their athletics program. They were Malcolm Burnside, Harley Clemons, J.W. Davis, Tom Gentry, Seth Hancock, Joe Holland, Tom Ligon, J.D. Reeves, Gene Sageser, Tom Ward and James

Lambert. Noticeably absent from that list were Albert Clay, a refugee from "The Great Indiana Caper," Warren Rosenthal, a fast food executive, who made one of his restaurants and his corporate jet available to the coaches, and a number of other good old boys.[363]

Singletary knew Hancock well from his large contributions to the athletics program and as his traveling companion on the Benson recruiting trip. The youngest son of Claiborne Farm founder Arthur "Bull" Hancock, he succeeded his father as the head of the farm where such famous stallions as Bold Ruler, Mr. Prospector and Secretariat stood at stud. Claiborne was a popular stop on Hall's recruiting trail, and employed a number of players during the summers. It wasn't possible to determine if Singletary knew Harley Clemons or not. Clemons was then the son-in-law of Hall of Fame trainer Woody Stephens, who trained a number of Claiborne's horses.[364]

It was impossible that Singletary didn't know J.W. Davis, whose tickets came from the allotment the president and Lancaster confiscated from Rupp when he retired. A prominent developer, Davis and Singletary traveled in some of the same social circuits. Three of the allegations involved athletes' illegal use of automobiles. Joe Holland, a member of Rupp's 1948 championship team and one of the Indianapolis Olympians, owned automobile dealerships. Tom Gentry was a party-giving, flamboyant horseman who it was impossible for Singletary not to know. Gentry later went to prison for money laundering and concealing assets in bankruptcy proceedings. J.D. Reeves, an officer in Lexington's largest bank and a member of the Wildcat Club, was a frequent guest in Lancaster's box at football games. Gene Sageser, a local businessman, also belonged to the Wildcat Club, but Singletary probably recognized the name. Tom Ward, a Versailles minister and legislator, corresponded with the president.[365]

One of the NCAA violations concerned athletes being furnished with gambling tickets and alcoholic beverages at a local bar. James Lambert was an owner of the Library Lounge, located near the campus. Lambert's close friends included John Y. Brown, Jr., famed Thoroughbred hostess and patroness of the wrestling team Anita Madden and Drew Thornton, a former Lexington narcotics officer who died after his parachute failed to open over Knoxville, Tennessee, with bags of cocaine strapped to his body. Lambert was said to be the man who accompanied football star, "Sonny" Collins, to Las Vegas.[366]

If Singletary didn't know Lambert, he certainly knew who he was. It was impossible to live in Lexington and not hear of Jimmy Lambert. His name was in the news regarding the missing sister of former Cincinnati Reds player Doug Flynn, Melanie Flynn, whose strange disappearance is still shrouded in mystery. The Flynn family lived in Lexington. In 1984, Lambert and Phillip Brock, a nephew of former governor Julian Carroll, were indicted in Federal District Court on sixty-seven counts of drug trafficking. In a related case, Lambert and Anita Madden were indicted on theft of grand jury materials, but were acquitted at their trial. Lambert, after appealing his case to the Supreme Court, was sentenced to five years in prison. He was described by Sally A. Denton in *The Bluegrass Conspiracy* as belonging to "The Company," a group of former Lexington narcotics officers gone bad, their close associates, and their alleged involvement in drugs, murder and other crimes.[367]

Ten of the violation related to assistant football coaches who arranged free flights for players' families to attend games, supervised the illegal practices, provided cash and clothing to athletes and made payments to players who performed certain plays on the field well. The money, the NCAA said, came from "A fund established by representatives of the university's athletic interests." Head trainer Al Green, the NCAA said, arranged free lodging for parents of injured players when they came to Lexington for their sons' surgeries.[368]

Hall's program had its share of violations. The NCAA said Hall and a former assistant provided improper gifts to induce players to sign with Kentucky. There was, of course, "The Great Indiana Caper." The program paid the expenses for a prospective recruit's father to visit the campus. For three years, Hall allowed his players to receive free gifts and movie passes.[369]

For the fifty-three violations, the NCAA gave Kentucky a slap on the wrist that included a public reprimand and censure, probation for two years and periodic reviews. Curci's football program was denied post-season play, televised games in 1977 and a one year loss of five grants-in-aid. Hall's program was restricted to three scholarships for two years, a loss of two each year.[370]

Of course, Singletary didn't want to appeal such light punishment nor call any more negative publicity to his athletics program run amuck. He was the one who accepted the athletics director's assurance each year that the football and basketball programs were in compliance with NCAA regulations and rules.

The NCAA's periodic reviews turned up only minor transgressions. In 1978, an assistant football coach was reprimanded for providing free transportation for friends of a recruit. In 1982, the tennis program gave nearly fifty percent more scholarships than they were allotted. In 1984, the women's basketball coach took a prospective recruit and her parents to lunch, and listed it on her expense account.[371]

During the Curci years Singletary never knew what was going to happen next. In March 1979, campus police arrested eight football players and charged them with the first degree rape and sodomy of a professor's daughter. From all accounts in was a gang-bang rape of the worst kind, and occurred in the football dorm. Curci suspended the players, and placed them on disciplinary probation until the case was solved. Nobody believed they would ever be tried on the charges.[372]

Susan Rice, director of the Rape Crisis Center, was furious about how the nasty charges were handled. "We may be the only agency working with the victim," she said, "that has any concern for her mental and physical state. People are looking for an out for these boys. I have never lived anywhere else where there was such an incredible sports mania among the general public." She was right. A Fayette County grand jury refused to indict the players. Curci suspended them for a year, but allowed them to keep their grants-in-aid.[373]

A year later, three other players, a former teammate and a co-ed pleaded guilty to stealing stereo and football equipment from Shively Sports Center and hiding it in the girl's apartment. In May 1981, two more football players were indicted on first degree rape charges involving a nineteen-year-old co-ed in the football dorm. As his teams' off the field conduct deteriorated, Curci's won-loss record slipped.[374]

Given more time, Curci might have turned his program around but the man who insisted he take the job, John Y. Brown, Jr., was elected governor in 1979, and wanted instant football success for his alma mater. During the 1981 Kentucky Derby, Brown began talking with former Washington Redskins coach, George Allen, about the head coach's job. The governor failed to mention that to Singletary, whose nose went out of joint when he heard it from the media. Singletary stiffly reminded Brown there was no vacancy and, when there was, a procedure was in place to handle it. Curci asked what all the fuss was about since he had three years left on his contract? Allen, caught between the governor and the university president, withdrew his name for a position that wasn't vacant.[375]

Brown blasted Singletary and his athletic officials, "We can look forward to continuing that great tradition of 30 years of losing." He charged the athletics board members were all from academics, "There's not half of the 22-member board that know a volleyball from a football." Brown said he entertained the idea of by-passing Singletary and hiring Allen anyway, but didn't carry through. Rumors circulated that Curci was finished.[376]

It was another athletics mess, but illustrated just how serious Kentuckians take their sports. All that kept the commonwealth from being at the bottom of the national educational barrel was Arkansas and Mississippi, and the governor was spending his time looking for a college football coach.

Singletary didn't have time for a talking paper so he appointed another ad hoc committee. This time he took no chances, and put Hagan in the committee chair to make a recommendation on Curci's contract. The committee advised the coach's contract be terminated. All the board members except "Happy" Chandler voted to buy out Curci's contract for $46,725 a year. Hagan telephoned Curci with the news.[377]

Unlike his predecessors, Curci didn't leave quietly, and had a few things to say. He reminded Singletary that Rupp wasn't fired when his team received the "sudden death" penalty in 1952. He labeled the board's decision to fire him gutless; said Hagan's telephone call had no class; called Singletary's ad hoc committee a kangaroo court and stated, "Now that I am buried in that famous graveyard at UK, along with some other wonderful coaches, I hope they say on my tombstone that while at Kentucky he was a decent person who was twice SEC coach of the year." Curci's eight-year record was 47-51-2.[378]

Curci took a banking position in Hazard with his good friend, William Gorman, did color commentary for games on radio and television , but kept some of his Kentucky connections. For years, Curci returned to Lexington to appear on the annual televised fund raiser for the Cardinal Hill Rehabilitation Hospital.

A new football coach was selected within two weeks and, by some streak of luck, the selection was outstanding. Jerry Claiborne, then coaching at Maryland, agreed to come back to Kentucky where he played for and coached under Paul "Bear" Bryant. He followed Bryant to Texas A & M and to Alabama before becoming head coach at Virginia Tech in 1961. There were a number of points in Claiborne's favor: he was a seasoned coach at fifty-three; his programs had never been investigated by the NCAA; most importantly, ninety-three percent of his players graduated. Claiborne's five-year contract paid him $50,000 a year, and the media estimated his income would top $100,000 with endorsements, camps, radio and television shows. His first season was an 0-10-1 disaster, but he was rebuilding a program that was the laughing stock of the SEC.[379]

# BOSS OF BUILDINGS, TYCOON OF TICKETS

If awards were given for audacity, Singletary would have had a closet full. While his basketball and football teams were still on probation from the 1976 investigation, he joined in a scheme to build them special housing clearly in violation of NCAA rules. He stonewalled implementation of Title IX, equal funding for men and women's sports, by holding the United States government at bay as long as possible without losing the school's federal funding. When it came to hoarding game tickets, he had few peers.

In May 1976 basketball coach Joe B. Hall wanted to build special housing for his team on university-owned property across the street from Memorial Coliseum. A lease-purchase arrangement failed because the gap between income and cost was too high. Hall had another idea. In only four years, he had cultivated enough of the deep pockets and good old boys that he took an architect's rendering of a the basketball house on the road and, in six weeks, collected commitments for over $650,000.[380]

Singletary asked law professor William Matthews to find a way around NCAA regulations prohibiting special housing for athletes so they could build the house. Matthews, to his credit, told him NCAA Recommendation Policy No. 9 was very clear: athletes were to live in the same facilities as other students. That wasn't what Singletary wanted to hear. The good old boys anted up over a half-million-dollars, and he had no intentions of disappointing them. Matthews hedged saying, in a technical sense, NCAA policies didn't exactly obligate an institution in the same way as constitutional provisions, by-laws or executive regulations. That was more acceptable to Singletary. Matthews did warn him that, since they were still on probation from the 1976 violations, to get NCAA clearance before proceeding with building the house. His advice was ignored.[381]

As UKAA architect of choice Don Wallace, of Lexington, put the final touches on plans for the house, athletic officials set up the non-profit Wildcat Foundation to receive the donations Hall rounded up. Thirty-six deep pockets gave cash, signed notes, made deferred payment arrangements or pledged amounts ranging from $5,000 to $50,000. There were other smaller donations of cash as well as in-kind contributions of paving, soil-treatment and ready-mix concrete.[382]

As the starkly modern, three-story building took shape, nothing was heard from the NCAA. It was indeed lavish for a college dorm. A Louisville firm of interior decorators used specially treated coal for the living room's huge fireplace to compliment natural wood paneling on the walls and leather furniture. A circular sofa in the meeting room could seat the entire team and coaching staff. The study featured a double hearth fireplace of Kentucky River stone with comfortable sofas and chairs. Bedrooms had extra-long beds and private bathroom fixtures were scaled to accommodate the tall athletes. Guests suites were equally lavish. All the telephone were blue and white, and there was a picture of Hall in every room. Basement recreation rooms, decorated in blue and white, had a wide-screen television, a pinball machine, sauna, projection room and another meeting room.[383]

There was a vast contrast between the basketball house, known as Joe B. Hall Wildcat Lodge, and the spartan institutional furnishings of the campus dorms that housed other students.

Hall's 1977-78 team won the SEC and NCAA championships, and media coverage showed them in the luxurious Wildcat Lodge. The coverage caught the attention of a disgruntled conference commissioner. The NCAA, who should have noticed the Lodge earlier if they had been conducting their periodic checks, conducted a secret investigation. In July 1979 they broadsided athletic officials with an edict to make changes in the Lodge before the first of August or any athlete living there would lose his eligibility.[384]

Robert C. James, Atlantic Coast Conference commissioner, told the NCAA about the Lodge. James, who apparently never saw the building, told NCAA executive director Walther Byers that Kentucky had remodeled a local mansion and turned it into a rich man's club for the basketball team. Byers quietly dispatched his investigators to Lexington.[385]

Singletary called it a disaster, and hastily called a meeting of athletic officials to decide on a course of action. They decided, as usual, to stonewall. Instead of admitting their mistake and correcting it themselves, they began to search for reasons to justify the Lodge. Larry Ivy, assistant athletics director, thought he found the answer at Kansas where athletes lived in special dorms. KU's football and basketball teams lived in one of four dorm towers owned by Phillips 66 Oil Company and leased to the school. That the occupants of the other three towers were students, not athletes, shot down Ivy's theory.[386]

Athletic official weren't taking any chances, and rushed to make the needed changes before August 1. Single rooms were converted for double occupancy; every other bathroom was locked; plush furnishings were removed and replaced with furniture similar to other dorms; black telephones replaced the blue and white ones; the wide-screen television was gone; basement fireplaces were rendered inoperative, and students, who weren't athletes, were brought in to equate the occupancy ratio in other university housing.[387]

Not good enough, NCAA director of enforcement William B. Hunt told athletics director Cliff Hagan. The two guest suites had to be converted into space for eight students. Private baths must be rendered inoperative not just locked. Fine art prints, not relating to athletics, had to be removed. Walls, denying occupants access to the first and second floor lounges, had to be built. "We assume," Hagan said sarcastically, "that this does not preclude student athletes' admittance for special functions of the department through other entrances."[388]

The lavish furnishing, not including the donated items, cost $75,000 in Blue White funds. They were auctioned off at a sale that drew little interest. University officials claimed they could find no record of the total amounts of the sale. Singletary later told Byers that forcing Kentucky to make those changes in the Lodge "Was the pickiest thing the NCAA ever did."[389]

Actually, the NCAA cut athletic officials some slack. They allowed them to keep the operation of the Lodge in the athletics department instead of placing it in university housing like other dorms. That later proved to be a big mistake.

Before the Lodge was finished, Curci began lobbying Singletary to build a similar structure for the football team. Gov. Julian Carroll offered Singletary and Curci $1 million in state funds for a football house. Athletic officials were confident they could raise the remainder from private sources. Wallace did another rendering of a 40,465 square-foot structure that would cost $2.2 million. They ran into all sorts of roadblocks, none of which should have been a surprise.[390]

None of Curci's teams had won a national championship. Public awareness of their adverse behavior off the field was mounting. Fund raising slowed, and Singletary and his minions lobbied Carroll, without success, for more money. They were unable to use the Wildcat Foundation for Carroll to channel the money through because it was a private entity. The ever creative Jack Blanton, vice-president for business affairs, suggested the university give the land to the state, let them build the football house and then give, or lease it back to the school.[391]

That wouldn't work for several reasons. The regional universities would demand equal treatment from taxpayers dollars. Singletary had spent a decade avoiding implementing Title IX, a federal law requiring equal facilities and programs for men and women. His time was running out. Blanton warned him, "Should the university be found out of compliance with Title IX, the shut-off of all federal dollars to this institution becomes imminent." Then, Blanton had another idea. He suggested they get around Title IX by housing both men and women in the football house with a wall separating them. Considering the problems Curci's players had with women off the field, that wasn't a good idea either.[392]

In June 1979 the media discovered plans for the football house, and a barrage of negative publicity resulted. Singletary started another talking paper to work his way through the mess. He complained that state funds were used for the football house at the University of Louisville, and no one objected. He blamed Curci for talking him into beginning the fund raising drive for the project in the first place. Not only did he hate to give the private funds back, but he could see Carroll's $1 million slipping away. "*UK only* institution that has not used appropriations$ (state money) for athletics program; hypocrisy, very selected outrage over spending taxpayers' $ for athletic budgets; make this apply to everyone, not just UK."[393]

Once again, Singletary forgot a few facts. Taxpayers' money provided the $3 million for the escrow account for debt payments on the stadium revenue bonds. If that amount continued to draw seven percent interest, over the thirty-year life of the bonds, then about $8.25 million, in state funds, went into the stadium. Gov. Wendell Ford sent $4 million through the university to the LCC when Rupp Arena was built for Kentucky basketball. More than $600,000 in state funds went into Memorial Coliseum.[394]

It was amazing the time and effort Singletary put into building the basketball Lodge and efforts to save the football house when he gave little or no attention to building an on-campus arena where the university would have benefitted from all the revenue.

Singletary was in another box he crafted. If he pushed for the continuance of the football house it meant a sure fight with the faculty and the student newspaper. The Council on Higher Education was just waiting to ambush him on the project. He finally decided the football house just wasn't worth the price. Losing Carroll's million dollars was sand in his craw as he complained, "Double standards, UK athletics program only one in the state not heavily subsidized by taxpayers."[395]

Had the football house been similar to the Aquatic Center, that Singletary called "A hole in the ground," he was fortunate it wasn't built. Title IX finally caught up with Singletary ten years after it was implemented. After numerous complaints, such as *Mernaugh v University of Kentucky*, were filed with Health, Education and Welfare's office of Civil Rights, Singletary finally capitulated over women's swimming in particular and women's sports in general. He pushed the envelope as far as he could, but he didn't dare lose the federal funds coming to the university.[396]

The school's only swimming pool was in the basement of Memorial Coliseum. The women's swim team was able to use the pool only when the men's team, faculty and staff were finished with it. Ray Mernaugh charged in his complaint that the men's swimming team had varsity status while the women's team was a club sport; men had a budget for travel, equipment and a coach while the women received $350 from campus recreation and used volunteer coaches.[397]

Nursing school dean Marion McKenna headed Singletary's committee on women's sports. It just looked better to have a woman in that position but, make no mistake about it, McKenna always followed Singletary's instructions. In 1981, nearly ten years after Title IX became law, McKenna saw no reason to elevate women's swimming to varsity status. The reason, McKenna told the athletics board, was a lack of funds. That statement resulted from one of three things: she was woefully uninformed; deliberately misled the board, or was following Singletary's instructions. When she made that statement, the UKAA, that had included women sports since 1978, had $7.3 million stashed in savings drawing interest.[398]

Singletary's attitude toward women's sports was at best slanted, and at worst chauvinistic. To give women equal footing with men grated on every shred of his athletic soul. He chaired a SEC committee on women's athletics, and his report stated that men's programs had to be protected at all costs. His report also suggested that if the administrators and managers of women's sports wanted a part in the SEC decision-making process they should relay their ideas to their male counterparts who would, if they so chose, discuss them in the conference setting.[399]

Regardless of those facts, Singletary attempted to influence his legacy in women's athletics. He ordered an institutional self study of the school progress in women's athletics in 1982. The results were amazing. "The merger of men and women's athletic programs under the UKAA came in advance of the mandates of Title IX, federal legislation requiring equal opportunity and financial supports for women's athletics," the report stated. That wasn't correct. Women's sports became a part of the UKAA in 1978, but, Title IX became law in 1972 and that move in no way related to equal funding then or now.[400]

It was another year after Singletary's in-house report was published before women's swimming was finally given varsity status. In 1984 Singletary boasted to the media that UK had just budgeted $1 million for women's athletics. "The university had done well in putting resources in that area," he bragged, "I don't think it's generally realized how much we've done with regard to women's athletics." Assistant athletics director Larry Ivy continued the dog and pony show, "The figure probably put us somewhere in the top five (programs) in the country. I'm not talking about the top five in the SEC, but in the country." At that time men's sports, including football, had a budget of $7.2 million.[401]

Singletary's decade-long delay in implementing Title IX put the university far behind other schools in funding women's sports. When C.M. Newton became athletics director in 1988, he began building up the women's sports program, but Singletary's ten-year delay in implementing Title IX put the school close to the bottom of the pile. In 1998, Kentucky ranked 264 among the 287 NCAA Division 1 schools in spending on women's sports as compared to men's athletics.[402]

Singletary reluctantly agreed to build the aquatic center in 1984. The pressure to implement Title IX gave him little choice. How the center was built was a perfect illustration of what happens when college athletics becomes mired in state politics. Don Wallace, the UKAA architect of choice for the aquatic center, was quite familiar with state construction projects. In 1978, Wallace's firm, Christman, Miller and Wallace, was suspected of running up so much expense in redesign fees there wasn't enough money to complete all the buildings in the Kentucky Horse Park's master plan.[403] The omitted structures were later built at an additional cost.

The architect's political connections were set in concrete, so to speak. Wallace left CMW and began his own architectural firm, DEW, Inc. In 1992 a state circuit judge revoked his firm's charter over Wallace's illegal corporate campaign contribution to first lady Martha Wilkinson's gubernatorial campaign on the same day her husband's administration awarded him the contract to design a 550-bed prison.[404]

The design for the aquatic center, as well, was set in stone. Swim coach Wynn Paul complained long and loudly about totally unacceptable features, but was forced to accept the design. The coach said the primary racing course went the wrong way; a bulkhead was in the wrong place; storage units were located at the farthest point from where the equipment was needed, and he pleaded for simple stairs to the diving platform rather than the design's elaborate spiral staircase.[405]

The cost of the center followed the same path. Only a month after the aquatic center's contract was let, trustees approved a $590,000 increase in the project, and that was the third time they increased the contract. While trustees were enlarging the scope of the aquatic center contract, athletic officials were deleting thirteen pool features totaling $435,000.[406]

Vice-president Jack C. Blanton was in charge of the aquatic center, but it became a project far out of control before it was finished years later.

There was no question of control when it came to game tickets. Singletary was a master at corralling those tickets. In his first year in office, Kentucky received 600 tickets to the NCAA mid-east regional tournament in Athens, Georgia. Students were allotted 316 of the tickets. Of the 284 left, Singletary had seventy-five plus his eight complimentary tickets.[407]

What happened to those tickets? A February 1976 letter to Singletary from Harry Lancaster provided a partial answer. The athletics director said he was holding the president's eight comp tickets for the NCAA regional tournament held that year in Memorial Coliseum. "In addition," he said, "we have twenty-six for you to sell." That quotation was underlined on Lancaster's letter that bore Singletary's initials.[408]

Apparently this was common practice because Rupp had tickets he sold. There were a lot of unanswered questions. Were the tickets sold for face value or were the prices inflated in the face of a state law against scalping tickets? Did the money go to the athletics program? Were the ticket swapped for political favors?

Kentucky basketball tickets, in Singletary's era, were powerful bargaining chips with many state legislators who, by virtue of their offices, received two free season tickets. Sen. Paul McCuiston was anxious to get good tickets in the new arena. "I know these things are going to be hard to get," he told Singletary, "I would appreciate it if you would put in a good word (for me)." The president was more than willing to oblige. "I have called Cliff Hagan," he told McCuiston, "and alerted him to the fact you're a good friend, and he has assured me you will be on the list." A few legislators refused the free tickets because they felt they were being lobbied with them.[409]

Fans were willing to go to extraordinary lengths to get basketball tickets. Paul Brown, from Princeton, asked former vice-president for business, Larry Forgy, then a Republican Party national committeeman, for help in getting Rupp Arena tickets. Brown, Forgy told an athletic official, "Hyperventilates when we are victorious, bleeds when we are behind and dies if we lose." Forgy, writing on a RNC letterhead, said if Brown could get tickets in the new arena he would change his political registration to the Democrat Party after he got the tickets.[410]

Singletary had competition in hoarding tickets from his own basketball coach. Joe B. Hall asked to be put on the committee allotting tickets for Rupp Arena. Singletary refused saying he could participate through athletics director Cliff Hagan. Instead of just participating, Hall cornered the market. Hagan gave Hall 412 tickets for choice lower level seats in Rupp Arena. "When the time comes," Hagan told Hall, "I hope you are prepared to face the flack with me and publicly defend the necessity of this distribution of seats for the continuance of our fine basketball program."[411] There were rumors that a prominent Lexington attorney brokered Hall's stash of tickets.

Horseman and philanthropist W.T. Young demanded and got some of the best tickets in Rupp Arena for himself and friends Alex Campbell and Robert L. Green. Young insisted Hagan reserve sixteen seats in the row behind Singletary and his guests for the three men. Young enclosed a check for $2,500, for his tickets, along with an arena drawing indicating the seats he wanted. Unhappy when he received his tickets, Young complained that he was assigned cheaper seats in another location. He pointed out to Hagan that he had the best seats in Memorial Coliseum, and expected the same in the new arena. Young left Hagan in no doubt of where he stood. "Cliff," he wrote, "none of this has any bearing on my university giving, but I do hope you will agree with my rationale that the best seats in the present Coliseum are those seats equivalent to Row A, sections 13, 14 and 15 as I have requested." Young also wanted two additional tickets since he and his wife were University Fellows, meaning each gave $10,000 to the school for that designation.[412]

Hagan got the message, "I feel we have broken so many of our ticket procedures by allowing you to get what you wanted, so that two more will not matter that much; I will see that you get tickets *somewhere* behind the rail in the section we discussed." Hagan added that he hoped the university could really count on Young "When it really gets rough around here."[413]

Young was a home-grown good old boy. His wealth began with the Jiff peanut butter fortune. He chaired the Royal Crown Cola board from 1966 to 1988; owned an enormous warehousing complex in Lexington; ran a trucking fleet, and his Overbrook Farm was an outstanding

Thoroughbred operation. A number of his race horses had the word, Cat, in their names. He was a member of Gov. John Y. Brown's administration when Humana, in which Young was a major stockholder, was allowed to build a new hospital in Lexington's already over-saturated market.[414]

When the university began raising money in the late 1980s to build a new library that most assumed would continue with the name, Commonwealth Library, Young gave the school $5 million and the name was quickly changed to the W.T. Young Library. Hagan's investment of basketball ticket paid a healthy dividend for the school.

Another Lexington businessman, whose pockets were perhaps not so deep, questioned Singletary about his inability to get basketball tickets while scalpers appeared to have plenty to sell at exorbitant prices. Ashby Neale, owner of A & N Rentals, joined the Blue White Fund to get football tickets, but, when he attempted to get Rupp Arena tickets, Hagan put his name in a lottery. Neale, who was willing to pay a premium price for his tickets, asked Singletary point blank what the ticket scalpers' source was. The president ignored the question and told Neale that he wasn't directly involved in allotting the tickets, but knew of the difficulties his staff experienced.[415]

One source of scalpers' tickets was students. As a graduate student, I noticed the same man was always standing in front of Memorial Coliseum when students' tickets were distributed. Students's tickets weren't transferrable, but their guest tickets were. The man always bought, in cash, as many of the guest tickets as he could. The number of guest tickets students could buy depended on the profile of the game. However, most of those guest tickets were in undesirable sections of the upper arena. Scalpers sold better tickets than students were allotted.

During reassignment of seats in Commonwealth Stadium, Hagan offended a former governor who stood by the school during the point shaving scandals and sudden death years. Lawrence Wetherby and friends, who were former trustees and judges, for years had fifty-yard seats in McLean Stadium. Hagan assigned the men, all of whom were elderly, seats at the top of the new stadium. Wetherby complained to Singletary that some consideration should be given to those "Who through the years, both good and lean, have been ardent UK fans." A cryptic note at the bottom of Wetherby's letter said, "Cliff agreed to call and talk with him." Wetherby's tickets were changed.[416]

Singletary had fourteen comp tickets for the new stadium, and an additional allotment of 132. Forty of those tickets went to the Lexington newspaper, an Ashland Oil Company executive, Guy Huguelet's son, a lieutenant governor and two Hazard bankers. I could find no accounting for the remaining ninety-four tickets in Singletary's allotment.[417]

# SWEETHEARTS, CONTRACTS THAT IS

Without those tickets, the next best thing for Kentucky fans, who bled Blue, was listening to broadcasts and watching telecasts of the games. That rabid fan base was a gold mine for game rights holders who increased their revenues by selling coaches' shows, and before and after game programming to stations in Kentucky and other states. One game rights holder made a cottage industry out of the broadcast and telecast rights, and other contracts he held on Kentucky athletics without competitive bidding.

Prior to 1965, individual radio stations made their own arrangements with the school for covering basketball and football games. When the broadcast rights were first put up for bids, the G.W. Johnson Agency, in New York, won the contract to broadcast basketball and football games for $39,000 a year for three years.[418]

The next successful bidder on the broadcast game rights was Jim Host, the former LCC consultant who ran a Lexington advertising agency. Host bid $52,750 a year for the three-year contract for the broadcast game rights. An aggressive promoter, Host had a UK degree in broadcasting, and called some games for the Standard Oil Sports Network established in 1951 by Claude Sullivan, the first "Voice of the Wildcats." [419]

Securing an agreement with WHAS, Louisville's 50,000-watt clear channel station, appeared to be the deciding factor in awarding the broadcast contract to Host. WHAS' Cawood Ledford, who succeeded Sullivan as the "Voice of the Wildcats," agreed to call the games.[420]

After his first season as the broadcast rights holder, Host bragged that he had increased the stations carrying the basketball games from twenty-five to forty-seven, and from twenty-nine to sixty-three for football. In his haste to increase his network, Host selected a Corbin station that operated only in the daytime. Many of the games were played at night. After months of squabbling, that included threats of lawsuits, Host selected another station the next year. Selection of individual stations carrying the games was left, by the contract, to the rights holder. [421]

Host, if he didn't go over the line, always appeared to skip just along the edge. According to his game rights contract, Host needed the athletics director's approval before hiring any on-air personnel. The announcement of an unapproved broadcaster earned Host a rebuke from Hagan. "This comes as a complete surprise and some embarrassment to me," he told Host.[422] The rebuke hardly made a dent in Host's armor.

Two years into his first three-year broadcast rights contracts, Host asked Singletary for a special favor. He wanted to substitute an irrevocable letter of credit for the performance bond required by his contract. It was unclear if the performance bond was ever executed. Singletary and the board approved the change. Host was again the successful bidder for the broadcast rights in 1977 for $85,000 a year for three years.[423]

In nine years, in-coming revenue from the broadcast right for football and basketball games more than doubled. Since broadcast rights were that valuable to a company outside the university, they should have been even more valuable to the school as both a source of revenue and a teaching tool for the college of communications. Singletary liked to refute the "Dr. Jock" image by saying his proclivity for athletics wasn't harmful to academics. If that was the case, the college of communications should have been equipped and staffed to handle the football and basketball broadcasts, and train students in their chosen field. Instead, the college of communications bounced in and out of accreditation during Singletary's administration.

Others certainly saw the value of the broadcast game rights. In 1980 there was a bidding war between Host and the Kentucky Network for the game rights. Host lost. His bid was $135,000, but the Kentucky Network bid $168,750. Not only did the Kentucky Network, a subsidiary of Financial Institution Services, Inc., in Nashville, fail the good old boy test, but their company headquarters were located in Tennessee, a hated rival in both sports.[424]

Host waged a bitter fight contending that , on the basis of experience, his low bid was the best bid. The Kentucky Network said their high bid was the best.

The contentious lobbying campaign Host waged was admirable. The fact that athletics officials even paid any attention to it was more telling. After all, they had a high bid and a low bid. That should have been the end of it, but we're talking about Kentucky. Host sent athletic officials a sixteen-page presentation outlining his broadcasting career. He argued the athletics board found no problems with his two previous bids. That was correct, but those were the high bids, not the low ones. He said the fact that he brought a second clear channel station, WCKY in Cincinnati, into the network should be a factor in awarding him the contract. He claimed, over the past three years, he had contributed $21,500 in cash or in-kind services to the UKAA, and in the past year alone had spent $27,000 promoting the sports broadcast network. There was no question about who Host was promoting. His corporate letterheads read, "University of Kentucky Sports Network, A Broadcast Division of Jim Host & Associates."[425]

Host contended his writing a manual for the NCAA on how to establish a sports network should be taken into consideration in awarding the bid. The most outrageous of Host's claims was that his broadcasts helped fill Commonwealth Stadium and Rupp Arena. He said the first year he won the broadcast rights, "Football was not selling out Commonwealth Stadium." The first year of Host's broadcast game rights contract was 1973, and the team played in the new stadium for the first time. End zone bleachers hadn't yet been moved from McLean Stadium into the new facility to fulfill the capacity of 57,800. He neglected to mention that.[426]

Host had a contract with the NCAA to broadcast their Final Four games with Cawood Ledford as the announcer. That was another reason, he said, that he should be awarded the contract despite his low bid. He challenged the Kentucky Network's ability to produce and originate a play-by-play network saying they lacked experience and qualification.[427] That wasn't Host's call to make.

When none of those arguments worked, Host began playing hard ball. He told athletic officials the Kentucky Network would arbitrarily take the game rights away from the small radio stations. There was no evidence of that, but it soon became apparent where the idea originated. Singletary was hit with a storm of letters from radio stations and the good old boy network. The letters were too similar and too timely not to be a part of a well orchestrated campaign. Jay Lasslo, sales manager of WSGS in Hazard, told Singletary that more money spent for a product didn't necessarily produce a better outcome. That was the same rhetoric Host used. Jack Mayer, manager of WDNZ in Clarksville, Tennessee, said he was shocked Host wasn't handling the game broadcasts, and that his station would make other programming plans.[428]

Then the good old boys kicked into high gear to protect one of their own. Don and Dudley Webb, Lexington attorneys and developers, strongly urged Singletary to renew Host's contract. In essence they were also telling him to disregard the legal process of competitive bidding. "We do not believe," they said, "that anybody can do the job as well as we all want it done without the deep feeling for UK athletics we know Jim Host has, but which we doubt any group from Louisville (the Network's Kentucky base) or Nashville will have." UKAA's architect of choice Don Wallace advised Singletary not to make a mistake, but to accept Host's bid. Warren Rosenthal, president of the fast-food company Jerrico, declared the broadcast rights should stay with Host. Rosenthal helped subsidize both the football and basketball programs.[429]

Even the game announcers got into the fray. Ralph Hacker, manager of the only Lexington radio station to carry the games, WVLK, advised Singletary that Host should continue as the game rights holder. Looking out for his own interests, Hacker added that he was available to continue as the color commentator on the broadcasts regardless of who got the contract. Cawood Ledford, the play-by-play announcer, did the same.[430]

A week before the broadcast rights were to be awarded, Host sent athletic officials and board members a memo with three legal opinions that he claimed supported his argument that the high bid wasn't necessarily the best bid. There was a certain amount of implied intimidation in the memo. He next turned his sights on Bernard Vonderheide, chairman of the radio and television committee that recommended the best bid to the athletics board. Host insisted that Vonderheide bring the committee for a tour of his broadcast facilities. Vonderheide ignored him.[431]

Singletary was under such pressure that he began another "talking paper" to reason his way through the confusion Host had stirred up. He noted that the Kentucky Network had no demonstrated ability in setting up a sports network, but added that Host was in a similar position when he first won the broadcast rights. Singletary acknowledged that the Kentucky Network had broadcast experience in operating a state-wide news network. He saw his position as being neutral, but couldn't overlook the additional money the Kentucky Network's bid represented.[432]

Host later accused Singletary of hunkering down when faced with difficult decision-making situations.[433]

Vonderheide's committee recommended to the athletics board the Kentucky Network's bid, based on their news production experience, be accepted. They offered a network of 123 stations, including WHAS and WCKY, with a program coordinator stationed in Lexington. Then, Vonderheide dropped a bombshell. He said the Kentucky Network's parent company guaranteed the payment of all fees, called for the in the bid, to the UKAA. It wasn't clear if that guarantee was specifically requested by athletic officials, or was volunteered by the company. Regardless, it was quite different from the amenities afforded Host in his first broadcast contract. Vonderheide's next remarks were directed at Host's high pressure tactics to keep the broadcast rights. He told the athletics board the committee took the Kentucky Network at their word just as they did six years earlier with another new bidder, Jim Host & Associates.[434]

Singletary let the athletics board meeting degenerate into disarray. That was rare since he usually handled those proceedings with an iron hand. He accepted a motion and a second to approve Vonderheide's recommendations before calling on the two bidders for a last effort to present their cases. After their presentations, and before voting on the motion on the floor, Singletary allowed board member and former NFL referee Tommy Bell to offer a substitute motion that was also seconded. Bell, who was also a trustee, proposed that both bids be rejected, and Host be awarded the broadcast and *telecast* (emphasis mine) game rights for one year at $86,318, the same amount Host previously paid for the broadcast game rights alone. Bell urged the board to approve his motion, and give Host the contract because "He's a fine Kentucky boy." Bell was an attorney, and should have known such actions would provide the Kentucky Network with a fine case for legal action against the university. Pushing the envelope, legal or not, was how the good old boys operated.[435]

The amazing thing was it almost worked. Instead of calling up the motions, for a vote, in the order they were made, Singletary first asked for a vote on Bell's motion, and the result was 6-8. He then called up the first motion, and the Kentucky Network was awarded the broadcast game rights for three years.[436]

Host was less than a gracious loser. He soundly criticized Vonderheide for not taking the committee on a tour of his broadcast facilities. One of his allies on the athletic board, faculty member Daniel Reedy, Host said, felt like he'd been taken down the primrose path by not having an opportunity to take the tour. That was pure hogwash. Then, Host complained that the Kentucky Network was trying to hire some of his employees. It wasn't clear exactly what he expected the university to do about that.[437]

Three years later, Host found himself out in the cold again. The Kentucky Network narrowly outbid him $319,000 to $317,000 for the broadcast game rights. The contract was awarded with little fanfare.[438]

Singletary handled televised game rights only slightly better than his management of the broadcast rights. That was unusual because he was an early proponent of televising games both on network and cable television. Athletic officials waited until December 30th, eight games into the 1975-76 basketball season, before taking bids on four televised games. WAVE, the National Broadcasting Company affiliate in Louisville, was the high bidder at $3,000 a game. Although athletic officials bitterly complained the station took advantage of them, they accepted the bid.[439]

The next year, there were many problems with the televised game rights. Paducah television executive Fred Paxton was quite angry about the way the school was handling the television rights. Paxton bought some games from the school that were also being peddled by the SEC on a live basis, and he had to pay additional fees for another Kentucky basketball game. "While the university has been in the business of selling rights at competitive bidding, it now finds itself in the embarrassing situation of not being able to deliver rights for which it advertised," he told Singletary. Paxton added the whole thing was most un-business like. The president was out of town, and Hagan made a stab at handling the situation, but Paxton still wanted to talk with Singletary.[440]

Lexington's Columbia Broadcasting System affiliate, WKYT, joined the Louisville station in 1977 in paying $92,000 annually for three years of the basketball games rights. The two stations rebid the same contract, for fifteen games, three years later for $86,318. WKYT manager Ralph Gabbard claimed the price reduction was because some of the best games were controlled and sold by the SEC. The stations were hardly losing money. They inserted a clause in the bid, that the UKAA didn't call for, to set aside $130,000 in commercial time to advertise the games' telecasts and secure network clearance for coach Joe B. Hall's weekly television shows.[441] The school accepted these extra items in awarding the contract with no problem.

Just as the furor over the Host-Kentucky Network altercation was fading, an all-out war erupted over bids on the televised game rights. In 1983 WAVE-WKYT bid $362,460 for three years to telecast eleven live and delayed games each season. Lexington's upstart American Broadcasting Corporation affiliate, WTVQ, bid $389,946. Both stations threw in promotional considerations not included in the bid call, just as WAVE-WKYT did earlier. The two stations weren't about to give up the televised game rights, they had controlled for twelve years, without a bloody fight. It was the classic confrontation of an insider finding himself on the outside, at least temporarily.[442]

Radio and television committee chairman Bernard Vonderheide allowed both stations to revise their bids on an item not even included in the original bid call. Consequently, the committee threw out both bids, and issued another bid call. It was clearly a move to circumvent WTVQ's bid in favor of WAVE-WKYT. That's how the ABC affiliate saw it, and filed suit against the university. WTVQ asked for and got a temporary restraining order on the new call for bids.[443]

Singletary's legal counsel, John Darsie, assured the president there would be no problem in convincing the judge to set aside the restraining order. That's how the good old boys operated, and they didn't fail Darsie. The legal counsel suggested three courses of action Singletary could pursue regarding the televised game rights: he could have new specs drawn up; consider renegotiating the contract instead of putting them up for competitive bids, or produce the games in-house.[444]

Darsie's second suggestion probably had some attraction for Singletary, but it was just a little too daring even for "Dr. Jock." It was likely, if Singletary had chosen to negotiate the contract, that WAVE-WKYT would have been the winners. Those stations had an aversion to being out in the cold.

Universities producing their own sports broadcasts and telecasts wasn't that far fetched. LSU began their pay-per-view telecasts of football games in 1985, and exclusive in-house broadcasts followed in 1988. Treva Tidwell, in LSU's electronic media division, said in a 1991 interview the school netted $750,000 annually from their football telecasts, and expected to clear $1.2 million that year from their in-house broadcasts. Like Kentucky, Tidwell said, LSU previously used private vendors for the broadcasts and telecasts. "We changed for two reasons," she said, "first, we get more money for the athletics department; our revenue increased thirty to forty percent. Second, we wanted more control of our own games especially relating to public relations and fees." She explained that LSU had problems with game rights' holders forcing stations, purchasing games from them, to buy additional programming. Such strong arm tactics, she said, reflected badly on LSU.[445]

With the impasse on the television game rights, it was an excellent time to consider in-house production of Kentucky games through the school of communications. If the college of communication's television division lacked expertise, Kentucky Education Television, bordering the campus, could have provided guidance.

There was some discussion of in-house production of the games. Vice-president Jack C. Blanton voiced his opposition saying there wasn't enough time. The first game was five months away, and that should have given them ample time. Apparently, nobody wanted to follow the in-house production route where the revenue would have gone to the school. The bidding stations certainly grimaced at the idea. WKYT manager Ralph Gabbard, who referred to the televised games rights as a "pot of gold," said the in-house idea had been kicked around for years, but was always dismissed. WTVQ general manager William Service said the idea of the school producing their own game telecasts was simply not viable.[446]

The television stations would have lost a considerable amount of revenue if the games were produced in-house. Even more important,

WAVE-WKYT would have lost the use of Kentucky sports in promoting their stations.

Angry about the entire mess, Singletary threatened, in a public interview, not to accept any bids for the televised game rights. Nobody believed he was serious. He told Blanton to come up with bid specifications that didn't have "A bunch of claptrap," as he called the extra items stations had added in the past. Singletary had no problems with the "Bunch of claptrap" in previous bids. Blanton knew just the person to solve their problem. He imported Ross Bagwell, a former producer of the *Tonight Show* who had a television production company in Knoxville. Blanton paid him $828 for the day's work. When a mandatory session was held for all prospective bidders on the televised game rights, there were so many problems with the bid specs that representatives from the television stations themselves straightened out the specs.[447]

When the new bids were opened, WAVE-WKYT had the high bid of $202,000 a year for three years. WTVQ's bid was $141,000 a year. WKYT's vice-president Jere Pique said their bid was a sacrifice. WTVQ's Jerry Fox said his competition "Deserved everything they got."[448]

Athletic officials were licking their chops over the additional funds the new bid brought the school. "Nobody raised hell before, during or after the bid process," Blanton told Singletary, "the Channel 36 (WTVQ) guy came up and said thanks for the opportunity to bid; obviously he wasn't very happy. I doubt this will save us from a blasting from their station, but it will save us from an embarrassing lawsuit about the handling of this contract. We are smiling all the way to the bank because of an approximate 100 percent increase in the rights fees the second time around."[449]

If Blanton was elated over the amount they collected from the televised game rights, he would have been euphoric over returns, such as LSU's, from an in-house production. In 1988, LSU's in-house production of football telecasts alone netted the school $750,000. The same year, Kentucky collected $326,000 from football and basketball telecasts.[450]

Management of the broadcast and telecast game rights paled in comparison to the handling of basketball and game program rights. Game program rights may appear inconsequential, but they were a good revenue source. Gone were the days when a simple mimeographed roster of players sufficed. Game programs in the late 1970s were on their way toward slick, full-color, 100-page bound books filled with advertising. Host had a monopoly on the game programs' rights, and the school made no effort to put them out for competitive bids.[451]

Singletary gave away the basketball game program rights in the negotiations of the Rupp Arena lease. Host was the LCC consultant who was a central figure in the negotiations. Host's firm was the only one allowed to contract for the basketball programs. There were not calls for competitive bids. From 1976 to 1980, the LCC kept Host's advertising firm on a $1,250 monthly retainer, and he did the game programs for a set production fee plus charges for photographs and net billing for out-of-pocket expenses. Host made it clear in the agreement he signed with the LCC that "This cost does not include the time of Jim Host who is donating his personal time to the center project."[452]

For the 1980-81 season Host produced 38,000 basketball game programs for $7,600. The next year he was paid $15,270 for 6,000 fewer programs. His 1985 contract with the LCC for the programs was extended to cover three seasons for $126,000 divided into annual payments. All the advertising and sale revenue went to Host.[453] The good old boys do take care of their own.

After two years of producing the basketball game program, Host went after the football game program. Through his firm, Lexington Productions, Inc., Host agreed to pay the UKAA a minimum of $55,000, or one-half the net income, which ever was greater, after *two years* (emphasis mine). His proposal was accepted with no calls for competitive bids.[454]

In his next two-year contract for the football game programs, also obtained without competitive bidding, Host furnished 40,000 football programs for $27,500 a year or half the net income. Host, of course, kept the books. Something happened in 1982 that moved Blanton to have Host sign a personal service contract instead of their usual one-page agreement. Although UKAA had a sports information staff that produced prize-winning, slick media information books, Blanton attested that "University personnel are not available to perform said function (producing the game programs)." The 1984 settlement for the football game program showed a total income of $178,291. After expenses, including $91,377 for printing in Host's plant, the remaining $70,311 was split evenly between the UKAA and Host.[455]

If was almost as if UKAA officials were brain dead when it came to stemming the flow of money from their athletics program into Host's pockets. It must have been an infectious disease because the practice not only continued but accelerated under the management of Singletary's and Hagan's successors.

# BENIGN NEGLECT

The politics involved in handling of media rights wasn't surprising, but their invasion into athletes' medical care was downright shocking. That opinion was shared by a nationally known sports figure. "Quite frankly, this is the most bizarre situation I have ever dealt with in my eighteen years of coaching," was basketball coach Rick Pitino's assessment of sports medicine at Kentucky. Pitino equated the attitude of the good old boy medical professionals to dealing with nine-year-old boys in his summer basketball camps.

Athletes health care had been a bone of contention between local physicians and the university since 1954 when Dr. Ernst Jokl, known as the father of modern sports medicine, was hired as a physiology professor to establish a rehabilitation center on the campus. The attitude was so typical of the Lexington mind set that said if we can't run call the shots, forget it. That was what happened with Jokl. The city's physicians were upset because they weren't running the rehab center. The breach between town and gown became even greater in 1962 when the Albert Benjamin Chandler Medical Center opened, and athletics director Bernie Shively refused to send injured athletes to the campus hospital. The reason was one of the members of the athletics board was a physician who practiced at another hospital.[456]

In 1984 medical center chancellor Peter Bosomworth wanted to create a sports medicine center, outside his own institution, for orthopedic surgeon James Andrews, then practicing in Columbus, Georgia.

Bosomworth's proposed orthopedic hospital, for Andrews to operate, would have been in direct competition with his own medical center's orthopedic department. The chancellor wanted a sports medicine practice that would gain national and international attention, but he wanted Andrews to head the effort. [457]

There was no indication Bosomworth ever consulted with Jokl, who lived a short distance from the campus, on his plans for the sports medicine center. Jokl, who died in December 1997, had all the credentials to develop the national/international sports medicine practice university officials claimed they wanted. He had advanced degrees from universities in Germany and South Africa; had held medical department chairs at German, Swiss and South African universities; conducted major international sports medicine research programs and, in 1942, was awarded the Buskton Browne Prize. The Prize was awarded every four years to the British citizen, outside of Britain, who made the greatest international contribution to medicine and public health. From 1952 to 1972, Jokl directed research surveys at the Olympic games, and twice served as one of the games' physicians.[458]

Four years after arriving in Lexington, Jokl and the Fayette Medical Society clashed over the rehab center. Society president Robert B. Warfield, after failing to remove Jokl from the rehab project with back room politics, attacked him in the newspaper charging that he and the university were practicing corporate medicine. The assumption was the rehab center should be controlled by local doctors such as Warfield. Furthermore, Warfield charged that Jokl had no Kentucky medical license. Few had deeper roots in the Lexington establishment than Warfield. His antecedents were some of the city's earliest settlers. An earlier family physician, Elisha Warfield, bred the famous Thoroughbred sire, Lexington. Warfield's judgment in selecting Jokl as an adversary was as flawed as his charges.[459]

Jokl was Gen. Jan Smuts' chief medical officer for ten years in South Africa, and was more than capable of responding to Warfield's charges.

He told Warfield his public attack was "Improper, impertinent and not in keeping with the general accepted standards of medical ethics." Jokl pointed out that the medical society was represented on the rehab board from the very beginning, and they had never questioned his credentials or indicated there was any problem. Jokl further scorched Warfield and the medical society. "In the country of my birth (Germany), I have experienced the advent of Nazism and therefore, know well the extent to which malice and greed can go, even on the part of educated men and women."[460]

Warfield was successful in closing the rehab center. He claimed the closure wasn't his aim, but that was little comfort to patients who had to travel to Cincinnati or elsewhere for treatment. Jokl said he didn't apply for a medical license because he wasn't practicing medicine in Lexington; he was establishing and supervising the rehab center. "I wanted to avoid the politics of it all," he said. Jokl concentrated on developing graduate courses in sports medicine, and directing doctoral dissertations.[461]

William Willard, the first dean of the medical school, received much the same reception as Jokl. Willard wanted the school's athletes treated at the medical center, not local hospitals. He said it looked peculiar that the university, with its own hospital, was sending its athletes to other medical facilities. An all-out war erupted between Willard and athletics director Bernie Shively with president Frank G. Dickey in the middle. Only after Willard agreed to a twenty percent discount for athletes treated at the medical center did Shively consent to a Dickey brokered deal to send injured athletes to the university's hospital.[462]

Dickey chaired an October 1962 athletics board meeting where the Willard-Shively pact, to have injured athletes treated at the medical center, was on the agenda. Dickey sat quietly as Shively told the board the university hospital's rates were higher than other local hospitals, neglecting to mention Willard's agreement to a twenty percent discount. Shively said he should decide where to send injured athletes. The board agreed with him, as Dickey continued to say nothing.[463] It was just another of those sweet-heart deals the good old boys created.

Athletes' medical care became a major issue during Charlie Bradshaw's coaching tenure. A former US Marine Corps drill instructor, Bradshaw conducted punishing practices. One of those practices sent thirty-four players to local hospitals. President John W. Oswald asked for an investigation, and Shively told him "Football players are only sent to the university hospital in cases of extreme emergencies."[464]

Sending injured players to local hospital, instead of the university's, was a practice that Shively and his successors, Harry Lancaster and Cliff Hagan, continued. During the intervening twenty-one years, the medical center gained a national reputation as an outstanding teaching and research facility. The center's head injury clinical and research program was among the best in the nation.

When Bosomworth began developing a plan for a sports medicine complex on the campus, with an outside physician in charge, he did his best to keep it secret. Meeting notes on the planning sessions were marked confidential. Singletary was kept in the loop as things developed.[465]

Bosomworth's plan called for a sports medicine practice to provide care for university athletes, be a referral center for other college, high school and recreational athletes, establish a nationally recognized sports medicine fellowship program, develop a recognized rehabilitation and physical therapy programs and conduct research relating to the biomechanics of motion. He expected the college of engineering, physical education department and the medical center's departments of orthopedics, physiology, biophysics and rehabilitation to participate in the practice.[466]

The chancellor's orthopedic dream facility included a free-standing 100-bed, $15 million hospital, and a $7 million research center on the campus. Both the hospital and research center would be headed by Andrews on a for profit basis. Thomas D. Brower, head of the medical center's orthopedics department, said, "This proposal shows more initiative then I've seen here in twenty years." Brower certainly didn't approve of the sports medicine facility being built outside the medical center. He suggested medical center orthopedists staff the facility, but Bosomworth had something else in mind.[467]

Apparently the connection between Bosomworth and Andrews occurred after the orthopedist operated on some Kentucky basketball players at Dr. Jack C. Hughston's sports medicine facility in Columbus, Georgia. Andrews was very interested in Bosomworth's plan, and retained James Cosgrove, a former Hughston Clinic administrator, to act as his agent in negotiations with the medical center chancellor.[468]

In1983, more than a year before documents show Bosomworth developed his plan, Andrews incorporated Kentucky Sports Medicine, Inc. A contract was prepared calling for the university to commit to a fifty-year lease for ten-acres of campus land for Andrews to develop and operate a for-profit sports medicine complex. No wonder Bosomworth wanted to keep his plans to gut his medical center's orthopedic department secret! Andrews' sports medicine complex would also have its own air transport service independent of the medical center's. Bosomworth was ready to lead a fund drive to raise the $7 million for the research facility attached to Andrews' hospital.[469]

Medical center physicians, who asked their names not be used, told me Bosomworth, for some strange reason, had an inordinate amount of animosity toward his own hospital's orthopedics department. If Bosomworth's plan had succeeded, the medical center orthopedists would have been forced to practice elsewhere. There was little or no consideration given to the charity patients the medical center orthopedists treated, or the important research the facility did.

Bosomworth kept Singletary in the loop because the president recommended the chancellor's sports medicine plan to the board of trustees at their April 1985 meeting. Trustee Albert G. Clay, a refugee from the "Great Indiana Caper," was a big booster of the plan to gut the medical center's orthopedic department. Clay had high praise for the plan and requested a proposal be developed immediately. Trustees passed the necessary paperwork.[470]

Bosomworth miscalculated if he thought his sports medicine plan would slip through without notice. Lexington orthopedists, many of them medical school graduates, had been acting as teams' physicians without pay. They all resigned when they heard about the Bosomworth-Andrews plan. The chancellor wasn't disturbed. He should have been. The Fayette Medical Society went after him with even more venom than they had exhibited against Jokl. They strongly suggested such a sports medicine complex be developed within the medical center, and asked Bosomworth to speak at their next meeting.[471]

The chancellor wasn't quite so cocky in his speech to the medical society. In fact, he scaled back the sports medicine complex plans. He spoke of a 35,000 square-foot facility built with capital raised by a private public organization. He even admitted such a complex would take patients away from his own medical center, and that getting state approval would be difficult.[472]

Hospitals were also opposed to Bosomworth's sports medicine plan. They wanted to know how he planned to get state approval to build another hospital when the local occupancy rate was only sixty percent. Bosomworth's own hospital had a daily average of 138 empty beds.[473]

Bosomworth had another card to play. If everybody was going to shoot down his plans for Andrews' 100-bed hospital, then he would bring Andrews into the medical center to establish a sports medicine practice there. Singletary approved the plan. The first step was to have athletics director Cliff Hagan name Andrews the school's team physician. Then, a slight hitch developed in their plans. Andrews decided to join a sports medicine facility being built in Birmingham, Alabama. Lexington native, Mary Lloyd Ireland, who did post-graduate work for Andrews, came to Lexington to establish the practice. When Ireland took a temporary leave, Andrews recruited Michael Ray, an Orlando, Florida, orthopedist, to replace her.[474]

Andrews elected to stay in Birmingham, with the giant Healthsouth Corporation that operated, in 1999, 124 medical facilities in forty-nine states. Among the five facilities Healthsouth operated in Kentucky was the Lexington Surgical Center. On Healthsouth's roster of physicians, Andrews was listed in 1999 as the Kentucky football team's physician.[475]

There was a war in the medical center over Bosomworth's attempts to bring Andrews's sports medicine practice into the facility. The breach was so divisive the chancellor went another route. In all my research, I was unable to find a definitive reason Bosomworth was so determined to deprive his own orthopedic department of the sports medicine center practice. Regardless, Bosomworth intended to have Andrews care for the school's athletes. The chancellor initiated contact between Andrews and Central Baptist Hospital for the purpose of establishing the orthopedist's sports medicine practice there to care for university athletes. A UKAA report on sports medicine attempted to sugarcoat Bosomworth's actions saying a quality hospital setting was needed for the sports medicine practice but, due to politics, it shouldn't be placed in the medical center.[476]

The report said Ray was unable to work with Andrews and Ireland any longer. He accepted a surgical appointment with the medical center's orthopedic department. It was a blow to the Bosomworth faction when basketball coach Eddie Sutton asked Ray to care for his team instead of Ireland, who was the football team's physician.[477]

Bosomworth kept Andrews informed about Ray's activities as he established the UK Sports Medicine practice in the medical center's orthopedic department.[478] It appeared the chancellor wanted a connection with Andrews above all.

Ray not only treated Kentucky basketball players but athletes from other colleges and universities. He set up a trainer outreach program for area high schools.[479] The Kentucky Sports Medicine practice eventually left Central Baptist, moved into their own building across town, but Ireland continued as the football program's orthopedist.

Singletary exhibited little concern about the conflict in sports medicine over athletes medical care. He gave Bosomwoth free reign to create a practice that was in direct competition with the medical center he headed. It was evident that Bosomworth ran the medical center with an iron hand. Just before the chancellor retired in 1994, a medical center employee, who asked that her name not be used, said,"After all, he's been a little dictator here for twenty years."

It was left to the next president to attempt to straighten out the sports medicine muddle because Singletary was focused on stonewalling another NCAA investigation of the basketball program initiated by a series of articles in the Lexington newspaper.

# BLACK OCTOBER

A shadow was cast over Singletary's athletic world in October 1985, when, in an interview with reporters, he learned the Lexington newspaper was preparing a series of articles detailing alleged illegal subsidization of Hall's basketball players during his entire thirteen-year coaching career at Kentucky. Thirty-five years had passed since the NCAA slapped the "sudden death" sanction on the school, and the same practice was occurring on the watch of "Dr. Jock," who achieved his ambition to be a major player on the national athletic stage.

Singletary dominated national college athletics the previous decade. He was president of the College Football Association for two terms, and directed the CFA's battle, in a legal skirmish all the way to the Supreme Court, to wrench control of football television revenue from the NCAA and split it among the participating schools. The CFA negotiated the first multi-million-dollar football television contract, outside the NCAA, while Singletary headed the organization. Twice president of the SEC, he chaired the National Association of State Universities and Land Grant Colleges' committee on athletics.[480]

He was a member of the American Council on Education's presidential committee on athletics and their ad hoc committee on reforming college sports. While sitting on the ACE committee, which favored the CFA's stand on football television revenue, he was an original member of the NCAA's presidents' select committee on athletics. Some thought it was a conflict of interest for Singletary to sit on both high profile committees which had opposite aims simultaneously. The NCAA was, of course, opposed to the CFA's stand on televised football revenue while ACE, for the most part, approved spreading the money among the participating colleges.[481]

Aside from his national prominence, Singletary was credited with laying the foundation for Kentucky's athletics program being one of the best financed in the nation. In achieving that goal, he became caught up in the "Dr. Jock" image, neglected academic needs and allowed the good old boys to become equal, and sometimes dominating, partners in the athletics program. Those were serious shortcomings.

Four months before the October interview, Singletary notified trustees he would retire in two years after his 65th birthday in 1987.[482] There was speculation he knew about the newspaper's digging into Hall's program before the interview. Lexington was a small, but gossipy, city where keeping a secret was difficult, especially about something as important as Kentucky basketball. There were rumors for a number of years that Hall's program was dirty.

Reporters told Singletary of thirty-three of Hall's former players interviewed, thirty-one said they were aware of improper activities while playing. Twenty-six said they received cash and gifts in violation of NCAA regulations. What made matters worse, the violations continued while the program was on probation from the 1976 violations.[483]

Hall bailed out leaving Singletary and Hagan to take the heat and the blame. In March 1985, after Kentucky's 70-86 loss to St. Johns in the NCAA western regional tournament, Hall suddenly resigned. He announced his resignation in Denver, Colorado. Making the announcement there, instead of back home in Lexington, limited his exposure for the media and their ability to question his actions. The previous April, Singletary had extended his contract for five years and extolled his accomplishments that included the 1978 national championship.[484]

There was, of course, much speculation about Hall's resignation from a job he fought tooth and nail to get in 1972. Some thought it was a simple case of burnout from the constant pressure of coaching Kentucky basketball, and failing to measure up to Rupp's standards. Hall's record of 297-100, eight SEC, one NIT and one NCAA championships was substantial. Rumors of health problems arose. Others speculated about Hall's large stash of choice Rupp Arena tickets, and a possible IRS investigation into the proceeds from the tickets' sale.

Hall's departure sent Singletary scurrying to Wildcat Lodge to assure the basketball players he would find them the best coach in the country. A sarcastic editorial in the Lexington newspaper was a harbinger of things to come for the president. "The university doesn't lose basketball coaches very often, but it loses good faculty members every year. So it's reassuring to think the next time the university loses an excellent teacher, an appropriate official will hasten to assure students that the university will seek the best available replacement...A commitment to excellence, after all, is a total commitment whether it applies to hiring and retaining good professors or the selection of a new high priest for the state's unofficial religion."[485]

There was no need to institute a national search. College basketball coaches from across the country would be in Lexington for the Final Four at Rupp Arena that year. Several nibbled at the vacancy. Lute Olson made his interests known until Arizona's deep pockets kicked in with more money for him. Vanderbilt's C.M. Newton, who lettered for Rupp in 1951, turned the job down telling Singletary how much he regretted missing the opportunity of working with him. Arkansas coach Eddie Sutton said he would have crawled to Lexington for the job, but that wasn't necessary as he was already in town. Singletary and Hagan, with little time for research into Sutton's background, gave him a five-year contract plus benefits from televison and radio shows, coaching clinics and shoe and apparel contracts.[486]

Sutton was an innocent by-stander in the allegations the newspaper made, but they doomed his program before it began. Just as Donovan and Shively did in 1951, Singletary and Hagan denied any knowledge of wrong doing. Hall was, of course, absent. Headlines from the first article,

"Boosters' cash, gifts line the pockets of UK players," sent the good old boys running for cover enmass.[487]

Former basketball players were evidently candid in the taped interviews with reporters as they discussed "Sugar Daddies," deferred summer job payments, selling their complimentary tickets at inflated prices. Each player received four season tickets that NCAA rules prohibited them from selling. NCAA regulations allowed athletes grants-in-aid to pay for tuition, fees, books and room and board. If they were financially strapped, they could apply for Pell Grants.[488]

Scott Courts, who only played as a freshman, described what happened during a pick-up game in old Alumni Gym. He said assistant coach Leonard Hamilton, now coaching the NBA's Washington Wizards, said something like, "Hey Buddy, if you ever have any money problems or anything, well, Don Webb might be able to take care of you...don't be advertising this now, but if you have a problem or something don't worry about it. Come and see me or Don Webb." Courts admitted he visited Webb a couple of times, and $500 was the most he ever received. "It wasn't like there was always money under my door from Don Webb," he told reporters, "he helped me when I ran short. I'd just say I needed a little help. And he would say, 'how much do you need? What do you need it for? Don't spend it all in once place.'" Courts sold this comp tickets that year for $2,250, and declared, "Thank God for those alumns."[489]

Webb was another of the ultimate good old boys. Native eastern Kentuckians, Webb and his brother began developing downtown properties in the 1970s, and eventually extended their empire across the country. The Webbs built the Vine Center complex, containing a 367-room hotel to lure the NCAA's Final Four to Lexington. On their initial trip the selection committee determined Lexington's hotel rooms were insufficient to host the tournament. When they returned for a second look, the Webbs rented a bulldozer, moved dirt around on the lot and put up a sign saying, "Coming Soon, 300-room Radisson Hotel.[490]

The Webbs contributed $5,000 of the $200,000 Lexingtonians had to raise to pay for NCAA officials' expenses while they were in town. Webb, unhappy about his ticket allotment, told Hagan, "I won't mention our other involvements in the Kentucky basketball program through the years because I don't believe it is necessary. I know the ticket problems are many, however, I don't think anybody else in town invested five years of hard work and $40 million dollars to get the NCAA tournament to Lexington as we have done."[491]

Webb later told a television news panel show that he had a letter from Courts denying he told the newspaper the developer gave him money, but he couldn't produce it because he'd sent it to the NCAA. His brother, Dudley Webb, flew to Denver, en route to California, and met with Courts, an investment banker there, on the day the first newspaper article appeared. Don Webb told the panel show that Hall introduced him to Courts and told the player that he (Webb) would be one on his best friends on campus. Webb claimed Hall was only making a general statement.[492]

By his own words, Webb indicated the depth of his involvement in the basketball program. "Joe would have said that to many other players and their parents that I've talked to," Webb declared, "that I've run into where they were recruiting people.[493]

Greasing athletes' palms was another good old boy, not quite on the Webb's level, Corbin physician Elmer Prewitt. According to the newspaper articles Prewitt gave $50 handshakes to Dirk Minnifield, Jay Shidler and three other players who asked not to be identified. Prewitt admitted visiting the locker room after games, but denied giving players money. "That's against the rules," he boasted, "I'm too smart for that. My support was in counseling and that sort of thing. I don't deal in money." Prewitt did deal in money. He gave $2,000 to help build Wildcat Lodge.[494]

One of the coal moguls was proud of his involvement with Kentucky basketball. "I'm a Big Blue fan from the word go; I love Kentucky basketball," Maynard Hogg told reporters. Hogg bragged he gave player Fred Cowan $200 anytime he wanted money. The money, Hogg maintained, was deferred payments from Cowan's summer job with his coal company. Cowan wasn't a member of the United Mine Workers' Union, but Hogg paid him as if he were. Apparently, another assistant coach, Dickie Parsons, introduced Hogg to Cowan.[495]

Kentucky basketball players were in demand as public speakers, and admitted to the newspaper they made as much as $3,000 from their appearances. Randall Stacy, an assistant in Sports Information who resigned in 1984, matched players with speaking and appearance requests, and was aware of the cash payments. "I think we would be terribly naive," he told the newspaper, "to think that wouldn't happen, but it was something I made sure I didn't get involved in."[496]

All-American Sam Bowie said he stayed away from the cash handouts because he was concerned about his reputation and future NBA career. Bowie, who played for the Portland Trailblazers and the Los Angeles Lakers, remembered Hall was constantly reminding players that taking cash and selling their tickets was against NCAA rules. Another All-American, Kyle Macy, wasn't so sure about that. "I'd say he was probably neutral on that," Macy said, "I just think he kind of looked the other way. Whether he knew what was going on, I don't know."[497]

Whether Hall knew what was going on or not was debatable. Hall's close personal friend, Cecil Dunn, who sat on the bench with the players during the games, was fingered by the newspaper as the person buying Jay Shidler's comp tickets for three years for $8,800. Shidler told reporters he was so naive his freshman year he didn't know the value of his comp tickets, and used them for family and friends. What made the Hall-Dunn-Shidler triangle so interesting was Dunn's profession. At that time Dunn was an assistant in the Fayette County attorney's office. That office was statutorily charged with prosecuting violators of Kentucky's ticket scalping law that prohibited selling tickets for more than the price printed on them. Dunn, the newspaper said, refused to comment.[498] Silence soon became a staple commodity among the good old boys.

Player Chuck Verderber summed up the situation, "It wasn't so much the players' problem, as it was the people surrounding the program. It became real greedy, I felt. It got so ridiculous, I was glad to get out." Verderber acknowledged taking money, but revealed no amount to the newspaper.[499]

When reporters asked Hall for an interview, he requested they submit written questions. Then, he refused to answer their fifty-three questions. Instead, he issued a prepared statement saying the reporters' questions were based on assumption and purported facts that he knew nothing about. Hall said he made every human effort to run a program reflective of its traditions in a manner that brought credit to the university and the commonwealth. "I am personally unaware of any NCAA rules being violated," he concluded, "I have not participated in any such violations and would not have permitted them had they been brought to my attention."[500]

Hall, well-known for his slow paced coaching style, knew the best defense was a stout offense. Apparently such illegal recruiting incidents as the "Great Indiana Caper" escaped his mind. Was it possible that his good friend, Cecil Dunn, purchased Jay Shidler's tickets without Hall's knowledge? Did Hall know nothing of the high jinxes of the Webbs, Prewitt, Hogg and other good old boys? Did he wear blinders in the locker room and fail to see the $50 and $100 handshakes? Singletary seemed to think so.

It was unreasonable, Singletary said, to hold a coach responsible for every problem facing a program. "I know you can generalize about that," he said, "but the fact is if something goes wrong in your program it doesn't necessarily mean that the coach has *done it* (emphasis mine). I think the players have to have some responsibility for his or her actions."[501]

There was a flaw in his logic as wide as the Grand Canyon. Any number of people could have done it. Where was Hagan, whose duties as athletics director were to supervise the program? He was the one who reported to the president that the basketball program was in compliance with NCAA rules every year. For that matter, where was Singletary while all this was occurring? He was wheeling and dealing on the national college athletic stage; going on recruiting trips as the "Great Indiana Caper;" opening the door for the good old boys to dominate the program; letting faculty know they really had no say in how the athletics program was conducted; hoarding tickets by the hundreds and allowing Hall to do the same; dipping into Haggin Trust funds to entertain politicians at lavish pre-game luncheons, and feathering his retirement nest.

Singletary more or less disappeared from the scene after the newspaper articles were published. He sent out his vice-president for public relations, Raymond Hornback, to take the bully pulpit the president previously used so effectively. Hornback called a news conference to reply to the newspaper articles, read a short statement, refused to take any questions and left the room. His statement said the school had notified the SEC and the NCAA of the content of the articles; legal counsel John Darsie was assigned to find out what evidence the newspaper had to verify the allegations; Hagan was to work with coaches on a reorganization of the program, and the faithful were banned from the locker room.[502]

Darsie, when he was refused access to the newspaper's materials, turned to the NCAA for help. Director of enforcement S. David Berst, after promising to complete the investigation in six months, said a decision would be made on issuing a formal request for the newspapers's source material. Berst, like Darsie, was simply putting the best spin on a terribly embarrassing situation. Both men knew there was no way the newspaper was going to let them have access to material that was protected by the First Amendment.[503]

Indicative of the negative national publicity on the way was the November 11, 1985 issue of Sports Illustrated. Dave Batton, who Hall tried to recruit, told the magazine, "Kentucky was illegal from day one." He said Seth Hancock, whose Claiborne Farm was a popular stopping point on Hall's recruiting trail, offered to invest Batton's future summer job earnings, $20,000 in a Thoroughbred. Hancock was one of the good old boys the NCAA asked the university to disassociate from their athletics program in the 1976 violations.[504]

Hancock, however, was welcomed back to the program when he put $250,000 into the Nutter Training Center, and worked to raise more money for that project and others. Hancock appeared to suffer from selective enforcement. He was a part of the "Great Indian Caper," but evidently had less impact than Albert G. Clay, who was up to his eyebrows in illegal recruiting violations. Clay wasn't mentioned by the NCAA, and certainly not the school. Neither were Warren Rosenthal, W.T. Young, Hilary Boone, William Sturgill, the Webb brothers nor Hall's good friend, Cecil Dunn, mentioned.[505]

Hesitant to stir very deep in making reforms, Singletary and Hagan institute only cosmetic measures. Habits were so firmly ingrained they were either unable or unwilling to make real reforms, or the appearance thereof. Two weeks after the newspaper printed the articles, Hagan announced the investigation was over, and new regulations were in place. Players' speaking engagements required coaches' approval and follow-up reports. Registration of athletes' vehicles had to be filed with the university. Head coaches were responsible for players' comp tickets being used only by designated relatives and students. Players' off-campus meals required a receipt. Guests, however, were still allowed to sit on the bench with the team during games, but they needed Hagan's approval.[506]

Singletary finally surfaced to address "The greatest furor over athletics that I can remember." He said he assumed the newspaper had reliable evidence or they wouldn't have printed the articles. He employed a kill-the-messenger approach in blaming the newspaper for his problems. "We may never be able to undo what you have done," he told them, "we may not be able to do that."[507]

Singletary had no apologies for his interest in athletics, even in the face of all the allegations. "It is commonly known that I enjoy intercollegiate athletics, and I do," he said, "I'm not apologetic about it. I like It. To move from that assumption to somehow that I have no balance about the proper role and importance of intercollegiate athletics is unacceptable to me.

Nobody knows how many meetings, dinners and lunches I've had with students who were not athletes here."[508]

Maybe it was wrong, but I assumed one of the roles of a university president was to interact with students whether they were athletes or not. Singletary was getting his sea legs again, and defending with an aggressive offense.

There were some on campus who agreed with him. Dental professor and athletics board member Charles "Chuck" Ellinger was a staunch defender of Singletary. "In my opinion," Ellinger said, "I think a lot of this progress is due to the leadership of Otis Singletary."[509]

Others disagreed, and were quite outspoken. English professor John Chubb said Singletary's administration did far too little to transfer some of the enthusiasm from sports to academics. Dental professor Emmett R. Costich said, "Some of the faculty, in jest, suggested we get an aerosol can of sweat and spray it around the medical center and he'd (Singletary) would be attracted to it like bees to honey." Costich said Singletary was unresponsive to his faculty's concerns when it appeared the dental school might be closed. Political science professor Lee Sigelman said Singletary was out of town on athletic business when a major mining research program was transferred to the University of Louisville. "I don't want to focus too much on that issue," Sigelman said, "but it is symptomatic."[510]

"That's a perception they're entitled to," Singletary responded, "but I've never been under any doubt about what the primary mission and function of this university is." When asked about the school being a good public university both academically and athletically, he replied, "I don't believe it's an either/or proposition. I don't believe the reason we don't have a good school is because we have a good basketball team."[511]

There was another picture of the university emerging, that of an institution whose academic reputation declined in recent years. Professors and staffs in mathematics and chemistry used their summer teaching salaries to purchase needed equipment for their departments. At the same time

Singletary had $8.1 millions in athletic funds stashed away in government bonds and certificates of deposit.[512]

The newspaper's refusal of Berst's request for access to their source material surprised no one. In January 1986 Singletary efficiently informed the board of trustees the university's internal investigation of the newspaper's allegations, based on forty-one interviews, was complete. The depth of the probe was reflected by the time the school spent on the investigation. The probe began in December, just as the fall semester and final exams were ending. It was completed in January as the spring semester was beginning. In between were the Christmas and New Year's holidays. Thirty-six of Hall's former players were contacted, and eight refused to be interviewed. Eighteen current or former university employees, thought to have knowledge of events, cooperated. Of the thirteen good old boys contacted, five refused to cooperate.[513]

It was as hard to pry that information out of Singletary as it would be for those opposed to the National Rifle Association to take a musket from Charlton Heston's "Cold dead hands." The media, when no information of the university's investigation was forthcoming, used the Open Records Act in an effort to get access to the paperwork. Legal counsel John Darsie replied that no paper work existed; that the report was transmitted orally to the NCAA.[514]

To accept the legal counsel's premise, one had to believe winged messengers were used instead of telephones; appointments were scheduled by extra-sensory perception; seventy-seven people were contacted by carrier pigeons, and the results of forty-four interviews were written in invisible ink. According to NCAA records, the university submitted, on May 19, 1986, a written report of its internal findings concerning the newspaper's allegations.[515]

The NCAA refused to accept the school's conclusions, and sent them back three times to gather additional information. Singletary left office long before the investigation was finally completed.

When Singletary's last employment contract was amended in 1985 to pay him $60,000 in Haggin Trust funds for each of his last two years in office, some other sweetheart deals were thrown in by school officials. He retained his tenure as a history professor drawing $75,000 a year until he reached the mandatory retirement age of seventy. Goodness no, he wasn't going to teach any history classes, but would assist in fund raising and write a history of his administration. It's been almost twenty years, and no book has appeared yet. Trustees gave him six months leave, with full pay, when he retired. His severance package was well over $500,000.[516]

For his post-retirement work, Singletary built himself an office in the archives of the M.I. King Library. For years, Special Collections was so pressed for space that many of their archival materials were stored twenty miles away in a former limestone quarry. Library shelving was ripped out to make way for Singletary's office, and the Haggin Trust paid the $50,700 bill. Another Haggin Trust account for Singletary, identified as the president emeritus, called for annual expenditures of $15,000. The trust was socked again for nearly $20,000 for Singletary's official portrait.[517]

The good old boys had their own rewards for Singletary, who came through for them on the downtown basketball arena. Gerald Headley, whose well-known family was prominent for their whiskey, racing and real estate interests, gave Singletary $100,000 to establish a discretionary fund for the next president. Floyd "Ratsy" Wright, a long-time athletics board member involved in the Lancaster-McCubbin affair, set up a trust fund for the medical school for Singletary to spend as he saw fit. The first payment in 1986 was $219,980. The Otis A. Singletary Fund for Excellence was established and, in 1989, had an account balance of $4.1 million. The new Fine Arts Center, build on the site of old McLean Stadium, was named for Singletary because, school officials said, of his strong support of the arts.[518]

Singletary's good friend from the "Great Indiana Caper," Albert G. Clay suggested trustees take $800,000 from Ashland Oil's $1 million gift, and establish the Otis A. Singletary Professorship in the Humanities. The athletics board create the $1 million Otis A. Singletary Graduate and Professional Fellowship Fund, and contributed $500,000. The fund enabled graduate students to continue their education as Singletary Scholars.[519] I didn't apply.

During his administration, Singletary paid the Washington lobbying firm of Cassidy & Associates $715,877 to help the university get $4.5 million in federal grants. Faculty members protested when Singletary became a lobbyist for the firm after he retired.[520]

At his retirement, the Louisville newspaper profiled Singletary as a "Charming, quick-witted, hard-headed, thin-skinned, soft-hearted, arrogant, aloof, arm-twisting visionary." The $250 million the state spent on community college projects showcased his political skills. He was a worn out genius, the newspaper said, who simply stayed too long on the job; a consummate politician who grew weary of dealing with professional politicians. The newspaper, unlike the university, addressed his current athletics scandal, and their source was quite close to Singletary. "That was a difficult time for Otis," Gloria Singletary said, "I think he was at the lowest ebb he's ever been…I thought he was pretty well battered."[521]

# A New Beginning

The solution to the latest athletic scandal was left for Otis A. Singletary's successor, David P. Roselle, to solve. Roselle, provost of Virginia Polytechnical Institute and State University, Blacksburg, became president in June 1987. A Pennsylvania native, his undergraduate degree was from Westchester College, and his doctorate in mathematics from Duke. After teaching mathematics at Maryland and LSU, Roselle went to VPI in 1974. He was no stranger to schools with high profile athletics programs.[522]

Roselle, whose pleasant dry demeanor tolerated no nonsense, initially depended on Singletary's crew of athletics investigators: legal counsels John Darsie and Joe Burch, law professor Robert Lawson and athletics director Cliff Hagan. After the NCAA's continued refusal to accept the school's findings in the investigation of the 1985 newspaper allegations, Hagan's ineffective management, and the appearance of the infamous Emory envelope, Roselle turned to an outside counsel to conduct a thorough investigation of Kentucky's famed basketball program. Not even during the point shaving scandals had the program been so closely scrutinized. Roselle ordered an internal audit of the UKAA finances; clamped down on the recruiting of academic deficient players; developed a model compliance program; fired his athletics director and basketball coaching staff; hired a snappy New Yorker to rebuild the basketball program, but he was unable to remove the influence the good old boys exerted in athletics. It is to his credit that he tried, but they continue to dominate the program.[523]

Roselle's first order of business was finding a solution to the NCAA's questions about the 1985 allegations of illegal subsidization. In June 1987, the school claimed protection under the NCAA's four-year statute of limitation, but did admit some violations occurred in the program prior to 1981. Those weren't the issue. The NCAA's committee on infractions said the university failed to develop complete information concerning the newspaper's allegations. The school was directed to answer five questions. Did Kentucky's investigative techniques help or hinder obtaining complete information? Had the school taken all reasonable steps to develop and confirm the articles? Were all potential sources of information interviewed? Did the school contend the newspaper articles were substantially incorrect? If so, why?[524]

In February 1988, Roselle told the committee on infractions that no president looked forward to meeting with them. "I do not relish it in the slightest," he said, "and assure you, if it is within my power to control the destiny of my institution, I will not be repeating the process." He stated he was there for a candid discussion of the issues, and had no intentions of dancing around the problems with subtleties and obscure generalities. How refreshing for a University of Kentucky president to make that statement. He added, "I have a major financial crisis back home and other critical issues that need my attention; I do not need a lingering problem with the NCAA."[525]

Roselle's financial crisis came from Gov. Wallace Wilkinson's refusal to increase state universities' budgets with new money from the Kentucky Lottery, the centerpiece of his gubernatorial campaign. Wilkinson called the university presidents "cry babies" for asking for more money for their institutions. A freshman college drop-out, Wilkinson was a multi-millionaire businessman from Lexington, whose administration ended in scandal. Community college chancellor Charles T. Wethington, his boyhood friend from Casey County, was the only other finalist in the search for a new president. That certainly put Roselle outside Wilkinson's circle that included that old hanger-on, "Happy" Chandler, and basketball coach

Eddie Sutton. Roselle, selected before Wilkinson was elected, was opposed for the presidency by Chandler.[526]

Partisan politics aside, Roselle was in an excellent position to look at the allegations without a bias. The school's investigation, for all practical purposes, was completed before he arrived. He said he had no reason to believe his investigators failed to follow any new leads, encouraged witnesses to be less than truthful, concealed information or suggested witnesses not speak with the NCAA. "We took extraordinary measures to get additional information and had mixed results," he said. "Some refused to be interviewed again, and others consented with ease and denied everything. It must be said in the final analysis, the case did not change in the slightest as a result of this effort."[527]

Three major obstacles stood in the way of continuing the investigation. Publicity caused those who could confirm or deny the newspapers' allegations to remain silent. Reporters may have been less than candid with the former players about the purpose of their interviews. The newspapers' refusal to relinquish their source notes ended the investigation. "I wish I could tell you the story in the newspaper is untrue," Roselle told the committee, "I can't. I can only say we made an honest effort to gather information, and reported to you what we found."[528]

Roselle had already met with football and basketball coaches and left no doubt in their minds that he held them accountable for their programs. He said publicly that honesty and integrity were more important to him than winning. Roselle characterized himself as being pro-academics but not anti-athletics.[529]

Sports columnist Billy Reed immediately drew a comparison between Roselle and Singletary. "Much as he hated the fact that his affinity for sports led some of his faculty members to call him 'Dr. Jock,' Singletary took a keen interest in his football and basketball teams. Don't expect Roselle to be so visibly involved." Reed predicted the new president would leave athletics alone as long as it was managed to fit his criteria. "He's so

satisfied with athletics director Cliff Hagan and the way the athletics association in being managed that he anticipates no major changes."[530]

Reed apparently didn't know that Hagan was already in deep trouble,
and that Roselle assigned others to do his job. An example was the F.W.
"Buddy" Schneider affair in January 1988. Schneider, a Lexington developer, asked Gov. Wilkinson to use his influence to get him a seat on the
athletics board. The request was sent to the governor's patronage man, Dr.
Floyd G. Poore. Poore contacted "Happy" Chandler about the appointment. Chandler backed Schneider saying he was a UK Fellow (meaning
he'd donated $10,000 to the development fund), and provided member-
ships in Spring Lake Country Club for coaches and players. Roselle heard
about Chandler's efforts on Schneider's behalf, and ordered legal counsel
Joe Burch to investigate the matter. The investigation revealed little except
that three former members of the football coaching staff, and possibly
some of the basketball coaching staff received free country club memberships from Schneider.[531]

Burch consulted with Lawson, the NCAA faculty representative, and
they decided it was wise to report the incident to the NCAA to show how
serious the school was about compliance. In the past, some of Singletary's
crew of athletic investigators appeared to be "lone rangers," going out on
their own, but all that changed with Roselle riding herd on them. Roselle
followed them every step of the way. [532]

Burch and Lawson decided to get Hagan involved. "It was felt," Burch
told Roselle, "that we could encourage Cliff Hagan to develop an attitude
of responsibility for his program by having him send the letter (to the
NCAA)." Hagan was fifty-seven-years-old, had been in athletics management sixteen years and he needed help to develop a sense of responsibility
for his own athletics program! Two weeks later the Lawson-Burch letter
for Hagan to sign went to the NCAA. Schneider got his seat on the athletics board, but not from Roselle.[533]

It was Lawson, not Hagan, Roselle told to investigate SEC and NCAA
concerns about football and basketball calendars, showing athletes with

remaining eligibility, being produced with profits going to the coaches, Jim Host, Cawood Ledford and others. Lawson admitted the calendars were a violation, but claimed Hagan knew nothing about them until the SEC began asking questions.[534] A source inside the athletics department, who asked not to be identified, told me Hagan knew about the calendars from the beginning.

The calendars, with one exception, were produced through Cawood Ledford Productions, owned by Host and Ledford. They had Sutton's agreement to publish the basketball calendar, but the team thought their group photograph was for publicity purposes. The profits were split between Sutton, Host and Ledford.[535]

The 1986 football calendar's photographs of players with remaining eligibility were furnished by the Sports Information Office. Profits from the calendar were shared by coach Jerry Claiborne and Sportstatic, Inc. Claiborne, however, used his portion to buy retirement annuities for his assistant coaches. In 1987, Host and Ledford worked out a deal with Claiborne to produce the calendar using photographs taken during spring practice. It was at this point, the SEC told the school, the calendars were a possible violation, and no funds were to be distributed on behalf of the football program.[536]

Lawson told the NCAA Hagan met with the coaches, and informed them the calendars were a possible rules violation, stopped all production and issued a memo prohibiting the use of photographs of student athletes with remaining eligibility on calendars and other similar items. Hagan's memo also prohibited anyone external to the school from using the institution's logo in the production of calendars. His memo also said any staff members involved in such publications had to get Hagan's approval before distribution.[537] The memo appeared to say don't do it but, if you do, my permission is needed.

The calendars turned out to be only a blip on the NCAA's radar screen. In December 1987, director of enforcement David Berst called the calendars a secondary violation that merited no further investigation. There was talk about the cozy relationship between the NCAA, Host, Ledford and the school. Sports Illustrated reporters Alexander Wolff and Armen Keteyian speculated that relationship was one reason Kentucky, one of college athletics' more productive cash cows, usually received light penalties for NCAA violations. The reporters pointed out David Cawood was a relative of Cawood Ledford, the broadcaster of Kentucky's games, and Host, who held the school's broadcast, telecast and game program rights, also controlled a number of lucrative NCAA printing and broadcasting contracts for the Final Four. "However far fetched their charges might be," Wolff and Keteyian wrote, "conspiracy theorists have noted the connections over the years as the 'Cats,' who seem to have nine lives, again and again dodged major penalties."[538]

If photographs of athletes with remaining eligibility couldn't be used for commercial profit by those outside the program, how did Host get away with producing the basketball game program containing the same? Nothing was said about that. It was a secret arrangement between the Lexington Civic Center and Host and, I suppose, they thought none would be the wiser. The NCAA certainly didn't go there.

Roselle again by-passed Hagan, and had Lawson investigate another possible violation connected to "Cawood on the Cats," a tabloid newspapers the radio announcer and Host produced. The paper's editor, Tom Wallace, was the scorekeeper for the Kentucky Prep All-Star Festival Sutton held in Memorial Coliseum in July 1987. Wallace, who was not working the event as a journalist, had several conversations with assistant basketball coach Dwane Casey. A month later, Wallace wrote an article for the tabloid quoting Casey, without his permission, on the athletic abilities of Festival participants Shawn Kemp, Chris Mills and Don McLean. Coaches aren't supposed comment on players they're recruiting.[539]

Lawson argued Casey didn't violate the NCAA by-law but, if there was a violation, he acted without any intent. Casey was going to get the blame either way. Hagan gently asked Cawood Ledford Productions to try to avoid violating NCAA regulations, but he slapped a reprimand in Casey's file.[540]

While delegating Hagan's responsibilities, Roselle kept close tabs on events. The mathematician was analytical in his approach to the program. He set priorities and examined athletics to see if they were being followed. His management style asked the following questions. Were athletics compatible and supportive of the university's academic mission? Were athletics providing a positive image with athletes meeting regular admission standards? Were the teams competing successfully under SEC and NCAA rules?[541] The obvious answers were, no.

Instead of building a stone wall around his athletics program, Roselle made changes necessary to insure athletics met his goals, not those of the coaches or the good old boys. He established his own compliance program that included an academic assistance program staffed with qualified professionals, and adequately funded to serve all athletes. Coaches were told to emphasize the importance of academics. Hagan reported directly to Roselle.[542]

The president wasn't too aloof to ask for advice on athletics. In November 1987, Roselle met with NCAA assistant executive director David Cawood to discuss his approach to managing a big time college athletics program. Guess who accompanied Cawood to the meeting? Jim Host. Cawood told Roselle his boss, executive director Richard D. Schultz, wanted to meet with him for further discussions. Plans for Schultz's visit included the Syracuse basketball game and reception and dinner at the president's home, Maxwell Place. UKAA staff and their spouses were on Roselle's invitation list, but not Host.[543]

Roselle instituted a secret audit of the UKAA's finances. The September 1987 Coopers and Lybrand report found no error or irregularities in the combined statement of revenue and expenditures. The audit suggested coaches' perks such as free dental service, clothing discounts, radio and television shows and the free use of dealer-owned automobiles be monitored by the school. In particular, the audit suggested the use of dealer owned automobiles by athletic department employees be reported as compensation to the Internal Revenue Service.[544]

Both head coaches of basketball and football and the athletics director had the use of two dealer-owned cars as part of their contracts. In May 1987, thirty-seven coaches of minor sports, assistant coaches, assistant athletics directors and department employees had dealer-owned automobiles. That list was compiled by assistant athletics director Gene DeFilippo. In 1995, I made an Open Records Act request for an updated list of athletic department employees who drove dealer-owned cars. It was a well-known fact the practice continued. George DeBin, the university's official records custodian, replied, "As to automobiles for 'other athletic department staff,' there are no such records." When asked for the source of his reply, DeBin's office replied that it came from associate athletics director Larry Ivy, whose name was on the 1987 list.[545]

The practice of athletic department employees enjoying the perks of using dealer-owned vehicles, changing every few months, occurred elsewhere. The Kansas athletics department reported to chancellor Gene A. Budig that donations from the Wheel Club, dealers who furnished athletics employees with cars, reached $175,00 at the end of the 1991 fiscal year. Former NCAA executive director Walter Byers called the practice a cars for tickets swap.[546]

Other portions of Roselle's audit, always marked confidential in his papers, included the financial involvement of various booster organizations. The K-Men's Association, made up of varsity lettermen, was the largest. It was the K-Men that Curci suggested routing money and property through when a NCAA investigation appeared imminent in 1975. The K-Men spent $44,580 for the program the previous year, and had a cash balance of $53,991.[547]

The Committee of 101 had $60,743 cash on hand, and the previous year spent $39,208 on the athletics program. The Wildcat Club had a cash balance of $21,326. The Lady Cats basketball booster club was way down the ladder spending only $3,261 on the program, and the amount the Volleyball Boosters spent was even less. Collectively, Kentucky's five booster clubs spent $104,535 on the program the previous year. Coopers and Lybrand pointed out they used only the figures the boosters furnished them.[548]

Soon after the audit was complete, assistant athletics director Gene DeFilippo organized a new booster group. "The Group of 50" was composed of many of the sons of the good old boys. The attraction of the Group was the exclusivity it would never exceed fifty members. It was quite successful with a waiting list of prospective members. For their $1,000 annual contribution, plus the cost of tickets, The Group of 50 were invited to football and basketball practices, attended away games, had special priority tickets to post-season games and socialized with players and coaches.[549]

Members of the Group of 50 included Bruce Bell, the son of former trustee, athletics board member and NFL referee Tommy Bell. Alex Boone was the son of horseman Hilary Boone who funded the tennis center and lent his private plane to the athletics program. Another insider was businessman Farra M. Alford, who previously received Rupp Arena tickets from coach Joe B. Hall's allotment. A father and his two sons, Buck, Henry and Thomas Hinkle, from Bourbon County were also members.[550]

Finally, in March 1988, the NCAA's committee on infractions announced their findings on the school's investigation of the newspapers' allegations about the basketball program three years earlier. The committee ruled the university failed to cooperate fully in the inquiry.[551] The negative decision reflected badly, not on Roselle, but on Singletary and Hagan who stonewalled the investigation from the beginning.

The committee found the program was lax in investigating allegations of players selling their comp tickets, and receiving excessive speaking fees. Evidently, there was no further investigation of the newspapers' allegation that coach Joe B. Hall's friend, Cecil Dunn, paid inflated prices for Jay Shidler's comp tickets for three years. The committee faulted the school for not using more leverage in forcing former athletes, who were in graduate school, to submit to further questioning. Letters the university sent to former players, unreachable by telephone, the committee said, implied the recipients' refusal to be interviewed was a satisfactory response.[552]

Kentucky's penalty was little more than a public reprimand. The school had to report in writing periodically to the enforcement staff concerning a comprehensive monitoring of the men's basketball program including economic audits of players' summer employment earnings, speaking fees, management of player's comp tickets and periodic NCAA inspections for three years.[553]

Roselle didn't appeal the committee on infraction's findings. He already had a model compliance system in place that legal counsel Joe Burch helped him develop. The program had four sections: a compliance officer on the athletics department staff, educational programs, monitoring the athletes and periodic audits. The compliance officer was responsible for the program adhering to all NCAA and SEC regulations, legislation and any changes; interviewing both newly enrolled and returning athletes at the beginning and end of each school term about summer employment rules, transportation, extra benefits, automobiles and other matters.[554]

The education portion of the plan focused on coaches, players and good old boys, especially those who employed athletes in the summer. Requests for players' speaking engagements went directly to the office of sports information who was responsible for expense reimbursements, and required approval of head coaches. Players had to provide a list of people they expected to use their comp tickets. If they included people who weren't family or students, the people had to be identified and reviewed. Detailed records of recruits' campus visits were to be kept, and the athletes weren't to be introduced to any of the good old boys. The faithful were banned from the locker room.[555]

Roselle was quite vocal in his opposition of coaches' recruiting players whose academic background failed to equip them for college work. The compliance plan called for internal audits of that portion by a person reporting only to Roselle. "The whole issue of basic entrance requirements for student athletes," he said, "rises from a concern that many young people who are unprepared for college work are being admitted to school to compete in college athletics."[556]

In January 1988, Roselle joined nine other SEC presidents in a review of the NCAA's Proposition 48 that required athletes to have a 15 ACT or a 700 SAT score, and a 2.0 grade point average in core curriculum of college preparatory courses. Roselle's problem was he had a basketball coach who, in less than three years, recruited five players who failed to meet NCAA admission requirements. John Pitman, from Rosenberg, Texas; Reggie Hanson, from Somerset; Eric Manuel, from Macon Georgia; Sean Woods, from Indianapolis, and Shawn Kemp, from Elkhart, Indiana, were all outstanding athletes, but academically ineligible to play their freshman years. Roselle wasn't happy with his coach.[557]

Sutton was responsible for recruiting those players, but some of the blame lay with university officials who admitted them in the first place. Pitman participated in summer work-outs and had a job at Crestwood Farm before admission officials just happened to discover he was ineligible to enroll in college. Hanson and Woods sat out their freshman season before joining the team. Kemp was admitted, but withdrew three months into his freshman year and transferred to Trinity Valley Junior College in Athens, Texas. Eric Manuel eventually presented the biggest problem to the school.[558]

Roselle instructed chancellor Art Gallaher to strengthen the school's admission policy for athletes. In February 1988, Gallaher told Hagan to immediately implement the new policy that clearly stated only those athletes with the ability and background to succeed academically could be recruited. An exception was made in the procedure the school used for handling athletes' academic requirements.[559]

Sutton apparently interpreted the exception to mean requirements were relaxed. "The policy change would make it easier for athletes who fail to meet Proposition 48 to enroll at UK in the future," Sutton told a news conference. Mark White, the admissions officer responsible for athletes' admittance, agreed with him. When Sutton's statement reached Roselle, he immediately instructed Robert Lawson to publicly refute the coach's remarks. "What we did, " Lawson explained, "does not change the standards of admission; we only changed the procedure where exceptions can be sought." Previously, only Lawson's approval was needed before the case for a questionable athlete went to the faculty exceptions committee. Under Roselle's rules, an assistant athletics director prepared the athlete's case, and his work was reviewed by the admissions director, Lawson and the athletics director. If two of those three approved the application, it then went to the faculty exceptions committee.[560]

It was difficult to determine how the talented, but academically ineligible, athletes were admitted since students' records were protected by federal law, the Buckley Amendment. There was a strong hint in Roselle's papers of collaborations between some coaches and the admissions office. Admissions officers failed to notice or call attention to the unusually wide gap between Eric Manuel test scores when he was admitted. "Our problem with Manuel's certification," Lawson said, "is partially traceable to our inexperience with athletic eligibility two years ago when that certification occurred."[561]

The school had been dealing in certification of athletes' eligibility since they joined the NCAA as a full-fledged member in 1936, and even before. The law professor was making excuses, but he demanded that someone who understood the rules had better be in charge of the admissions office to avoid "Another mistake like the one (Manuel) we made two years ago." Lawson told vice-president Edward Carter and admissions officer Joseph T. Fink, III, such errors,"could result in worse consequence than we presently face. With the NCAA death penalty in our future, a major violation of NCAA rules will put our basketball program on the sidelines for two years. Should that happen, of course, the three of us along with president Roselle would be well advised to get out of Kentucky as soon as possible."[562]

# A Good Old Boy Loses Out

Correcting lax admissions standards for athletes, instituting a model compliance program and searching for funds to expand the university and increase faculty salaries kept Roselle busy. Straightening out some of Singletary and Hagan's athletic buildings, such as the aquatics center, took a back seat. Roselle did, however, find time from putting out fires to keep an eye on athletics director Cliff Hagan.

The aquatics center was in total disarray when Singletary left office. One contractor took bankruptcy during the prolonged construction. Severe weather caused other delays. A fire, caused by spontaneous combustion of paint supplies, damaged the entire structure and impeded completion for five months. The aquatics center was truly a Murphy's Law project: if anything could go wrong it did. A turf war developed with vice-chancellor Jack C. Blanton and architect Don Wallace on one side, swim coach Wynn Paul on the other and nobody was refereeing.[563]

About the only thing everybody agreed on was naming the building after the late athletics director Harry Lancaster. As trustees' continued to expand the scope of the center's contract, Blanton continued to delete some features necessary to the building. Paul objected to many of the center's features including the elaborate stairs to the diving tower, a bulkhead placed in the wrong section of the pool, the depth at the shallow end and many more. The more Paul spoke out, the angrier Blanton became. Finally, he told Paul, "When the project is complete and the contractor turns the pool over to the university, it will be possible to initiate new projects that will make the facility satisfactory to you." In essence, Blanton was saying nothing was going to change the politics of the building regardless of how much more money was required. Just another day in the life of Kentucky athletics. Finally, he told Paul, "Keep your powder dry and your swim trunks on in anticipation of additional funding needed for this project. You also ought to be extra nice to Mr. Hagan and the athletics board members, me included."[564]

From July 1986 to March 1988, trustees' approved $146,208 in changes for the aquatics center, and that didn't include the nearly $750,000 they authorized in previous orders. In April 1986, alternations to aquatic center features amounting to $835,000 were made that included the scoreboard and the diving tower, but still not the elaborate spiral stairs. Finally, Paul told Hagan, the architect's plans for the diving tower were "So grandiose and extravagant that I recommend we would be better off waiting until the building is released to the UKAA, and then hire another contractor to build the tower for $50,000 rather than trying to come up with the $130,000-$200,000 required to fill in the one in the plans."[565]

When the aquatics center was finally turned over to the UKAA, Blanton told Hagan an additional $557,661 would be needed to get the facility Paul wanted. Blanton low-balled the estimate. UKAA accounting director J.R. Hisle said it was necessary to spend another million dollars to modify the center before swim meets could be held. Those modifications included additional bath facilities to meet health regulations, new lane graphics to replace those that failed to line up properly, a new deck surface was required because swimmers were unable to stand when they got out of the pool, timing clocks, the scoreboard and functional stairs to the diving tower.[566]

It was absolutely amazing that no one in authority, that I could find, showed any concern over the excessive expenditures for the aquatics center, or asked what happened to all the money. At the same time the school was pouring money into the aquatics center, floor boards were collapsing in Frazee Hall, a classroom building; concrete was peeling off Paterson Office Tower; engineering and architect buildings were fire traps; faculty members were leaving in droves, but it was mandatory to keep an even keel in athletics.

The 51,587-square-foot Lancaster Aquatics Center, whose initial completion date was March 1985, was dedicated four years later. Paul, who fought an admirable but futile battle, said, "It doesn't bother me anymore; there are always going to be delays in a huge project like this."[567] Paul never had a chance to get the facility he wanted.

With the aquatics center soaking up funds like a sponge and athletics money going for Roselle's priority of academics, Hagan's plans for expanding Commonwealth Stadium were shelved, but the athletics director held out to the bitter end. He proposed stadium expansion in 1979, six years after it was built, and continued until he resigned.

With Roselle delegating many of Hagan's management duties, he had plenty of time to spend five months in 1987 perfecting his fund-raising plan for the stadium expansion. Hagan wanted a surcharge of $50 for each season football and basketball tickets sold. He argued Kentucky's priority seating costs were the lowest in the SEC, and had the figures to prove it.[568]

Somehow, Roselle's signature found its way on a September 1988 Blue White Fund solicitation letter asking for funds to expand the stadium. An accompanying brochure said an addition 8,000-10,000 tickets could be sold with proper marketing. The plan was to build permanent end-zone seating to connect with sidelines' stands with sky boxes between the decks. The expansion would seat 73,000. Vice-president Edward Carter sent the mailer to Roselle with a note saying, "I see you now support stadium expansion."[569]

Hagan's sky box idea came from his SEC survey. Alabama had no sky boxes in 1988, but made $625,000 from selling press box seats. LSU collected $750,000 from a similar arrangement. Florida sold their sky boxes for $1.5 million, and had a waiting list of people ready to shell out another $700,000 for priority seating. Auburn reaped $1.5 million from sky boxes selling for $30,000 each. Tennessee collected $700,000 and Vanderbilt $150,000 from their sky boxes. Georgia, Mississippi and Mississippi State had no sky boxes. The good old boys got in line for sky boxes at an initial cost of $36,000 each. They included horseman Seth Hancock, businessman Labe Jackson, Jr., developers Don and Dudley Webb, bank president Wayne Smith, automobile dealer Frank Shoop and media mogul Jim Host.[570]

There were objections to the stadium sky box idea from within the university. Chancellor Art Gallaher, hesitant to voice his objections since Roselle removed athletics from his office, asked his vice-chancellor Jack C. Blanton to convey his message to the president. Blanton was happy to convey the message, but blundered by contrasting Roselle to Singletary. "Singletary, whom many perceived as 'Dr. Jock,' would not allow these vanity boxes to be built and neither would Art," he told Roselle. The sky boxes, Blanton continued, had the potential to fulfill the expressed social needs of twenty-six businessmen while annoying the sensibilities of 56,000 others on game days. If the boxes had to be built, Blanton suggested any profits go to academics. He was resentful the idea hadn't been discussed with the athletics board, himself included.[571] Blanton was the same administrator who guided the aquatics center building blunder.

Roselle commented to Carter on Hagan's suggested surcharge plan, "Cliff Hagan will come to visit: please have this revised prior to then." What Hagan got, when Roselle was finished with his plan, was a one-dollar increase in ticket prices, and a ten-dollar surcharge on season tickets estimated to bring in $850,000.[572]

Hagan had no opportunity to expand the stadium although he and assistant athletics director Larry Ivy continued to meet with architects and a design team. In April 1988, Roselle took the last of the designated $4 million from athletics for the school's general fund. Hagan told the board he hoped the practice wouldn't continue. "We've had difficulty keeping up with the Joneses in the conference," he whined, "we don't want to lose ground. Should our attendance dwindle or our financial support erode, we could find ourselves in financial trouble."[573]

Roselle ignored Hagan's protests, and told the board he appreciated their approving the transfer of funds without any objections. Board member and strip mining mogul William B. Sturgill, Singletary's friend from the Haggin Trust episode, said it was the proper thing to do. Nicholas J. Pisacano, medical school professor, was gleeful, "It's probably the most noble action I've seen this board take, and I've been on the board for twenty years."[574]

Hagan's days were numbered. He repudiated rumors circulating about new NCAA allegations, and denied Kentucky received only a slap on the wrist for the 1985 violations. "The fact is that neither the university nor the NCAA could substantiate many of the (newspaper's) allegations," he said. Roselle let him call a news conference in August 1988 to extol what he called his thirteen years of athletics accomplishments. Hagan included the newly installed compliance program that was created by legal counsel Joe Burch and Roselle. He bragged about Kentucky's $13 million budget and virtually no debts while other SEC schools, such as Alabama, owed $34 million. At that time the UKAA owed $8 million on the stadium bonds.[575]

Hagan refused to elaborate on the condition of athletics beyond his written statement. Sports information director Chris Cameron said Hagan worked on the statement for three days. "It's his words," Cameron said, "but we helped in terms of sentence structure and editing."[576]

There were no documents in Roselle's papers to indicate his true feeling toward Hagan, but his statements to others about the athletics director spoke volumes. Juanita Johnson told Roselle her opinion of Hagan's ineptness in hiring women's basketball coaches. "I think you need to take a close look at your athletics director as he does a good job of one thing and that is looking pretty," she added. At the top of her letter, Roselle wrote "Art (chancellor Gallaher), one of Hagan's fans. You should, I think, show him the letter." Clarence R. Durham, of Anchorage, grumbled to Roselle about the seemingly lack of support the athletics director gave football coach Jerry Claiborne's fund raising efforts. Durham said Claiborne personally raised half the money to build the Nutter Training Center, and no other SEC coach was required to be a fund raisers in addition to all their other duties. On Durham's letter, Roselle wrote, "Cliff, want to try your hand at a reply."[577]

Hagan's failure to appear at an October 1988 news conference, where new NCAA allegations against Kentucky were announced, signaled his departure. He protested that he was in Baton Rouge for the LSU-UK football game performing his duties as athletics director. When Roselle yanked him into his office for a two hour meeting, the athletics director said was a shock to him. The president held him responsible for the conduct of the basketball program. "To hold me responsible for what are only allegations seems premature and unfeeling," Hagan moaned, "that's the unfairness of it, the administration has control."[578]

After wheeling and dealing with Singletary on athletics for twelve years, it probably was a shock to Hagan to discover he was no longer in charge and was subservient to a president who valued responsibility.

Bernard Vonderheide, public relations director, said the university saw nothing unfair in holding the athletics director responsible for the lack of institutional control in monitoring the men's basketball program. Hagan understood his now insecure position, and only made lame excuses such as, "I've put a lot of energy into compliance with NCAA rules' there's very little else you can do except have faith in the people you've hired."[579]

By November, Roselle and Hagan worked out an arrangement where the athletics director would resign immediately. He was given a newly-created post as special assistant to vice-president Edward Carter at the same salary $84,150 a year. Hagan supposedly had an office in the basement of the Administration Building, but there were few if any sightings of him on campus. The next year, his salary was reduced to $62,853, and he took early retirement. Hagan's retirement was the only occasion I found when

Roselle dipped into Haggin Trust funds for athletic purposes. Haggin Trust funds of $102,192 eased Hagan into retirement.[580]

There was little public outcry over Hagan's departure. Students cared little for him because of his dictatorial control of tickets, and many were glad to see him leave. "Happy" Chandler and former UK athlete, E.P. Grigsby, promised to fight any move to fire Hagan. Chandler contended coach Sutton, who had been on the job for three years, was more responsible for any wrongs linked to basketball than Hagan, whose association with the school covered thirty-seven years. Chandler's prophecy, that thousands of Kentuckians would fight for Cliff Hagan, never came true.[581]

Hagan, however, remained a sports icon to many. Sports columnist John McGill wrote, "Hagan's management style was perhaps largely a result of his tenure under Dr. Singletary, who as school president, apparently ran the athletics department as much as Hagan did."[582]

"The saddest of all," McGill continued, "is the very real possibility that Hagan's greatest failing was simply the inability to perceive the enormousness of his role. A failure to realize that when it came to overseeing the integrity of coaches and their programs, the buck indeed stops at the AD's desk. If that was Hagan's greatest failing, the fear is that he could be lumped among people whose hands might be far more dirty. By all accounts, he shouldn't be. Blame him for holding the reins too lightly, but blame him not as a mastermind of corruption."[583]

McGill was correct about Hagan operating in Singletary's shadow, but he was also a clearly visible major college athletics director on the national scene. As for Hagan not being a party to corruption, there were apparently many things the columnist didn't know. Hagan's had his own stash of basketball tickets, and arranged for coach Joe B. Hall's 412 choice lower arena season tickets. There were the deals with the calendars for the profit of coaches and Jim Host. Hagan not only cut a deal with Host to deduct $100,000 from his television rights contract, but allowed the broadcaster to go months beyond agreed upon rights payment dates. Hagan refused to discuss athletes' medical care at the university hospital. There may have been other incidents, but when Hagan left the UKAA few files remained with any reference to his actions.

Roselle immediately named Joe Burch as interim athletics director, and a national search began for a new athletics director. Among the forty applicants were Burch, Larry Conley, one of "Rupp's Runts" and a television commentator, and another of Rupp's former players.

Charles Martin Newton, Vanderbilt basketball coach and assistant athletics director who lettered for Rupp in 1951, was back for another look at his alma mater after turning down the head basketball coach's job three years earlier. Newton, a native of Rockwood, Tennessee, who played in the New York Yankees minor league system, was the unanimous choice of the committee, the athletics board and trustees. Newton coached at Transylvania from 1956 to 1968, when he moved to Alabama. He was an assistant SEC commissioner for a year before going to Vanderbilt in 1982. Newton's bachelor and master degrees were from Kentucky.[584]

Newton's four-year contract, at $106,000 a year, allowed him to earn outside income and included a controversial supplemental agreement. If Newton kept Kentucky athletics clean through 1994, he would receive a $150,000 annuity. He was annoyed at media questions about the annuity, "there was never any talk of if we run a clean program, we are going to run a clean program. Hell, that's an expectation. The intent there is not necessarily to get the benefit; I'm going to get the benefit. The intent is if I'm not here or if I don't do my utmost to keep the program in good shape, I don't get the benefit."[585]

If the annuity had been revealed for what it actually was, partial compensation for leaving his higher paying job at Vanderbilt, no uproar would have occurred. In 1992, another $50,000 was added to his annuity to keep the program clean through 1996, and his annual salary was increased to $131,000. Newton's income from radio shows and endorsements was unavailable.[586]

The annuity created a minor flap in the SEC. Mississippi athletics director Warner Alford scoffed, "That's what you're supposed to do; I don't understand having an incentive for doing what you're supposed to do." SEC commissioner and former Vanderbilt basketball coach Roy Kramer said he had mixed feelings about whether or not schools should offer inducements for playing by the rules. Kramer had several incentives that drove up his salary and benefits as conference commissioner in 1996 to $354,000 a year.[587]

With Newton's appointment came a series of new athletics buildings and renovations, some of which were actually completed on schedule. They included a $850,000 renovation of Memorial Coliseum, the first since it opened in 1950; a 133,000-square-foot indoor practice facility, plans for an on-campus arena and, once again, stadium expansion. New locker rooms, a state of the art training facility and a meeting room were built on the first floor of the Coliseum with UKAA administrative offices and basketball coaches' on the second floor. The renovation, reducing Coliseum seating to 8,000, was completed within a week of the scheduled date.[588]

Newton's office in the Coliseum was plush with Oriental carpets and reproductions of antique furniture. Sitting in the main conference room was a bronze bust of Adolph Rupp sculpted by alumnus Bill Burton of Owensboro, Cliff Hagan's hometown. The day after Hagan was fired, Burton wrote Roselle of his concern that the bust remain in the Coliseum. "The bust," he told Roselle, "was intended as a gift to the university, not Mr. Hagan personally. In light of Mr. Hagan's recent resignation, it is important for me to know it will stay at the university." Roselle assured him it would.[589]

Newton found some new deep pockets ready to open their checkbooks for the Coliseum renovation. They included Howard Settles, president of Century Offshore Management, Inc., of Lexington and Metairie, Louisiana. Settles told Newton that the basketball team "Has been a point of pride and symbol of excellence for our often maligned state." He gave $3,000 to the Blue White fund, $75,000 over three years for the Coliseum renovation, and wanted a sky box when the stadium was expanded.[590]

What contributors, such as Settles, expected for their donations created a problem. Newton planned to take fifty-six lower level Rupp Arena seats from the students' section. Bruck A. Rector, student trustee and son of a prominent Lexington real estate agent, wrote Roselle protesting the loss of the tickets. Rector was angry that athletics officials waited nearly two months after the Coliseum renovation began before announcing the ticket change. He said attorneys told him the action was possibly illegal. "In the past," Rector told the president, "fund-raising projects involving tickets have been used to (1) raise money and (2) line the pockets of athletics department officials. This, combined with the 'hush-hush' nature of the project, has made UK students, faculty and administrators wonder if anything really changed in the UK athletics department." Newton blinked, and the students kept their tickets.[591]

Newton's indoor practice facility, that began with a $7 million price tag, didn't fare as well as the Coliseum renovation. At the ground breaking in October 1991, Newton estimated construction would take about a year. The facility, with an elaborate system of nets below the seventy-two-foot ceiling, provided the football team with a full-sized artificial turf field and contained configurations for baseball, track and field, soccer, golf and gymnastics. There was the usual excuse of bad weather delaying the completion. What was expected when the project started in November? Construction errors in the grand Kentucky tradition and problems with the complicated system of nets delayed the practice facility's opening three times. The facility finally opened in September 1993, at a cost of $8.5 million, and was named for Ervin J. Nutter, an Ohio industrialist and engineering alumnus, who contributed $1.5 million to the building.[592]

With the practice facility completed, Newton turned his attention to expanding the stadium. He had a base of 38,000 sold season tickets on which to build. Renovation of plumbing, permanent end-zone seating, four new elevators, forty private boxes with rest rooms and food preparations areas, a year-around novelty shop and upgraded press box facilities were supposed to be completed in time for the 1998 season. That didn't happen. Athletic officials bragged they had the state's permission to spend $24 million on the stadium. Associate athletics director Larry Ivy said revenue bonds would be sold to finance the renovation. He boasted the original revenue bonds, financed by the state, would be paid off in 1997, five years early.[593]

If they were paying off the original revenue bonds five years early, they had indeed tapped into some very deep pockets. Another Open Records Act request went to the legal counsel's office. The controller's office replied those bonds would be paid off on the original schedule that ran through 2002. Ivy was referring to, but didn't elaborate in the media, the UKAA's plan to use the $3 million, the state placed in escrow for debt payment on the bonds in 1973, to pay off the remaining debt of $3.1 million. Official records custodian George DeBin said the state agreed, from the beginning, the athletics association could keep the $3 million when the bonds were paid out.[594]

Never let it be said that taxpayers' dollars don't find their way into Kentucky athletics.

# FAKED OUT

Athletic officials weren't the only ones using cunning footwork and parsing words. Medical center chancellor Peter Bosomworth did the same in his efforts to keep athletes' medical care with an outside physician instead of in the sports medicine practice in his own department of orthopedics. Bosomworth found a willing partner in the new athletics director. The strategy Bosomworth and Newton formulated was straight out of the good old boys' playbook.

When Roselle came into office, Mike Ray's UK Sports Medicine practice supervised the basketball team and treated athletes from other sports, except football, and those from other universities and colleges in the region. Ray instituted a trainer outreach program for area high schools and, for a time, it appeared he and other orthopedists would build the sports medicine program they envisioned.

Claiborne wanted the sports medicine practice of Mary Lloyd Ireland, an associate of surgeon James Andrews, to care for his football players. A conflict between the two practices was inevitable. Bosomworth was in a position where he could achieve his aims by two roads. If he couldn't send all the athletes to Andrews and Mary Lloyd Ireland, then he would bring them into the medical center.

Singletary's departure gave the medical center orthopedists some hope of a fair hearing of their sports medicine plan before Roselle, but they had to circumvent athletics director Cliff Hagan who refused to discuss the matter with them. The orthopedists were concerned about the proper time to approach Roselle because, going through the chain of command, they had to have Bosomworth's approval. Orthopedist department chairman Thomas Brower heard that Andrews and Central Baptist were exploring the possibility of establishing a sports medicine center similar to the one Bosomworth planned two years earlier.[595]

"All of these plans," Brower said, "seem to be predicated on the continued reputation gained by the care of the football team. This is the linchpin of the whole operation." He suggested they get busy and make their presentation to Roselle. "Such a maneuver is going to run into a very powerful individual and that is (head) athletic trainer Al Green; most people on campus are not fully aware of this man's power structure," he added. Green was one of the architects of Bosomworth's original sports medicine plan to build Andrews a 100-bed hospital on university property.[596]

Green's close connections to the Andrews-Ireland practice at Central Baptist Hospital was best illustrated in the events following a tragic accident at the Kentucky Relays in 1987. Scott Hartman, a Tennessee athlete, was hit in the head by a hammer thrown by Berea College's Alan Mills. Although the Relays were held almost in the shadow of the medical center, Green, a university employee, sent Hartman to Central Baptist Hospital nearly an hour after he was injured. The athlete was paralyzed. Medical center physicians were appalled since the school had developed one of the best head injury clinical and research facilities in the nation. Kay Hartman, the athlete's mother, filed suit against the UKAA, but legal counsel John Darsie claimed the athletics association was an arm of the university and as such was immune from legal action. The Sixth Circuit Court of Appeals said otherwise, and the school's insurance carrier finally paid the family $1 million after making them wait for five years.[597]

Ray's trainer outreach program was growing in popularity and covered several high schools in the area. The outreach program provided services of orthopedists, trainers and physical therapists. He was asked to make a presentation about the program, that cost schools one dollar a year, to the Woodford County (Versailles) Board of Education. UK head trainer Al Green was also at the meeting, apparently as a representative of the Andrews-Ireland practice's trainer outreach program that cost $11,000 a year. The board initially decided to go with Ray's program until a local man, Jim Gay, protested. Gay, whose son was associated with Andrews-Ireland's practice, offered to pay the $11,000 cost, and that tilted the decision.[598]

Ray and medical center physicians were furious that Green, a university employee, represented a competing sports medicine practice. Green's presence at the meeting gave them the perfect opening to approach Roselle. Bosomworth had little choice but to agree to the meeting where the orthopedists would present their plan to Roselle for treating all athletes at the medical center's sports medicine practice. They told Roselle that both the athletes and medical center would benefit since an accredited sports medicine program had to be associated with a residents' training program.[599]

Green's presence at the board of education meeting representing an outside practice got Roselle's attention. He told Hagan to immediately investigate the sports medicine problem. Since he earlier refused to even discuss athletes medical care with the orthopedists, Hagan apparently felt he had to do something. He sent a memo to football coach Jerry Claiborne relaying Roselle's concerns that a university employee on his staff was soliciting business for an outside medical practice. Claiborne replied immediately, "This is in response to Dr. Roselle's inquiry into one of the members of my coaching staff being on Central Baptist Hospital's payroll and going around 'bad-mouthing' the UK medical center; no one on my staff is on that hospital's payroll." That wasn't precisely what Roselle asked about.[600]

At best Claiborne was splitting hairs, and he went on to defeat his own argument. "Al Green, head athletic trainer, is a paid consultant to Central Baptist's sports medicine program," the coach continued, "he began his consulting work before the medical center announced their sports medicine program." Claiborne claimed Green was not involved with the day-to-day affairs of the Andrews-Ireland practice. "He has informed me," Claiborne said, "he has not spoken negatively about the medical center's sports medicine program in public as part of his consulting duties." Claiborne's failure to explain Green's presence at the board of education meeting indicated just what the trainer was doing there. That wasn't the first time Green was accused of making negative remarks about medical center physicians. Two years earlier, vascular surgeon Edwin J. Nighbert complained to Singletary about disparaging remarks Green allegedly made about the institution's medical training.[601]

Attached to Claiborne's letter to Hagan was a report on the UKAA's medical services policy. From all indications, the report had been hurriedly assembled to address Roselle's concerns about athletes' medical care, and defend athletic officials' actions. The football coach claimed, in the report, there was no need to change medical care for the school's athletes. With the completion of the Nutter Training Center, specially designed for the football team, Claiborne said he would rarely need either sports medicine practice. The coach's ties to the Andrews-Ireland practice were clear. He said it was time to sit down with Roselle to discuss the history of the situation and resolve it.[602]

Roselle was far ahead of them. He instructed Hagan to see there were no further conflicts of interest between Green, his trainers' staff, the Kentucky Sports Medicine practice at Central Baptist Hospital or any of the physicians connected with either organization. Green and his staff were to make no arrangements outside the university without Hagan's approval. Hagan's contribution was to send memos, containing Roselle's edict, to all the athletic trainers. It was clear Hagan had no intention of following Roselle's orders. Several weeks later, the Kentucky Sports Medicine practice conducted a symposium on football injuries with the final session held at the Nutter Training Center on campus. A symposium brochure identified Ireland as the "Kentucky Team Physician." Medical center orthopedists doubted they would have been allowed in the Nutter Center. They were correct.[603]

After Burch became interim athletics director, there was some discussion, in the form of scribbled notes, of attempting to iron out the dispute over athletes' medical care between the two practices. Roselle told Burch to settle the differences between orthopedist Mike Ray and trainer Al Green. Nothing I found indicated any serious effort was made. Instead, Burch had another idea.[604]

Since UK Sports Medicine, in the department of orthopedics, had no intention of giving up the fight to bring all athletes' medical care into the medical center, Burch decided they were right. But, he decided athletes would be cared for in the medical center, not in Sports Medicine, but in Student Health under the supervision of internist John Perrine. The fix was in big time! Medical school dean Emory Wilson abandoned the orthopedists, and asked Perrine to submit a proposal, worked out in advance, to treat athletes in Student Health and then refer them, if necessary, to the appropriate specialists. The conflict over athletes' medical care was so great that Wilson sent his letter to Perrine's home instead of his office in the medical center.[605]

Although Wilson conceded Student Health couldn't maintain a presence at all athletic events, he played ball sending the plan to Bosomworth with his blessings. It was obvious that athletes' medical care took a back seat to the politics involved. The transfer of all athletes' medical care to Student Health was no more than a ploy to bring Andrews and Ireland into the medical center.[606] It appeared Bosomworth and his administrators could have cared less about the athletes, they were going to have their way come hell or high water.

Wilson suggested he and Bosomworth meet with the new athletics director to discuss the transfer to Student Health. Bosomworth had other ideas. He waited until Roselle left, and met with C.M. Newton alone. By then, the interim president, whom everybody saw as the next president, was none other than Gov. Wallace Wilkinson's good friend and "Happy" Chandler's protégée, Charles T. Wethington.[607] The fix was truly in place.

Bosomworth bowed and scraped to Newton telling him he was willing to work with whatever medical group the athletics director wanted to care for the athletes. He and Newton set up a committee, composed overwhelmingly of deans and division directors, to formulate their plan. It was a smart political move as it eliminated most of the medical center orthopedists from the loop.[608]

Proof of that was found in one of the many memos Bosomworth wrote about his discussions with Newton on the subject. The two men talked about naming medical school professor Nicholas Pisacano to the committee since he had been on the athletics board and was hospital board member. "Newton thinks," Bosomworth wrote, "putting Nick into the committee structure will help keep Nick from stirring the pot out side the institution to get the attention of the athletics association. I tend to agree with that. If properly managed, Nick would be a very positive force in this process."[609]

While Bosomworth and Newton were hatching their intrigue, Ray and his associates formulated a ten-page plan to consolidate medical care for all the school's athletes, varsity, intramural and club, into UK Sports Medicine. The plan was sent to medical center director Frank Butler who, of course, passed it on to Bosomworth. Ray, an orthopedic consultant to the US Olympic cross-country ski team, pointed out that all the clinical services needed to treat athletes' injuries were in the medical center. He proposed that sports medicine-trained physicians hold clinics in each sport's training room for two hours each morning; provide coverage at all games and events, both at home and away; designate certified athletic trainers to work closely with intramural and club sports. Such a relationship between the medical center and athletics, he emphasized, would be an advantage to both. Athletes would receive the best of care, and the connection would enhance the residents' and fellows' programs in teaching and training physicians in the treatment of sports-related injuries.[610]

Regardless of the best interests of the athletes, Ray's plan didn't have a chance. In July 1990, Wilson sent Newton a copy of the Perrine plan that not only returned all athletes' medical care to the campus, but included faculty appointments for both Andrews and Ireland in the medical center. Andrews' malpractice insurance would be paid by the medical center. Perrine would coordinate the sports medicine program from Student Health. During the transition period, athletes would continue to be treated by both practices. Afterwards, Wilson expected Ray and his UK Sports Medicine physicians to be involved to some extent.[611]

Newton not only approved the plan, but wanted any extra benefits that might be there for him and his family. In Wilson's plan, physicians would accept athletic and student health insurance as full payments for medical treatments. It seemed that Ray had been making house calls for coaches and their families without charge. Newton liked the idea of no out of pocket expenses for himself and his staff. That nifty little item caught the attention of Roselle's watchdog for athletics, Edward Carter, who told Bosomworth in no uncertain terms that athletic administrators, coaches and their families weren't included in this plan for athletes. Carter pointed out those people had access to the same insurance coverage as all university employees. The chancellor had no choice but to nix those benefits.[612]

Bosomworth chaired a meeting with the medical school dean Emory Wilson, surgery chairman Byron Young, orthopedic chairman Herbert Kaufer, Ray, Andrews, Ireland and Newton to discuss incorporating both medical practices into the care of athletes in the medical center. Conspicuous by their absences were Perrine and his associate from Student Health, Spencer Turner. During the transition, each practice would continue to treat athletes. The medical center orthopedists were led to believe they were getting their chance.[613]

The most astounding part of the meeting was the announcement that Ray and his associates, residents and fellows in UK Sports Medicine would have access to the Nutter Training Center, to all sports-related surgeries performed at the medical center as observers or assistants, they would be allowed to stand on the sidelines at football games and there were to be no verbal confrontations or accusation made in front of the athletes.[614]

Medical center orthopedists had long complained they were forbidden access to the Nutter Training Center, and Bosomworth's announcement confirmed that. Evidently, UK Sports Medicine physicians had been denied access to the medical center's operating rooms while surgeons from the other practice were operating. Ray, by far, performed the most procedures of any orthopedists on the staff. The medical center's orthopedists being forbidden to stand along the sidelines at football games was ridiculous. If verbal confrontation hadn't occurred between the two practices, why did Bosomworth ban them in the future? The chancellor really had things in a mess.

When Bosomworth's plan was implemented to move athletes' medical care to Student Health, the UK Sports Medicine physicians found themselves effectively eliminated. They weren't the only ones. Perrine was shuffled out as the head man in Student Health, and replaced by Spencer Turner as head physician for sports medicine. Turner had a great resume for running a sports medicine program. His medical center appointment was in the department of preventative medicine, and his speciality was in environmental health. It was easy to tell where Turner's priorities were. He was concerned about having his and his associates' photographs in the basketball and football media guides. Turner also wanted an identification tag as the chief team physician, and a shirt with similar wording.[615]

The medical center orthopedists were furious. Ray, who was then chairman of the SEC's sports medicine committee and whose research on sports-related injuries had produced countless journal articles, said Turner made no effort to discuss athletes' medical care with him and his associates. He was absolutely correct in accusing Turner of attempting to establish a good old boy club in sports medicine without the proper credentials. Kaufer and Ray protested to Bosomworth to no avail. Wilson tried to convince the orthopedists the move was to their advantage. That was similar to getting gored by a bull and then being convinced it was to your advantage. One of Ray's associates, Henry Striene, was unable to order lab work for his patients in Student Health because "He didn't have admitting privileges in that department." Turner, quite taken with his new position, informed Ray that he should no longer call his section of orthopedics sports medicine because he (Turner) was UK sports medicine.[616]

Bosomworth had sports medicine in such a mess, he did his best to ensure it never reached public view, and it didn't. The chancellor's plan was approved by Newton and the athletics board, but needed the endorsement of the medical center board. Attached to a copy of the agreement sent to medical center board member, Jerome A. Stricker, of Covington, was a note warning him not to discuss the proposal and to keep it confidential.[617]

In a June 1994 Open Records Act request, I asked to examine the agreement that both public boards ratified and any other contracts or pacts concerning athletics medical care and the physicians, practices and/or institutions involved. The legal counsel's office sent my request to associate athletics director Larry Ivy, who passed it on to head trainer Al Green. Green replied, "There were and still are none (agreements) with any of our physicians or medical facilities that I am aware of." Newton wrote Green in January 1991, thanking him for his part in the transfer of athletes' medical care to Student Health, an act that required the approval of both the athletics board and the medical center's board.[618]

Ray and David Caborn, another orthopedic surgeon in UK Sports Medicine, asked Bosomworth why Turner, who had no formal training in sports medicine, was selected to head the program. They asked who recommended him, why he excluded their sports medicine practice from athletes' medical care and why did Ireland's orthopedic fellows had access to athletes and medical procedures in the university's hospital when residents and fellows from the medical center didn't? "It's truly an injustice," they told Bosomworth, "when administrators compromise not only the quality of care (for athletes), but also the education of medical students, residents and fellows." The chancellor apparently refused to answer their questions, because he referred the letter to his medical center director Frank Butler.[619]

To absolutely no one's surprise, team physician assignments for the UK Sports Medicine doctors were few. Turner, Perinne and Kim Clawson, the daughter of a former medical center vice-chancellor, made up athletes' medical staff. Ireland had the majority of teams, Ray and Caborn had a few, and the rest were divided among doctors whose specialities ranged from allergy to obstetrics to psychiatry.[620]

Turner promised to cut the cost of athletes' medical care. He required sick or injured athletes to hobble across the campus to student health instead of their training rooms as Ray's plan outlined. Whenever possible, he advised emergency room treatment not be used for athletes's sickness or injuries. If, by chance, an athlete went directly to a specialist's office, Turner told consultants to send them back to student health immediately. He planned to soak athletes' parents for as much of their medical cost as possible. "Most students' (parents) have some form of health insurance," Turner said, "and we may be able to take advantage of that for expensive tests, particularly for non-athletically related concerns."[621]

The cost of athletes' medical care soared under Turner's management. In the six years prior to Turner's implementing Bosomworth's plan, local orthopedists charged an annual average of $54,234 to care for the football team. After Andrews and Ireland took over the team, the annual average cost climbed to $180,180. Cost of medical care for the football team alone was $236,879 in 1989. From 1979 to 1984 the average annual medical costs for the basketball team was $10,646. After Ray took over the average was $17,446. Athletes' medical care under Turner soared to $424,053 in 1993, but was down to $256,099 in 1995.[622]

Basketball coach Rick Pitino wanted Ray to continue caring for his team, but was powerless, under his contract, to protest Newton's decision. Ray resigned in April 1992, to open his own orthopedic practice in Clermont, Florida. In addition to his work with the US Olympic ski team, he accepted a position with the Russian Olympic ski team. Caborn, who received some of his training in Scotland, replaced Ray as director of UK Sports Medicine, and had little use for the good old boys' politics.

Kaufer and Brower, nearing retirement, remained. Kaufer had the guts to call Newton to task for his failure to combine both sports medicine practices into athletes' medical care. He criticized the athletics director for omitting his orthopedic physicians' photographs from the football and basketball media guides, where Turner, Andrews and Ireland were publicized as the teams' physicians.[623]

Newton didn't take well to Kaufer's charge that he didn't play fair in integrating both practices into athletes' medical care. Newton replied claiming he failed to remember any agreement where physicians from both practices would provide care. After all, that was his and Bosomworth's intentions from the beginning. "I honestly am having a problem understanding why a group of professionals cannot work together to provide quality medical care for an outstanding group of student athletes," he told Kaufer.[624]

Kaufer replied suggesting Newton show him where the medical center orthopedists were treated fairly, and he would withdraw his complaint. There was quite a flap over Kaufer's daring to challenge Newton. Dean of medicine Emory Wilson apologized to Newton for Kaufer's remarks saying it never ceased to amaze him how grown men sometimes acted. What was amazing was the school of medicine dean bowing and scraping to an athletics director. Newton's feelings were massaged with the apology. He told Wilson, "I had grown weary of the 'childishness' so I reacted. I think Frank (Butler) and Spence (Turner) and all are doing a great job."[625]

None of the essential questions were answered: why medical center officials ignored an acclaimed sports medicine practice to place athletes' medical care in student health; what was Turner's association with Andrews and Ireland; had Turner done any sports medicine research or contributed any journal article on the subject? An Open Records Act request went to the legal counsel's office for Turner's answers to those questions. Turner displayed his distaste for the inquiry in his reply, "It has always been my policy not to be involved in commentary on internal personnel and organizational matters with the news media or other research efforts. I simply have no comment on these issues." Rather than press the legal request, I decided to let Turner's own words stand. They more than adequately reflected both his attitude and the sports medicine situation.[626]

Caborn, when faced, like Ray, with similar political shenanigans, was said to have threatened to leave the medical center and take his large patient following with him to another orthopedic practice. Administrators quickly retreated, but there will probably be similar upheaval as long as the good old boy attitude prevails, even in athletes' medical care.

# Two of a Kind

Nowhere was the good old boys' attitude more prevalent than in athletic contracts. Jim Host's sweetheart contracts not only continued under Newton, but proliferated. Roselle, enmeshed in a new and demanding NCAA investigation, had little time to keep an eye on the wheelings and dealings in Memorial Coliseum.

In 1989 Host recaptured the broadcast game rights, in public bidding, to add to the telecast rights he already held. Throw in the game program rights for both football and basketball and video season highlights, not put out for bids, and it was clear Host made a cottage industry out of Kentucky athletics.

It's obvious that Kentucky's athletics program was the base for the sports communication and marketing empire Host built. While his company was privately held, it was difficult to determine who the stockholders were. Congressional financial disclosures in 1995 revealed the Rep. Jim Bunning, (R-KY), a former baseball pitcher held Host stock worth between $100,001 and $250,000. Host was the political consultant for Bunning's unsuccessful 1983 gubernatorial campaign. Host's expansion in the 1990s included a contract with Rawlings Sporting Goods to push their products in joint promotions with corporations, and a $75 million pact with the NCAA. Bull Run Corporation, the Atlanta-based diversified holding company that purchased WKYT-TV in Lexington, held thirty percent of Host stock in 1997.[627]

Despite the national expansion, Host's grip on Kentucky athletics tightened. Negotiation for the basketball game program rights occurred only once during Roselle's administration. Athletic officials weren't involved since Singletary gave the game program rights to the Lexington Center Corporation in 1976. With no call for public bids, Host's was the only one submitted. From 1985 through 1988, Host paid the LCC $126,000 for the program rights. Retail price was two-dollars, but subjected to an increase during the contract period.[628]

Figures for the game program rights were available for only one season, 1986-87. Host's accounting showed income of $222,129. Included in the $123,919 expenditures was a $2,000 contribution, no recipient listed, and $21,713 in "Host only inside sales' commissions." Host charged $84,508 for printing the program in his own plant. UKAA files revealed Host cleared $24,497 for rights he paid $42,000 annually.[629] You can bet he cleared a tidy profit on printing the programs.

The basketball team was 18-11 that season, and in the middle of still another scandal, and the program sales' may have suffered. It was doubtful the game programs' advertising sales declined as they were predicated on coach Eddie Sutton's SEC championship the previous season and an appearance in the NCAA's Elite Eight.[630] Using the conservative 1986-87 season's figures, Singletary gave away approximately $5.3 million in gross revenue from the game program rights over the twenty-four years the basketball team played in Rupp Arena.

Host's next basketball game program contract with the LCC expanded from three years to five for a total price of $325,500. For that price Host furnished a 100-page, perfect bound program with fifty pages in color and a 65-35 advertising-editorial ratio to sell for three-dollars each. Host retained the right to raise the program price by one dollar, and the rights of first refusal to renegotiate with the LCC at the end of the contract. He also had the right to charge the UKAA the full retail price for each of the 200 programs the association purchased for each game. During the life of the contract, if that clause was followed, the UKAA paid an estimated $50,000 for their own basketball game programs.[631]

Football game program rights brought Host into sharp conflict with Roselle. In August 1989, sports information director Chris Cameron notified Herald-Leader circulation director Mike Kujawa the newspaper was prohibited from selling their papers around the stadium on game days. Cameron explained, "Our football game program contract does not allow outside vendors to sell or distribute printed material in the aforementioned area on game days."[632] It was unlikely that Cameron, in mid-level management, made that decision alone. He was obviously following orders.

The newspaper took exception, and Roselle told athletics officials they made a mistake. That didn't sit too well with Host. He asked Roselle to reconsider "A decision which I understand the university had made regarding allowing the Lexington Herald-Leader to sell newspapers around the football stadium and on the premises of the University of Kentucky Athletics Association's controlled property before and during games this fall."[633] What Host was really protesting was his two or three-dollar program being clobbered by the thirty-five-cent newspaper's game rosters.

His grumbling continued, "The end result, Dr. Roselle, is that they are in it for the economic gain for themselves while at the same time hurting the athletics association's bottom line." He accused Roselle of caving in to the newspaper's influence. Host wisely shied away from an open conformation. "The airing of disputes of this nature in a public forum could be embarrassing to all concerned," he continued, "but I think it is inherently unfair for the newspaper to be granted this right to the economic detriment of the University of Kentucky Athletics Association and its rights holder, Host Communication, Inc."[634]

Host wasn't finished, "The newspaper used the argument that since the university grounds are public property, to prohibit them from selling the newspaper or giving it away (and in fact they are selling it) would be a violation of their Constitutional rights is, in my judgment, a sham of an argument."[635] He expected his sweetheart contract, not obtained through a public bid process, to supersede the United States Constitution!

The arrogance didn't stop there. Not only did Host want Roselle to change his mind, but wanted him to do so before the next home football game. The president took his time to reply, and was critical of athletic officials handling of the issue. Roselle told Host that Cameron's letter, from deep inside the bowels of athletics, was a dumb move.[636]

Host back-pedaled somewhat saying he wasn't questioning the newspaper being an important supporter of the university. His concluding argument to Roselle could have easily been turned around and used against him. "The bottom line," Host replied, "is I just don't think you can allow one entity, regardless of how important they may be to the university, at the exclusion of everyone else and that is the genesis of my argument."[637]

Roselle tersely informed Host that he missed the point. He hadn't concluded the newspaper could be sold at the stadium, but that the argument athletic officials used were beyond the pale. The president said the school owed the newspaper the courtesy of a meeting to discuss the matter. Roselle added, tongue in cheek, "now that we have that tidied up, I expect we will pursue some mutually acceptable resolution." It was never in doubt that the newspaper would continue their Saturday sales at the stadium. Total revenues for the 1989 game programs were $190,557. Expenses of $127,252 included $87,402 for print in Host's plant. The sixty-forty split netted the UKAA $37,983, and Host pocketed $25,322.[638] Using that figure as a conservative average, Host netted around $500,000 from the football game programs over twenty years.

Associate athletics director Larry Ivy speculated the UKAA might have to put the 1990 football game programs out for competitive bidding. Perish the thought. Nothing happened, and a letter from Ivy to Host served as a contract for that year. The net profits were about the same. In May 1990, Host signed a personal service contract to furnish the game programs, and there was some discussion about a total concept idea.[639]

Ivy was quite taken with the total concept idea, and apparently Newton was also. It was another of those beautiful sweetheart contracts. In 1992 the football game program contract with Host was amended, retroactive to 1991, and extended to 1995. The kicker was the UKAA threw in Host's unlimited use of the official Kentucky logo, along with the football game program contract, for a flat fee of $42,000 a year. From 1979 to 1989, the UKAA income from game programs averaged around $35,000 a year. That meant Newton and Ivy were giving Host the unlimited use of the Kentucky logo for only $7,000 a year. Items with Kentucky's official logo sold unbelievably well. From April 1995 through June 1996 (the Pitino national championship year), Kentucky received $2.4 million from Collegiate Licensing Company for use of their logo on various items.[640]

The deal smelled so sweet, I couldn't wait to see what happened when the contract was renewed, privately, of course. Another Open Records Act request went to the legal counsel's office in December 1996 for a copy of the new football game program rights agreement. It was really no sunrise when official records custodian George De Bin replied that the agreement for the 1996-97 program "Had not been completed yet." The 1996 football season was over a month earlier without a contract for the game programs. "No payment has been made for the 1996 football season," DeBin continued, "Mr. Hisle (UKAA accounting director), in the accounting office advised that it could be spring or early summer before payment is received." Apparently, Newton allowed Host to use the money belonging to the UKAA for months without asking for payment.[641]

Not only was the usually frugal Newton generous in allowing Host to use the association's money without calling for payment, but he was very generous in his praise of the businessman. Some of his letters of recommendation sounded like he was soliciting business for Host. He was lavish in his recommending Host's companies to University of North Carolina athletics director John Swofford.[642]

The Kentucky game programs' rights were only part of Host's vast accumulation of exclusive deals. In addition the NCAA's Final Four program,

Host produced conference tournament programs for the SEC, ACC, SWC, Metro, Big 8, MCC, Sun Belt, Missouri Valley, WAC and for the Big 4 Classic. His other publications included Texas football, NCAA football and basketball reviews, SEC football and basketball guides, the official NCAA championship guide, football and basketball programs for Texas, Tennessee and Notre Dame.[643]

Radio programming controlled by Host included the NCAA radio network, broadcasts of men and women's Division 1 basketball championships, the NCAA College World Series and College Sports USA. Covered under his basketball umbrella were Auburn, Florida State, Tennessee, Texas, Kentucky, Notre Dame basketball and the Keeneland (Race Course) Network. Host produced basketball and football television shows for Auburn, Florida State, Kentucky and Texas. His Video-Seat, pay-per-view division, carried college football games.[644]

At Kentucky, Host's deals were indeed sweeter with each administration. He worked out an exclusive deal with athletics director Cliff Hagan to produce and market season video highlights of the games. Of course, there were no calls for public bids. The deal not only continued under Newton, but it got even sweeter.

Records of the early season video highlights were sketchy. In 1987, the UKAA received $2,611 from Host. No records pertaining to the videos were found for the next few seasons. A settlement for the 1990-91 season highlights videos was made in December 1992, and showed 5,860 videos were produced, 1,140 remained unsold. Host listed income of $82,944, and production costs of $40,849. The settlement indicated each of the blank tapes cost $6.97, and sold, after production, for around $19.00. The tape-buying public paid less than that in retail outlets for blank video tapes, and surely Host received a discount for purchasing the tapes in bulk of more than 5,000. Host and the UKAA split the net profit of $28,783 equally, but the association paid David Combs a fee of $3,000 out of their share. There was no explanation of the Combs' fee.[645]

In 1992 Host informed UKAA officials their earlier marketing arrangements for the season video highlights weren't in compliance with NCAA regulations. The correspondence not only illustrated that Host was as much on the inside as Newton, the leader of the program, but reinforced the theory the Sports Illustrated reporters advanced about the school receiving light penalties from the NCAA due to Host's involvement.[646]

"I received this (an enclosed copy of NCAA regulation 12.5.17) interpretation while at the NCAA convention," Host told athletic officials, "all we need is for C.M. (Newton) to designate us to receive orders and that he approves the sales and distribution activities." Newton's approval, of course, was forthcoming immediately.[647]

The regulation Host mentioned said any agency, other than the institution, could sell and distribute video season highlights containing names and pictures of enrolled student athletes, with remaining eligibility, with the written approval of the athletics director.[648] The season videos contract became even sweeter.

A letter between Host and the UKAA served as the video highlights contract for the 1992-93 season where they continued the fifty-fifty split of the net profits. Unable to find the contract for the next season, I sent another Open Records Act request to the legal counsel's office. Associate athletics director Larry Ivy replied to the request in January 1994 saying, "The 1992-93 agreement (season video highlights) was a verbal one between Coach Newton and Jim Host." [649] Ivy's letter confirmed what many suspected, Host's input in the program's management was almost equal to that of the athletics director.

Control of season video highlights turned ugly after Pitino's team won the NCAA national championship in April 1996. State media had big plans to produce various items commemorating Kentucky's first national championship in eighteen years. Two Lexington television stations planned to market video of post season celebrations including the team's arrival at Blue Grass Airport and raising the championship banner in

Rupp Arena. Kentucky's two largest newspapers had books on the season and championship tee-shirts ready to sell.

The UKAA caught everybody by surprise with an announcement of a cease and desist campaign against the media plans. Their premise was such marketing threatened the eligibility of undergraduate players. Make no mistake, the cease and desist campaign was all about money, not eligibility. The loud smell of special interests being protected by the school tainted the post season. The media reported the story with few comments, and certainly did no research on the school's declaration.

Sandra D. Bell, UKAA director of compliance, said, "According to NCAA rules, the school must take steps to limit the commercial distribution of undergraduates' names and pictures that are used without the athletes' permission." Bell continued, "The institution is required to take steps to stop such activity in order to retain his or her eligibility." Bell, in attempting to institute the cease and desist campaign, cited NCAA regulation 12.5.17, the same section Host used four years earlier when he was arranging another no-bid contract with Newton for the season video highlights.[650]

Bell's statement to the media immediately brought First Amendment rights into the picture. Athletic officials apparently had little regard for the media rights of editorial production. Earlier, Host told Roselle the newspaper's claiming their Constitutional rights to sell their product at the stadium was a sham of an argument. Bell denied the school was attempting to curb media rights, and said she "Did not think the university's actions presented a First Amendment concern.[651]

Kentucky fans went wild when their team beat Syracuse for the national championship. That translated into a huge market for all items relating to the championship, including videos, shirts and books. Any videos sold, other than those covered by Newton and Host's tidy oral contract, if it was still in effect, cut into their profits. It was never the school's president, Charles T. Wethington, Newton, Host or the NCAA's director of enforcement David Berst who proclaimed the cease and desist campaign, but Bell in athletics' middle management. Pounded by the media, Bell lamely defended the school's action, "We really would like to play basketball next year, that's all we're trying to do."[652]

Most of the media ignored the cease and desist campaign. WKYT-TV, a part of Host's Sports Communications entity that held the media game rights, folded and honored the school's request. WLEX-TV produced their video, sold it for $10 and gave any profits to charity. The Lexington newspaper sold their book, "Bravo Blue," for $12.95, and put out a tee-shirt. The Louisville newspaper's book on the season, "Journey to Greatness," sold for $19.95.[653]

Athletic officials weren't contented by attempting to intimidate the local media. They went national. Dave Mingey, senior publicist at Sports Illustrated, confirmed his magazine received a letter from Kentucky athletic officials requesting they halt publication on the annual special edition on the national basketball championship. "Sports Illustrated had never received a similar letter concerning one of its collector issues," Mingey said, "which this year included a commemorative of the University of Nebraska' football team and it's quest for a national title. It's the first time as far as I know that this has happened." Mingey added that the magazine's attorneys advised them to publish the issue on Kentucky since it was an editorial product protected by the First Amendment.[654]

The school's efforts to halt publications and souvenirs sales had nothing to do with protecting undergraduate athletes' eligibility. It was all about the money athletics officials feared would be lost to other publications and videos.

Sports Illustrated's "Return to Glory, Kentucky Wildcats, 1996 NCAA Champions," was a ninety-six page commemorative issue that featured undergraduates as well as the four seniors on the team. Near the back of the magazine was a two-page advertisement for "SI Insider Authentics" selling shirts, jackets, caps and plaques with the Kentucky's official logo and the "Official 1996 NCAA Championship Video" for $19.95.[655]

Every order that SI received took money away from Host's and Newton's deals. Host's video, "Untouchable: The 1995-96 National Championship Season Highlights Video," also sold for $19.95. Host also produced his own book, "Untouchable: The Crowning of the Commonwealth," selling for $39.95. A May 1996 check of Lexington's largest bookstore revealed that Host held copyrights on at least five books and four videos on Kentucky basketball.[656]

Sports columnist Billy Reed, who once worked for Host, questioned the university and the NCAA using a double standard in their attempts to discourage the media from selling commemorative books, videos and clothing connected to the championship. Since the free enterprise system was open to all, Reed asked, "By what rights does the NCAA presume to control them" It was surprising that Reed bought the cease and desist campaign as coming from both the school and the NCAA.[657]

The entire cease and desist campaign positively reeked of special interests being protected. What gave it all away was no public statements from Newton, the NCAA, the university president and Host remaining in the background. From all indications Host preferred to remain out of the spotlight, and keep his business as private as possible.

Host's holdings were a conglomeration of corporations. Sometimes a settlement with the school of a contract held in the name of one company was paid from another. That occurred in the 1994-95 season video highlights settlement. A Host Communication Inc., statement indicated revenue of $105,432, with a profit of $24,302 split between the company and the school. In July 1996 the UKAA received a check for their share, $12,151, from Sports Communications. Sports Communications was the group Host put together to handle media rights, and included WKYT-TV, WVLK radio, Clear Channel Communication and Host Communication.[658]

Host extended his sports marketing horizons in December 1996 by signing an exclusive five-year, $75 million contract to market NCAA trademark events such as the Final Four and fan festivals. The pact enabled

Host to sign contracts with corporations for the use of the NCAA trade-mark on various products. His previous NCAA broadcast and tournament program rights were included in the contract.[659]

The relationship between Host and the NCAA's assistant executive director David E. Cawood became even closer in 1997. After twenty-three years as the NCAA's number two executive, Cawood resigned to become a vice-president of a Host affiliate, Universal Sports America, in Dallas. Cawood's work was in marketing and advising sports publications. [660]

Host was required to enter into public bidding for the school's television game rights. He was less than successful in his $496,000 contract for television game rights from 1986-87 through the 1988-89 seasons. That time frame encompassed coach Eddie Sutton's disastrous last two years. Athletics director Cliff Hagan was more than generous in helping Host solve his problems. In January 1988, the second year of the contract, Host told Hagan he lost $251,953 on the contract's first year television rights. The letter Host wrote Hagan indicated the previous year's rights possibly hadn't been paid yet. Host said he didn't want to show a loss for the 1987-88 season on his books. His proposal to Hagan, "Which you have (already) accepted is to pay a total this year of $382,726 for the football and basketball (television game rights)."[661]

This occurred while Roselle was searching for additional funds for the university. It was doubtful if he knew Hagan cut $113,272 from Host's previous year's payment that was already past due. Host asked to make the $382,726 payment in three installments of $127,575. The first was included with his letter to Hagan. The second was due in January and the third by March 31st. In April 1988, UKAA accounting director J.R. Hisle told Hagan he'd received only the January payment. "I was under the impression," he told Hagan, "that we were to receive the second install-ment in February and a final payment in March."[662]

In March 1989, Host won back the game broadcast rights from the Kentucky Network, who held them for nine years, with a bid of $902,000. The game rights fees were divided into six annual payments, beginning in December and ending in April. With that arrangement, the football season was over before the first payment was due. Given the latitude Host enjoyed with the UKAA allowing him to go months beyond the payment dates, it was possible payments for the basketball game rights weren't made until December after the prior season ended.[663]

A new twist was added to the next call for bids on radio and television game rights. The contract covered four years instead of three, and included the exclusive rights to produce and market the coaches' shows and their endorsements. Host had the high bid of $1.5 million. In 1996 Host bid $2.3 million for the same rights through April 2000.[664]

Nothing more was heard about the school producing the broadcasts and telecasts in the school of communications. If they were worth $2.3 million to Host, weren't they worth even more to the school in profits and experience for their television and broadcast staffs and students to learn by working in the field?

Kentucky's televised football and basketball games had no copyright protection until 1988. Cable television systems paid fees for the games to the Copyright Royalty Tribunal in Washington, DC. The Tribunal paid the schools through the NCAA. Host's company asked the UKAA to share cable television revenue, $58,399, from eleven 1988 football games. A clause in Host's contract with the UKAA read, "The (Athletics) Association shall receive one-half of any rights fees resulting from broadcasts of the games by cable operators emanating from the signal of the contractor (Host)."[665]

Athletic officials sought counsel from Bernard Vonderheide, chairman of the broadcast and television committee. He wanted nothing to do with it, and passed it on to legal counsel John Darsie. Darsie, at first, said, Host wasn't due any money because the clause in question was inserted in the contract to encourage the contractor to sell Kentucky games to cable operators to bring in more money. Darsie pointed out the games in questions didn't arise from any sales. If Darsie drew up the contract, then the actual wording and his purported definition were at odds. Eventually, the legal counsel told Vonderheide to divide the revenue from ten, not eleven, games with Host in the interests of being absolutely sure the contractor received all sums due him.[666]

Despite the money rolling in, all wasn't sweetness and light in the land of Kentucky broadcasting. Cawood Ledford retired as the "Voice of the Wildcats" in 1992, and sold his interest in his and Host's production companies to Host. WVLK general manager Ralph Hacker left his color commentary slot to replace Ledford. Hacker was widely criticized and complaints poured in from across the state. After his first season doing play-by-play, the Lexington newspaper did an extensive article on Hacker, who refused to be interviewed. "Hacker's detractors have bombarded the (radio) call-in shows, both post game and the weekday variety, with their laundry list of complaints," John Clay wrote, "They insist Hacker had no feel for play-by-play, that his broadcasts are riddled with errors, his descriptions are fuzzy and tardy and that his lone talent is for saying the wrong thing at the wrong time."[667]

Newton and Host rushed to Hacker's defense. "I've not had any letters complaining about basketball, absolutely none," Newton said. "I've had some letters about football but not very many." That wasn't quite correct. A Danville dentist, T. Clay Stuart, wrote Newton in July 1993, four months before the newspaper article appeared, complaining about Hacker's calls in both sports. Newton sent Stuart a terse note and forwarded his letter to Host for a more detailed reply. "I don't agree with you regarding his basketball calls," Host told the dentist, "I thought he was excellent and so did literally all of those from whom we heard."[668]

Newton tried to shift the responsibility for Hacker to Host. "The way our contract is; it's Jim Host's call as to who he hires," Newton explained, "I'm not going to put Jim in the seat that I'm in to hire a basketball or football coach, so I'm sure not going to sit in his seat to hire the broadcaster." Once again, Newton's parsing the explanation wasn't correct. The athletics director's approval, as spelled out in the contract, was required for all on-air personnel. Newton's attempt to wiggle off the hook came back to haunt him.[669]

Hacker had another problem. He organized "Republicans for Wilkinson" during Wallace Wilkinson's gubernatorial campaign, and was rewarded with the vice-chairman's slot on the Kentucky Lottery board. The lottery was a big advertiser on the broadcasts and telecasts of Kentucky games. Hacker ran WVLK, the only radio station in Lexington allowed to carry the games. The station was one of the four entities that made up Sports Communications, and shared in the profits from the games. In essence, when the lottery bought time on the games' telecasts and broadcasts, Hacker was implementing a contract with himself. After Wilkinson left office in 1991, newly elected state auditor Ben Chandler, grandson of "Happy" Chandler, found the lottery paid Sports Communications $650,000 for advertising for the games the previous year. Chandler said he found no record of the time purchases being discussed in lottery board meetings. "State law," he said, "requires lottery board members to avoid even indirect involvement in any undertaking with the lottery's interests."[670] Young Chandler had his sights set on the governor's chair, and wasn't about to rock the boat.

There were other allegations about Hacker and the lottery. They included a round-trip charter flight from Louisville to Nashville, paid for with lottery funds, when a Governor's Council meeting caused Hacker to miss the team plane; a $5,000 lottery contribution to the Ralph Hacker Scholarship Golf Tournament; $1,000 in lottery money paid for a table for the luncheon commemorating the fifteenth anniversary of Kentucky's 1978 national championship. In 1992, newly elected governor Brereton C. Jones booted out the entire lottery board, Hacker included. A month later, Jones was being interviewed, over a state-wide radio network in Louisville, and he was critical of the previous lottery board. Listeners to Hacker's station, WVLK, instead of hearing Jones listened to seven minutes of silence. Hacker, noted for his thin skin when criticized, denied pulling the plug on the governor's broadcast, and claimed the silence was due to technical difficulties.[671]

Host made it clear that Hacker was on the broadcasts to stay, but a new face appeared on the telecasts. Martin Newton, son of athletics director C.M. Newton, was hired by Host to do color commentary on the games' telecasts. Newton was ill at ease, inexperienced and mumbled his words the first season, but later improved. His father defended Host's selection of his son. "When Jim came to me," Newton said, "my first reaction to that, and I have not said this publicly, was 'no, I don't need this and he doesn't either.' Then I got to thinking, if they think he's good enough to do this and want him, why should I not approve." It took nepotism to rear its ugly head for Newton to admit his approval was required for on-air personnel for the games' broadcasts and telecasts.[672]

Game broadcast and telecast rights were powerful tools for those holding the contracts. That was illustrated after the 1996 basketball championship. Associate journalism professor and news director of the campus radio station Cindy Hosbein was critical of all the puff pieces local television stations produced as well as the newspaper's excessive coverage. "Lexington's television news media should provide in-depth coverage, but they crossed the line of journalistic responsibility, integrity and professionalism," she said, "objectivity was thrown out the door and it's a shame."In her commentary, Hosbein included the comment of WKYT-TV news director Jim Ogle, "It's not important to be objective; it's just fun." WKYT-TV, of course, was the only Lexington television station to carry the games. Ogle claimed Hosbein's remarks about him were inaccurate, and yanked his station's news broadcasts from the campus station, WUKY. Two other local television stations offered their newscasts for campus broadcasts.[673]

Inability to take criticism found another victim in Hacker's thin skin. Disapproval of Hacker's football calls not only continued but intensified.

After five years as the play-by-play announcer, Hacker stepped down from the football broadcasts, but remained on the basketball games. Hacker was replaced by his own station' news director, Tom Leach. Most thought it was a vast improvement.

# FOLLOW THE MONEY

The game rights favoritism was minuscule compared to what happened in April 1988 when Roselle received a call from Los Angeles Daily News reporter, Eric Sondheimer. An Emery Air Freight envelope, sent by assistant basketball coach Dwane Casey to Claud Mills, the adoptive father of recruit Chris Mills, came open at the company's Los Angeles terminal allegedly revealing $1,000 in fifty-dollar bills. The envelope, taped shut by Emery employees, was delivered to Mills who denied receiving the money. The newspaper learned of the incident through an Emery employee, John Zaverl, whose brother-in-law, Adam Bratt, worked for the publication.[674]

Two months after telling the NCAA's committee on infractions he never wanted to appear before them again, Roselle was faced with the school's most serious allegation since the sudden death penalty in 1952. No bunker mentality was employed, Roselle met the problems straightforward. He ordered Burch, Lawson and Hagan to make an immediate and thorough investigation. Casey, in Pittsburgh when the story broke, was questioned several times, in the space of a weekend, by athletics officials. The assistant coach said he put a tape cassette for Mills in the overnight envelope, left it in the basketball offices to be picked up by Emery but didn't remember sealing the envelope. "I never put any money in any package," Casey said, "and I'll say that until I die."[675]

Burch and Lawson called Emery supervisor Paul Perry in Los Angeles, and he confirmed the reporter's disclosure that the company found money in the envelope. Lawson asked Casey and his lawyer, Joe Bill Campbell, if the assistant coach had access to any unusually large amounts of money in the past six months, or if anyone had given him substantial amounts of cash. Casey said, "No." The answer came back to haunt him. Campbell said he would make Casey's bank records available to them.[676]

Roselle gave legal counsel Joe Burch ten days to complete interviews, from Lexington to Los Angeles, with all concerned. Those interviews, conducted jointly with NCAA investigator Charles Smrt, included basketball coach Eddie Sutton; Casey; Larnette McDowell, the temporary employee in the basketball offices who mailed the envelope in question; five Emery employees, Claud Mills and his sons, Chris and Terry. Burch was under specific orders from Roselle. "My instructions were to stick with it, (the interviews) and him (Smrt) until he went back to Kansas City and I came back to Lexington," Burch said.[677]

Using all his available resources, Roselle asked Hagan to supervise the investigation, but later changed his mind. Hagan's explanation was a few days after the president asked him to handle the investigation, legal counsel John Darsie called him and said Roselle had hired an outside investigator. Hagan was shocked, and speculated Roselle's actions had been prompted by the way the school handled the 1985 investigation of the Lexington newspaper's allegations of infractions. Hagan was asked, under oath, if there was a taint on those who handled the previous investigation? He evaded a direct reply, "I think we had a new president that was insecure and didn't know who to handle the situation."[678]

Roselle was anything but insecure. He certainly didn't handle the situation in Hagan and Singletary's management style. Roselle had a different story for Hagan's removal from the investigation. He said he needed somebody to handle the matter immediately and, after he asked Hagan to handle the matter, the athletics director went out of town. "The point was," Roselle added, "we needed an experienced investigator and we needed someone who was in town."[679]

The appointment of former Court of Appeals judge James Park, Jr., as the school's independent investigator/counsel not only shocked the faithful, but illustrated Roselle's independence. No university president had ever dared go outside the school to find a person to conduct a NCAA investigation. Park came from a Lexington establishment background. His father was a founding partner of the Stoll, Keenon and Park law firm headed by Richard C. Stoll, the school's first power broker who influenced university decisions, both athletically and academically for a half century. James Park, Sr., had a stubborn streak. When then athletics director John J. Tigert denied Park had played baseball for a semi-pro team in Richmond. The athlete confirmed the accusation although it resulted in another SIAA suspension. Park, Jr., left his father's firm to join Brown, Todd and Heyburn, one of Kentucky's largest law firms.[680]

Three university lawyers, legal counsels John Darsie and Joe Burch and law professor Robert Lawson, were dispatched to assist Park. Darsie, a Versailles native, had degrees in English and law from the school, and was very much of the establishment. Lawson, a West Virginia native, held degrees from Berea College and the university law school. He joined the law school faculty in 1966, and was the principal drafter of the Kentucky Penal Code and wrote the Kentucky Evidence Handbook in 1976. Burch, a Covington native, had economy and law degrees from UK. He held posts at the school ranging from dean of men to acting associate director of the US Tobacco and Health Research Institute. Burch made a career of holding positions in just about every university department. He and Lawson were the most productive of the three lawyers.[681]

While Roselle was getting his investigative team in place, Darsie was busy preparing vice-president Edward Carter to handle the media's Open Records Act requests. Darsie, a veteran stonewaller from the 1985 investigation, bragged about how he handled the media. "At UK," he explained to Carter,"we have usually made copies of the requested records and provided them to requesters at a central point because we did not want them mucking through our files." Mucking is the term used to describe the removal of manure from horse barn stalls.[682]

Unlike Singletary, who vanished from the scene in such circumstances, Roselle practiced early damage control. While public relations director Bernard Vonderheide was releasing the president's statement to the media about impending NCAA violations, Roselle was meeting with editors of the commonwealth's two largest newspapers, David Haup at the Courier-Journal and John Carroll at the Herald-Leader. Vonderheide explained Roselle's absence from the news conference, "This was an important story, and we wanted people who were going to be editorializing on it to know from the beginning what we were doing." In times of Kentucky athletic crisis, this was an unheard of move, a first.[683]

Emery refused access to their employees for depositions and, from their perspective, with good reason, but legally it couldn't stand. The UKAA and Casey petitioned US District Court asking that Emery be forced to make their employees available for depositions. Federal judge Eugene Siler ordered Emery the next day to make their employees available for the discovery process. That cleared the way for depositions of Eric Osborn, Paul Perry, Steve Nelson, Richard Flanders, David Jones, Derwin Dawson and Clarence Bullerman who worked for Emery's security firm.[684]

Ever thorough, Burch kept detailed summaries of his early interviews with Emery employees, and they were invaluable. There were inconsistencies between Burch's summaries, the newspaper story and information obtained in depositions. Eric Osborn, according to the newspaper article, found the open package and saw the money. Burch's summary quoted Osborn as saying "He looked inside without making much effort and saw a tape and the money." During his deposition, Casey's attorney, Joe Bill Campbell, handed Osborn twenty five-dollar-bills and asked him to place them in the envelope where he said he found them. "To tell you the truth," Osborn said after making the effort, "I can't even get your money out now."[685]

Burch's summary of David Jones' interview was even more startling. Jones told Burch, "Eric showed it (the letter) to him and he handled it. The package was not open. He turned away for a moment, and Eric said something about the package containing a tape and money." In his deposition, Jones, a five-year Emery employee, said the package in question was at least partially open when Osborn showed it to him. He didn't deny his earlier statement to Burch about the package not being open when he first saw it.[686]

Supervisor Paul J. Perry, an eighteen-year Emery employee, told Burch and Smrt the money was sticking out of the cassette sleeve when Osborn showed it to him. Perry said, "Oh, shit." Burch's summary revealed "There was immediate talk by people in the dock area about the money, UK basketball and the Mills kid." When Park asked Perry about the terminal gossip during his deposition, he waffled and claimed not to remember. He didn't, however, deny his earlier statement to Burch. Perry said he took the envelope to supervisor Steve Nelson's office and left. When he returned, it was his impression security had counted the money, in used bills, put them back in the envelope and sealed it with tape.[687]

Nelson confirmed Perry's account of the incident. Clarence Bullerman, who worked for Security Experts, Nelson said, made notes on his clipboard. Nelson called Mills to verify the address, make sure someone was there to sign for the package and requested that he make sure the sender didn't place cash in future packages since it was against Emery regulations. When Mills asked what the money was for, Nelson said, "I don't know maybe it's a bonus." Nelson bristled when Campbell asked him if he saw Perry and Bullerman put the money back in the envelope and tape it closed. "When it was taped up," Nelson said, "I didn't see them put the money back in. But, I'm sure as hell not going to blow a $45,000 a year job for a thousand dollars.[688]

Bullerman was unable to explain why he failed to copy the serial numbers from the bills for identification or make a damage report except to say he saw no need. He denied he made any notes of the incident. A twenty-five year veteran of the Chicago police force, Bullerman told Burch such Emery packages regularly came open. In Burch's summary, Bullerman said he didn't see Paul put the money back in the envelope and failed to recall the package being taped shut. During his deposition, Bullerman swore he watched while Perry put the money back in the envelope and re-taped it. Asked to explain the differences between his statements, Bullerman replied he was under oath for the deposition.[689]

Richard Flanders, an Emery dispatcher, told Burch he spoke with Claud Mills who wanted to know when his package would be delivered, and appeared irritated when told there was money in the envelope. Flanders, in his deposition, failed to recall Mills saying he didn't want the money and that he (Flanders) could stick it up his ass."[690]

Derwin Dawson, manager of Emery's Lexington operations, said the overnight envelopes were designed to carry twenty sheets of paper, not video cassettes. He added that previous packages, with video tapes, hadn't come open, but pointed out that he hadn't seen all of them. When asked if he was a Kentucky basketball fan, Dawson replied, "You cannot succeed in business in Lexington without being one."[691]

Mills told Burch he was expecting Casey to send him two cassette tapes that one of his son's team mates wanted to send to a college coach in hopes of getting a scholarship. Mills filmed all of Chris' games and analyzed his moves. Mills said he had to pick up his sister from work and called Emery to find out when the package would be delivered. When the delivery hadn't been made before Mills left, he woke Chris up and told him to sign for the package. The package was on the table, Mills said, when he returned unopened. Mills said when he opened the package there was only one tape and no money. Mills talked with Casey, after his weekend interviews with athletics officials, and said the coach revealed that he had been asked to resign.[692]

Many suspected Casey had been asked to resign. University officials avoided the subject of Casey's resignation. There was no mention of Casey's resignation, at that time, in the school's Response to the NCAA. It was surprising that Mills' comment wasn't deleted from Burch's summary notes.

Chris Mills, with his father present, was grilled by Smrt and Burch about why he failed to pay more attention to the envelope. He said he was asleep when his father got the telephone call from Emery. The player denied receiving any money from Casey or knowing anything about it. Burch described how Smrt was leaning on the athlete to admit knowledge of the cash. "When pressed to tell the truth to save his basketball career," Burch's summary revealed, "his story did not change, although he did become visibly agitated and went outside for a while."[693]

Mills was livid about Smrt's treatment of his son. He later told Park he doubted if Smrt would have asked such questions in a white man's house in Beverly Hills or Bel Air. "I felt like he was accusing me; he hadn't even talked to Casey, nobody in Kentucky and he didn't believe what Chris said. That really hurt me."[694]

The NCAA, on July 25, 1988, told Roselle they were conducting an official inquiry into the allegations surrounding the Emery envelope; it was likely the school would be found in violation of the rules; ten additional allegations would arrive within the next month. It was the very situation Roselle pledged to avoid. Hagan attended the news conference, made no comment and left. Sutton issued the usual disclaimer of responsibility for any wrong doing.[695]

A NCAA supplemental inquiry, the second of a total of twenty-four allegations, inquiries and questions, arrived in October. Park advised Roselle to act with care in releasing names of those mentioned in the inquiry. The former judge advised the material, of a personal nature, might or might not be true. There was no legal problem as the material was the part of an on-going investigation, and protected under the Open Records Act. Roselle followed his advice and released a summary.[696]

His actions, however, opened the door to shield the faithful. The university's investigation of the NCAA's twenty-four allegations, inquiries and questions produced 138 interviews, statements and depositions from eighty-three people believed to be involved. Investigators focused on an Ohio basketball junkie, and a Los Angeles sports agent/attorney. That was a method of producing guilty parties without really involving the good old boys. Somehow, both the school and the NCAA failed to interview one who was in the middle of the Emery envelope mess.[697]

Roselle made some efforts to curb good old boys' involvement in the athletics program. He clamped down on coaches' and athletic officials' use of horseman Hilary Boone's airplane. The arrangement probably had been a good deal for Boone, whose largess to the school included the tennis center and the faculty club. The UKAA paid Boone for the use of his plane, the horseman then donated the same amount back to the Blue White Fund, which was tax deductible. Roselle told athletic officials that any request to use Boone's plane had to be cleared with his office.[698]

Investigators tip-toed carefully around coach Eddie Sutton's good friend Jimmy Hamilton, who lived in Lexington at the posh Griffin Gate development. Hamilton's name cropped up constantly in the Emery investigation. Hamilton and Sutton met through Alcoholics Anonymous and became friends and business partners in an Ashland shopping center. Hamilton, whose choice Rupp Arena seats were near those of Patsy Sutton, the coach's wife, owned substantial mineral rights, real estate, and Lexington's only taxi company run by his son, John Kennedy Hamilton, who later had a scandal-ridden tenure as Kentucky's secretary of state.[699]

Jimmy Hamilton was in the basketball offices the day the Emery story broke, had a long meeting with Sutton and was described as looking shocked and more emotional than usual. Joe Bill Campbell, Casey's attorney, said Hamilton's brother was bragging in their hometown of Springfield about Jimmy putting money in the envelope while it was on a secretary's desk. Hamilton later offered to get Casey the best lawyer money could buy. Casey refused the offer which was understandable since Sutton and the other assistant coaches cut him out of meetings and gatherings after the scandal broke.[700]

Campbell compiled an affidavit alleging Hamilton's involvement in the scandal and sent it to the NCAA. He alleged Hamilton was in the basketball offices, as he frequently was, the day the Emery letter was shipped.

On the day the story broke about the Emery envelope, Campbell quoted Associated Press reporter Mike Embry, who was also in the offices, about Hamilton appearing nervous and anxious to see Sutton. Casey's lawyer used the affidavit as an argument that university officials should have interviewed Hamilton.[701]

According to Campbell's affidavit, he learned only two weeks before the committee on infractions was to meet that university officials hadn't interviewed Hamilton, whom he referred to as "Eddie Sutton's bag man." He continued emphasizing that Hamilton made every effort to control the selection of Casey's attorney.[702]

Instead of questioning Hamilton themselves, the NCAA asked Burch for an explanation of why the man wasn't interviewed. Burch wrote Hamilton in September 1989 requesting an interview. He accepted Hamilton's decision that nothing positive could be achieved by responding to what he termed Campbell's defamatory and ludicrous statements.[703] Hamilton, however, didn't file suit against Campbell.

"I see no reason to offer my assistance to the University of Kentucky which I believe unjustifiably betrayed my friend, Eddie Sutton," Hamilton told Burch in his reply. He said he was incensed that anyone would believe that he was foolish enough to put cash in the Emery envelope. Hamilton denied that he placed the money in the Emery envelope, or furnished money for that purpose. His denial, about furnishing money, appeared limited to the Emery envelope in question.[704]

Burch explained Hamilton's tender treatment to the NCAA. He said the university chose not to disassociate Hamilton from their athletics program for a number of reasons: his reply to the letter requesting an interview wasn't a total lack of response; there was no evidence he committed any improper acts; with Sutton gone, Hamilton had no further ties to the program.[705]

Burch didn't discuss Hamilton's involvement in securing $10,000 honorariums for assistant coaches James Dickey and Casey. The honorariums weren't illegal, but the assistant coaches' failure to report them as outside income was a violation of NCAA regulations. Sutton had the luxury of reporting his outside income orally to the athletics director or school president in order to keep it confidential. Assistant coaches had no such protection. Casey and Dickey were disturbed when their outside incomes in 1987 were reported in the media. School officials thought they had redacted all references to the source of that money in the Response to the NCAA, but they overlooked one in Park's March 1989 interview with Dickey.

An example of the Response's redactions occurred in Park and Burch's 1989 interview summary with Casey. The first redacted name was labeled "B" and the second "D." Concerning the honorarium, Park asked Casey if Sutton or someone else contacted him about additional resources available for assistant coaches?

Casey: "Yes. He did contacted me and said that he had someone who wanted us to do some speaking engagements in the area. He introduced me to a gentleman, I think by the name of_. He's the one who asked me to speak to some civic groups and also some school there in _____."

Park: "Did you meet?"

Casey: "Yes, I did."

Park: "And where was that?

Casey: "He came by practice."

A few lines later they were discussing the $10,000 check and Park asked Casey if he received it?

Casey: "Yes, I did."

Park: "And how did you received it? Did you receive it directly from _____ or _____ did you receive it from somebody else?"

Casey: "I received it, I think, from _____ is who I received it from."[706]

From all indications, "B" was apparently Hamilton, and "D" was multi-millionaire western Kentucky businessman David Reed.

Assistant coach James Dickey said Hamilton was the person who arranged his $10,000 honorarium from Reed Crushed Stone Company in

1988. David Reed's operation, located in Gilbertsville, was sold in 1990 to Vulcan Materials, Inc., for $137 million.[707]

Dickey also received an $11,000 check from Nike as part of Sutton's contract to hold clinics in 1987 for the shoe company. He thought Casey received about the same amount. Dickey appeared to receive more money from Sutton's basketball camps than Casey whose income from that source ranged from $5,000 to $7,000. [708]

The origin of Casey's $10,000 honorarium wasn't discernable, but he cashed the check at the bank on which it was drawn and made deposits into his Lexington bank account the same day.[709]

Dickey had another honorarium from International Spike, a Lexington company headed by Labe Jackson, Jr., another of the good old boys. The assistant coach thought he spoke to a group of people from Walmart or K-Mart for the money. He said he was contacted directly by Jackson and was unaware if Sutton or Hamilton were behind the request.[710]

Hamilton's name continued to surface after the NCAA penalties were announced in 1989. Marta McMackin, Sutton's administrative assistant, suspected Hamilton was the man who put the money in the Emery envelope, and said so in her deposition in Casey's suit against the company in US District Court. When asked for an explanation of her statement, McMackin replied, "Because he's crazy enough to do something like that." She told of Hamilton being in the basketball offices often, and walking about flipping through large rolls of money. While being questioned by H.L. Riggs, Jr., attorney for Emery's security service, McMackin's testimony took an unusual turn.

Q: "Do you have any knowledge of whether Mr. Hamilton was a user of controlled substance or drugs?"
A: "I had heard that, you know, I don't know for sure."
Q: "Had you heard that coach Sutton used drugs?"
A: "Are you putting alcohol in that?"
Q: "Not right now. I will in my next question."
A: "Okay, yes."

Q: "Do you have any knowledge of Mr. Sutton and Mr. Hamilton ever using drugs together there at the basketball office.?"

A: "I never saw them."

Q: "When I say drugs, is there a particular drug that you are thinking about?"

A: "Cocaine."[711]

Sutton took great exception to Hamilton being suspected as the source of the money in the Emery envelope. He said he knew Hamilton well enough that he would never do that without asking him first. Sutton expressed doubts there was ever any money in the envelope and, if there was, it could have been put there in Emery's Los Angeles terminal just as easily as in the basketball offices. Sutton's memory was murky about Hamilton being in the basketball offices the day the Emery envelope was sent to Mills.[712]

Casey, whose depositions and statements filled 1,300 pages, talked about how vague everyone seemed to be about Hamilton being in the basketball offices the day Emery picked up the envelope in question. He alleged that Hamilton was a major supplier of cash and other benefits to Sutton's program. Emery attorneys had more interest in Hamilton's connections to the scandal than the school and the NCAA did, and wanted to make him a third party to Casey's suit against them.[713] The case was settled before the judge could rule on their motion.

# COLOR MADE A DIFFERENCE

Compare the treatment Jimmy Hamilton received from university and NCAA investigators with that of Barbara Brown, Shawn Kemp's mother; Mary Manuel, Eric Manuel's mother; Claud Mills, the father of Chris Mills. Not only was Hamilton one of the good old boys, but he was white, rich and well connected. Brown, Manuel and Mills were black, of modest means and lived outside Kentucky. Sad to say, but race appeared to determine how individuals were handled.

Their sons were outstanding basketball players and, if things had followed the normal course, all would have probably had successful careers in the NBA. As it turned out two of them did well in the NBA, but the third was hung out to dry regardless of the fact he led his teams to two national collegiate championships.

Brown was harassed unmercifully. The NCAA strung together a thin line of circumstantial evidence in an attempt to prove assistant coach Dwane Casey gave her money at different times. Their biggest leap was the assumption that Casey was the possible source of the monthly extra income Brown listed on Kemp's application for a student loan. That income came from Social Security benefits Kemp received from a disabled father until he was eighteen.[714] Never let it be said the NCAA doesn't leap before it looks.

The NCAA alleged Casey sent Brown an Emery overnight letter on October 22, 1987, and two days later she paid cash for an airline ticket from South Bend, Indiana, to Lexington, for a campus visit. Nobody wanted to believe Brown used her own cash for her airline ticket. University investigators, after demanding twice that Brown produce copies of her airline ticket, said they found no evidence of the charge.[715]

A month later, the NCAA alleged Casey sent Brown another Emery overnight letter, and three days later purchased a car for her son. Brown said she had long planned to give her son an automobile on his eighteenth birthday. She discussed her plans with his Concord High School coach, Jim Hahn, in Elkhart, Indiana. Hahn warned her that whatever school Kemp attended would likely be accused of giving him the automobile regardless of the circumstances. Brown went ahead with her plans, and purchased a 1987 Cavalier for $12,500 from Tom Naquin Chevrolet in Elkhart. She had a problem with the down payment, but eventually worked that out.[716]

Investigators wanted records of all her telephone calls and correspondence with Casey. They asked for copies of her average annual income for the past two years as a secretary in the radiology department of Elkhart General Hospital. They also wanted the copies of the sales invoice indicating the price of the car, her financing agreement with GMAC, a record of her payments, the loan agreement for her daughter's car and amounts she paid on that vehicle. Finally, Brown told them her relationship with her daughter was none of their business. She assured them she made each monthly payment on Kemp's car.[717]

Investigators were so convinced that Casey provided Brown with money for Kemp's car's, especially the down payment that Park and one of his attorneys went to Elkhart, Indiana, to interview the salesman who sold Brown the car. Park was still following the same path a year later when Brown agreed to an interview, with her lawyer present, in her home. Park spent considerable time laying the groundwork to ask Brown if Casey, or anyone else at the university or a representative of the school's athletic interests, suggested that she would receive cash if Kemp attended Kentucky. Then, Park got to real purpose of the trip. Where did Brown get the money to make the payments on Kemp's car? She explained that she had saved everything from her income tax refunds to small amounts each month.[718]

Park switched tracks, and began to question Brown on how she expected to pay for Kemp's freshman year expenses when he was a partial qualifier unable to get a grant-in-aid. She replied that she was relying on a student loan, which investigators knew all about, and a Pell Grant, available for financially-strapped athletes. For any additional money, Brown was relying on her recently retired mother for assistance.[719]

Brown then turned the tables on Park, and talked about how her son was treated at Kentucky. She talked of the time he had to spend alone; the school's failure to tell her about his academic problems until after he left; how he was encouraged to stay when he shouldn't have been there in the first place. "We're suffering from that," she told Park, "and I don't know when or if we'll ever get over it."[720]

Kemp may have been an academic deficient student, but he was a phenomenal basketball player. His departure from the campus was under strange circumstances. Basketball coach Eddie Sutton was under pressure from Roselle to halt recruiting Prop 48 players like Kemp, who were academically ineligible in their freshman year. In September 1988, Sean Sutton, the coach's son who was a guard on the team, reported two gold chains, worth $700, stolen from his Wildcat Lodge room. Police recovered two gold chains from a downtown pawn shop. Pawnbrokers were required by state law to photograph the person pawning items.[721]

Sean Sutton first said the chains in question were his, but later recanted. No charges were ever filed against Kemp. The chains could have been Kemp's. When photographed, he would have known a record of the pawned items existed. Kemp abruptly left the university to enroll in Trinity Valley Junior College in Athens, Texas. He was later drafted by the Seattle Supersonics, and was an All-Star in 1992. A 1994 contract extension with the Supersonics put his salary at an estimated $46 million through the 2002-03 season. Kemp was traded to the Cleveland Cavaliers in 1997.[722]

Barbara Brown must have received some satisfaction that her son's earning power far eclipsed that any of the investigators would ever achieve, but she was unlikely to forget her Kentucky experience. Neither would Mary Manuel or Claud Mills.

Mary Manuel's skirmish with NCAA investigator Bob Shrout illustrated the absolute arrogance of the organization. Sutton deserves credit for protesting the way she was treated, but he got nowhere. Manuel said Shrout showed up at her Macon, Georgia home with no warning. Because of a previously scheduled appointment, she told him she was unable to answer questions at that time. Shrout, according to her recollections, demanded to know where her appointment was. She told him it was none of his business.[723]

Regardless, Manuel took time to answer some of his questions. She said Shrout came back the next day asking the same questions. She replied that she had answered those questions the day before. Manuel said Shrout responded, "You're going to answer my questions, all of them. And you're going to answer them because you're lying and Eric's lying, and neither of you is telling the truth." She tearfully recalled that she asked him to leave her home three times before he finally left. Shrout stood in her yard, she said, and shouted, "I'll tell you what, Eric will pay for this. He will be the one hurt by all this." Taking time to compose herself, Manuel said, "Those were his last words as he walked out of the yard, 'Eric will be the one to suffer.'"[724]

Eric Manuel and his family did suffer. Manuel lost his eligibility and sat out his sophomore year. The school allowed him to continue to attend classes and kept his grant-in-aid active. The dark clouds were too much for the quiet, unassuming young man, and he enrolled in Hiwassee Junior College in Madisonville, Tennessee, then transferred to Oklahoma City University, an NAIA school. Even there he was hounded by his Kentucky past. The NAIA wanted to honor the NCAA's lifetime ban on Manuel's ever playing college basketball, and disputed his eligibility. Mark Hammons, an Oklahoma City lawyer, took up Manuel's cause pro bono.

He filed suit against the NAIA, and won his case in Federal District Court. While the NAIA appealed the decision, Manuel led his OCU team to back-to-back national NAIA championships. Manuel received his degree from OCU, and Clay Stoldt, the school's sports information director said "He was so very proud to graduate."[725]

The taint from the Kentucky scandal, however, appeared to follow Manuel wherever he went. He played basketball in Europe, but the NBA wasn't in his future.

The Mills home, in legal counsel Joe Burch's April 1988 summary of interviews, was described as a small apartment in a building with eight units. The apartment's contents were designated as being fairly worn. It was a description found in no other documents relating to interviews during the investigation.[726]

When Park interviewed Claud Mills two months later, he told the former judge he was upset with Burch about the way NCAA investigator Charles Smrt treated him. Mills quoted Smrt as telling him, "I think you received the money. I think one of your sons maybe did something with the money and didn't tell you." He told Park that Burch just sat there through Smrt's remarks. "He hadn't even talked with Casey, nobody at Kentucky," Mills continued, "he didn't believe what Chris said. And that really hurt me. And he didn't believe what my younger son said." Actually, Mills was incorrect about the discussions with assistant coach Dwane Casey. University officials questioned Casey repeatedly and immediately after Roselle heard from the Los Angeles reporter.[727]

Mills said he felt his treatment was prejudiced. "Deep down within me, what I really felt, because he hadn't told me no black guy at Emery he had talked to," he continued. Mills said Smrt told him he felt he and his sons were guilty. In another interview session with Burch and Smrt, Mills said maybe it was time for him to go to court, ended the dialogue and called his attorney.[728]

Chris Mills transferred to Arizona to play out his eligibility. He was drafted by the Cleveland Cavaliers and later played for the New York Knicks.

The NCAA had a strange manner of handling their interviews with Barbara Brown, Mary Manuel and Claud Mills as opposed to easing around the good old boys like Jimmy Hamilton. NCAA investigator William Satum wanted to interview "Cats' Pause," a Kentucky sports publication, publisher Oscar Combs about one of the allegations relating to prospective recruit Lawrence Funderburke. Combs, with an independent streak, didn't quite fall into the good old boy network, but came to Lexington after selling his weekly newspaper in Hazard and was successful with his specialty publication. There was nothing illogical about Combs' request that his interview with Satum be recorded. The request, however, threw the NCAA in a tail spin. Satum called his Kansas City headquarters for instructions, and the interview was canceled. Combs wasn't going to let them off that easy. He called a news conference and said he wanted to cooperate with the NCAA, and offered to pay a court stenographer to record the interview. Satum again called NCAA headquarters, and the interview was canceled a second time.[729]

In the face of all the publicity about the Combs' interview, NCAA director of enforcement S. David Berst provided a convoluted reason the organization didn't tape their interviews. Berst's explanation indicated the NCAA had practiced spin control long before the Clinton administration took office. The reason Berst gave for his investigators not taping their interviews was "To assure some confidentiality and to give us time to review the information to check accuracy. I think it is the correct policy to go about our business reasonably discreetly." Berst claimed the interview method they used allowed them to provide those interviewed with their version of the discussion to agree or disagree with. It was doubtful if Barbara Brown, Mary Manuel or Claud Mills were afforded that luxury.[730]

If the NCAA taped their investigative interviews, it might be difficult for them to put their particular spin on the results, and that might hurt some of their cash-generating schools, and their deep pocketed backers if they were caught in blatant violations.

Combs had the wherewithal to call the NCAA's hand on their failure to tape their interviews. The Browns, Manuels and Mills, overwhelmed by the school and the organization, were certainly treated differently. For that matter assistant coach Dwane Casey, who was also black, was treated differently from his white counterpart.

# REPUTATIONS ON THE LINE

By the end of October, the NCAA had twenty-four allegations and inquiries of violations for the school to answer in the next three months. Roselle, Park, Burch, Lawson and associates kept long hours. The result was the *Response of The President of The University of Kentucky to The National Collegiate Athletic Association.*

The more serious allegations were the money in the Emery envelope; charges of academic fraud in connections with player Eric Manuel's ACT test in Lexington; improper control of players' comp tickets, especially after the 1985 scandal, and the conduct of assistant coach Dwane Casey.

Allegation No. 1 concerned the Emery air freight envelope Casey prepared to send to Claud Mills and the alleged $1,000. The university concluded, in its twenty-six page answer to the allegation, the $1,000 was in the envelope when Emery employees examined it in Los Angeles. They also acknowledged that Casey prepared it for shipment, and Larnette McDowell, a temporary secretary in the basketball offices, completed the shipping instructions. McDowell saw no money in the envelope, but didn't look in the cassette sleeve. There was no evidence, the school said, that a third person placed the money in the envelope after it left the school, and pointed out that Emery failed to document the money was in the package when it was delivered to Mills. The university concluded it was unable to respond to the allegation with any certainty.[731]

There was a problem. Casey denied he had access to any substantial sums of money early in the probe, but the school found he received the

$10,000 honorarium on February 2, and used cash to pay his Greentree Marriott Hotel bill in Pittsburgh the first week of April when he was on a recruiting trip. The problem with their assumption was Casey had received at least four salary checks in the interim, and they could have been the source for the cash. In a January 1989 interview with Park, Casey said he used the honorarium to pay his debts and expenses. He actually took a cut in pay when he moved from Western Kentucky to UK. In describing his financial status when he received the honorarium, Casey told Park, "At that time, judge Park, I had just gotten rid of a house I bought in Bowling Green and I had taken a loss on it, which was close to $12,000. And also at the time I had a friend I had co-signed a note with who had bought a car. He joined the service and left me with the note in Bowling Green, and I had to come up with the money, which was I think like $2,500 at that time. So I was in a pretty tight situation financially at that time."[732]

Park asked Casey, "Did you have anything left over from this $10,000 after you paid your debts, were you sending it out or could have been sending it to anybody else?" Casey replied, "No, I did not." Park continued, "At any time did coach Sutton or __ or __ (Names redacted in the Response) or anybody else suggest that this $10,000 was to be used to provide benefits for recruits?" Casey answered, "Never."[733]

The NCAA believed Casey put the cash in the envelope. Their reasoning, based on Emery employees' statements and university documents, accepted Emery employees finding money in the envelope, and delivering it to Claud Mills. The NCAA gave another reason for their conclusion: inconsistent statements supplied by Casey, McDowell and Mills. The enforcement staff said, "It appears Casey had cash available during this period to provide $1,000."[734]

There seemed to be a double standard employed by both the school and the NCAA when judging Casey and another assistant coach, James Dickey. Dickey received a similar $10,000 honorarium, and didn't report it to the NCAA. From all indications, Dickey, who was white and much closer to Sutton, made more money than Casey. Dickey had to recant denials of additional money, $1,600, that he kept in the basketball offices from the previous summer's camp.735

Granted, Casey left the Emery envelope in the basketball offices to be mailed, and he did have access to a large amount of money. But, so did Dickey who wasn't asked to account for how he spent his honorarium and what use he planned to make of the basketball camp funds stashed in an office desk. That theme continued with the Eric Manuel situation.

When it came to Manuel it appeared all the rules were tossed out the window. Students' grades and grade point averages are protected by the Buckley Amendment, a part of the federal Family Educational Rights and Privacy Act. In August 1988 Park's investigators discovered considerable differences between Manuel's three efforts to pass the college entrance tests. Suddenly, his grades and test scores were public knowledge. He scored the American College Test equivalent of a three and a seven on his first two Scholastic Aptitude Tests, and a twenty-three on the ACT he took in June 1988 at Lafayette High School in Lexington. The highest possible scores were 1600 for the SAT, and thirty-five for the ACT. In October 1988, Sutton announced to the media that Manuel had a 2.41 grade point average, and shouldn't have to take the ACT again. By the time Manuel obtained the services of legal aid attorney Edward Dove, it was too late to protect his legal rights under the Buckley Amendment. Dove did succeed in obtaining a federal court order to keep twenty- five items relating to Manuel's student records under seal and out of the Response when it was released to the public.736

Park asked Manuel to sign a release so the ACT could make a statistical analysis and comparison of his answer sheet with that of Lafayette student Chris Shearer, who sat four or five feet away from the athlete during the test. Park and the NCAA threatened Manuel but, from all evidence I could find, he refused. However, Park met with ACT vice-president Ann V. York in Iowa City in September 1988, and received the analysis. Of the 219 questions on the test, 211 of Manuel's matched those of Shearer.

The ACT said the chances of that happening, without fraud, were two in a million.[737]

How did officials know to compare Manuel's answers to those of Shearer out of the numerous students that took the test? Even more importantly, how did they handle the physically impossible question of Manuel copying Shearer's answers when the Lafayette student, who wrote right-handed and sat several feet to the athlete's left, without attracting the attention of any of the four proctors who patrolled the aisles? Nobody wanted to answer those questions simply because the answers failed to uphold their conclusions.

Lafayette counselor Terry Guion, one of the proctors for the test, said other students told her Shearer boasted around the school that he helped Manuel get into Kentucky. Mary Manuel and the athlete's high school coach, Don Richardson, said Manuel told them he signed his name twice the morning of the test, once on the answer sheet and again when someone asked him for an autograph. Lafayette officials were careless with Manuel's test answer sheet. Guion told investigators that another proctor wanted Manuel's autograph for her son, and she, (Guion) copied the player's answer sheet, and cut off his signature. Dove said he investigated where the test answer sheets were stored from the time they were collected after the exam on Saturday until Guion mailed them to the ACT on Monday morning. "We worked that area to death, followed every lead and did everything possible," Dove said, "UK believed he was guilty and Eric took the fall." Chris Shearer's father refused Dove's request to interview his son.[738]

What really happened with Manuel's answer sheet was the biggest mystery of the entire investigation. Again, it was physically impossible for Manuel to copy Shearer's answers considering the distances between the two students and four proctors observing them. None of the proctors reported any irregularities during the four-hour test.

Many, except the university and NCAA investigators, believed Manuel signed two answer sheets and someone, who knew Shearer was an excellent student, copied his answers on a second answer sheet. That opinion was voiced by a university marketing professor Thomas E. Whittler, but nobody paid any attention. Whittler, who had administered over a hundred such tests, said it was impossible for Manuel to have copied Shearer's answers. "I'm inclined to believe," Whittler said in an op-ed article he wrote for the newspaper, "that Manuel's 211 of the 219 copied answers may be attributed to another source, namely adults. It is only through adults' devious efforts that cheating on this examination is possible. It is interesting that the university and the NCAA placed the blame on a young unassuming athlete, but then again, it is easier to attribute fault to young people who may not be able to defend themselves than to attribute fault to successful adults who can."[739]

The shame was the university's and the NCAA's placing all the blame on Manuel, and ignoring all the questions that pointed elsewhere. Almost as an afterthought, the prestigious Lexington law firm of Greenebaum, Doll and McDonald entered the case. Two of their attorneys, Danny C. Reeves and Richard C. Stilz, Jr., became co-counsels with Dove. University records revealed that Bobby Stilz lettered in Kentucky basketball in 1967. Dove was surprised by the firm's entry into the case. "Defending Eric," Dove said, "was much like rearranging the deck chairs on the *Titanic*."[740]

Without a doubt, I believe investigators not only were careless in Manuel's case, but also looked the other way, as much as possible, on the allegations concerning players' comp tickets. The NCAA found those comp tickets were handled with little supervision. Players received four comp tickets for each game. During 1987-88, 543 regular season and 283 post-season tickets weren't used by players. Those 826 tickets were a tempting morsel. The school admitted, "During the 1987-88 academic year members of the basketball staff utilized unused student-athletes' complimentary admissions approximately 100 times." The school didn't list the number of the players' comp tickets the basketball staff used, only the number of times. There could be a great difference. The school claimed they put the remainder of the unused players' comp tickets on sale to the public. Basketball coach Eddie Sutton was unhappy with the number of his ticket allotment, and was vocal about it. When Hall resigned in March 1985, he still controlled 384 of the 412 season tickets Hagan allotted him in 1976. After Sutton was hired, the athletics board, in responding to all the publicity about Hall's large number of tickets, reduced the basketball coach's number of tickets to sixty-four. "I have nothing to do with tickets," Sutton charged in a July 1988 sworn statement, "I got screwed when I came here with tickets. That's on the record, isn't it? I don't have enough tickets. Let's put it that way." Six months later, Sutton had a different attitude. In a January 1989 interview with Park, Sutton said, "I don't think we could have done a better job in monitoring the tickets than we have done. Coach Dickey was responsible for that, but I certainly oversaw it. I looked at it to make sure and stressed the importance of doing it properly."[741]

What the university did answered the question of who was protecting whom in the matter of the athletes' comp tickets. In their reply to the NCAA allegation about abuse of players' comp tickets, the school found eight violations. Eric Manuel, the school said, violated the rules on comp tickets six times, and Derrick Miller violated the rule twice. Miller's eligibility was restored in February 1989, Manuel left school and the basketball staff was told to clean up their act.[742]

Just as there was never an answer about coach Joe B. Hall's friend, Cecil Dunn, and his alleged purchases of player Jay Shidler's comp tickets earlier, there was only a smattering of information about the 100 times the basketball coaching staff used their players' comp tickets. The school chose to lay the blame for the comp tickets abuse on Manuel and Miller, who were both black, rather than the coaching staff.

Sutton often asserted that he wasn't named in any of the NCAA's allegations, but he was. In an amendment to Allegation No. 11, Sutton's actions came into question. Assistant coach Dwane Casey, Manuel and the coach's son, Sean Sutton, initially told NCAA investigators the players drove to the ACT test site, Lafayette High School. But, Casey made arrangements with Lafayette basketball coach Donnie Harville to drive Manuel to the test site. The two players were getting into Sean Sutton's car when Harville drove up, and they rode to the school with the coach. The NCAA said Casey, Manuel and Sutton provided false information that was contrary to ethical conduct since Harville's transporting them was no violation. Here's where Eddie Sutton comes into the picture. Casey informed Sutton about what he and the two players told the NCAA. Sutton's administrative assistant, Marta McMackin, was present at the conversation. Sutton, according to the Response, instructed Casey to contact Harville and let him know what they told the NCAA before investigators questioned the high school coach. Casey didn't. There was a second conversation between Casey and Sutton about the matter, and McMackin was also present. According to The Response, Sutton was upset, "Because the conflict in the statements make it appear that the two young men had been lying." Casey and Sean Sutton said they simply forgot about the transportation arrangements. Manuel said he initially gave false information because he thought Harville's driving them to the test site was a violation. The university said Sutton denied the second conversation with Casey about the incident. The enforcement staff said they were concerned that Sutton's efforts to provide Harville such information would hinder their efforts to obtain candid and truthful information in their interview with the high school coach.[743]

In March 1989, while trying to keep his coaching job, Sutton proclaimed he wasn't named in any of the NCAA's allegations against Kentucky. From all indications, Sutton had some kind of assurance from NCAA executive director Richard Schultz saying he was not charged with any violations of the organization's rules and no penalty would be assessed against him and he would be free to coach at another school.[744]

There appeared a nebulous area in the relationship between Sutton and Schultz concerning the allegations. Transcripts of Sutton's sworn statement in Park's office in July 1988 provided a hint. In addition to the coach's attorney, Park and his staff, there three NCAA investigators were there for the statement. Sutton demanded to be the last person interviewed in the investigation. When NCAA investigator Charles Smrt told him that wasn't going to be the case, Sutton said, "Well, then, I'm not going to talk to you. I —I—that's what I told you wasn't it? I wanted to be the last person interviewed on this investigation." At Sutton's persistence, Smrt suggested the NCAA could make an additional allegation against the school for the coach's refusal to be interviewed. "Hey, I don't care," Sutton said, "I already talked to Dick Schultz a week ago today. Do you understand? So, you can do anything you want to do." Faced with Smrt's continued threat, Sutton consented to the interview.[745]

When the interview was over, Sutton asked Smrt how long the investigation would continue. Smrt didn't give him an answer. Sutton was concerned over damage done to his recruiting, his assistant coaches' reputations and his own. "My reputation has been hurt," he said, "I might not be the Olympic coach in '92 or '96. I don't want this thing drug on. My request is for them to bring this thing to a close. Get it over with. Penalize us. We'll live with that. But don't drag it into next year." Without giving Smrt a chance to reply, Sutton continued, "I mean, Chuck, I mean that's all I ask. That's what I told Dick (Schultz) out there (in Kansas City) a week ago. I said, 'Dick, get this thing over with. Don't drag it on. If we're guilty penalize us.'"[746]

Schultz himself fell under the shadow of Park a few years later when the NCAA retained the former judge as an independent investigator to determine if Schultz was involved in giving interest-free loans when he was athletics director at the University of Virginia from 1981 to 1987. Park apparently mined a rich lode of information. After Park made his report to the organization, Schultz immediately resigned as executive director in 1993.[747]

The NCAA's other allegations against Kentucky included irregularities in Sutton's summer basketball camps, players living rent free in the summer in Wildcat Lodge when they weren't enrolled in classes, recruiting violations by Casey and Dickey and giving financial aid to ineligible athletes.[748]

# CHANGING OF THE GUARD

As Roselle assembled answers to the NCAA's allegations, basketball coach Eddie Sutton denied rumors of his departure and football coach Jerry Claiborne quietly contemplated retirement.

Sutton's 1988-89 13-19 season was the school's worst record since the 1926-27 team, coached by the school's first All-American Basil Hayden, which was 3-13. Rupp, always the standard by which Kentucky coaches are judged, had his worst season in 1966-67 with a 13-13 record. Sutton might have survived that season except for the NCAA investigation, rumors of personal problems and the fact that his slow style of offense was wearing thin with the "faithful."

A guard for coach Hank Iba at Oklahoma State, Sutton used his old coach's deliberate style of play that was quite a departure from Rupp's brand of "race horse basketball." Callers to his radio show begged him to use the enormous amount of talent he had to increase the games' tempo. He refused. Some of his players, such as Rex Chapman, weren't happy at having to make seven or eight passes before shooting regardless of the looks they had at the basket. Chapman, referred to as the "Kentucky Wonder" of high school basketball, left after his sophomore year, and was the first player selected by the Charlotte Hornets in expansion NBA draft.

Rumors abounded about Sutton's drinking problems. An oft heard phrase was, "Eddie, Kentucky fans like their Bourbon and their hair straight." Sutton's hair often looked as if it were permed. Broadcaster Cawood Ledford speculated the coach's drinking problem was the reason

Sutton failed to receive the customary contract extension at the end of his first year when he took the team to the Elite Eight, and he was the Associated Press' coach of the year.[749]

Sutton didn't want to turn loose of the coaching job he said he would have crawled all the way from Arkansas to Lexington to get. In a meeting with Roselle, Sutton refused to resign. Two days later Roselle told him he was calling a meeting of the athletics board, and he had the votes to fire him. Sutton resigned in April 1989, and the school bought out the remaining year of his contract for $150,000.[750]

Roselle later said he regretted the turmoil that led to Sutton's resignation, but circumstances created a need for a change that was in the school's best interests. "Sutton wanted to stay," Roselle recalled two years later, "I and others thought he should leave. The wisdom in what we did ought to be apparent to everyone including coach Sutton." He pointed out Sutton was in a better situation. "He's talking about getting over all his problems," Roselle added.[751]

Sutton, who spent a year holding clinics for Nike before taking the coaching job at Oklahoma State, had a different opinion of those troubled times in Lexington. In 1991, Sutton, a coach of the year candidate who took his Oklahoma State to the NCAA tournament while Kentucky stayed home, said, "That was a very severe penalty Kentucky was given. If it (the investigation) had been handled in a different manner, I think they'd be going to the NCAA tournament today. I just think it should have been handled differently."[752]

High on Roselle's list as Sutton's successor was Richard A. Pitino, the dynamic coach of the New York Knicks. Pitino had a reputation, earned at Boston University and Providence, for turning troubled college basketball programs into successes, and Kentucky was in deep trouble. The newspaper, still heady from their Pulitzer Prize for the 1985 basketball expose, welcomed Pitino to Lexington with a re-hash of stories of NCAA allegations at the University of Hawaii, when he was in his first job as an assistant coach there. The allegations included providing tickets for players to fly to the mainland, and extra benefits in cars-for-tickets exchanges. Pitino told the Hawaii newspaper in 1977 that he was guilty only of handing out coupons for free meals at McDonald's.[753]

The newspaper kept hammering on the subject for days with front page stories. Pitino called a news conference to defend his record."No one in this business has more integrity than Rick Pitino," he said. "The Hawaii problem is no problem because I've already been a head coach at Boston U. and Providence. I'm not an assistant coach fighting for his first job."[754]

"It was an old story," Pitino later recalled, "but in light of Kentucky's tarnished past, I had no reluctance in dropping out after C.M. (Newton) visited us after dinner and told me he thought it would be best to cancel the process. C.M. felt Kentucky didn't need any more negative publicity, and that the Herald-Leader would make it difficult for all of us." Apparently, Roselle had a chat with Newton about who was calling the shots. At 7:30 the next morning Newton knocked on Pitino's hotel room door to do an about face. "He (Newton) had spoken with David Roselle," Pitino said, "and told me the president was not concerned about the Hawaii incident. 'He's totally comfortable with what you stand for and, if you agree, wants to proceed with the interview.'"[755]

The media, however, has continued to give Newton, not Roselle, the credit for bringing Pitino to Kentucky. Newton has continued to accept accolades for Pitino's hiring.

Roselle told Pitino he'd done a thorough check into his background at Boston and Providence, was confident he had been totally compliant with NCAA rules and the job was his. Roselle told Pitino the Kentucky program could do all the things that his alma mater, Duke, was doing both academically and athletically. He gave the coach four to five years to rebuild the program.[756]

In June 1988 Pitino signed an eleven-paged contract for $105,000 which included all the usual perks of health care, insurance, funded retirement benefits and two cars. Like his predecessors, Pitino received a bonus of a month's salary if the team won the SEC or qualified for

NCAA tournament play. Unlike his predecessor's, Pitino's contract listed thirteen specific SEC and NCAA violations that would invalidate his hiring. The coach participated in decisions on travel, scheduling and such, but athletics director C.M. Newton always made the final decisions.[757]

One clause of his contract irritated Pitino, and another caused him considerable embarrassment. Sutton's basketball camps were a mess with some athletes apparently attending free. Some high school coaches were given excessive fees as speakers and instructors. Pitino's contract included all the specifics for operating his camps including room rates in the dorms. Everything went smoothly for the first camp. The second year, he noticed there was a big hike in room rates. An investigation revealed school attorneys, drawing up Pitino's contract, used the wrong room rates. The UKAA made up the difference the first year, but Newton put his foot down the second year. Pitino protested that he was trying to avoid making it a camp for rich boys only, but Newton was unmoved. When his contract was renegotiated in 1993, room rates for his summer camps were removed.[758]

Pitino's engaging personality made him an ideal candidate for a sports marketing and endorsement gold mine. Somebody recognized that. It may have been Newton, but more likely it was Jim Host who held the broadcast and television rights to the games. No other coach was required to have an agent to handle his endorsements, but Joe B. Hall and Eddie Sutton's endorsement potential never reached that of Pitino's. An addendum to his first contract, named the agent selected by Newton. To absolutely no one's sunrise the agent was Jim Host. The addendum called for the agent to maintain accurate records of all income and expenses relating to the coach's shows and commercial endorsements, and allow an institutional inspection of his books.[759]

Since Host, not the athletics association paid Pitino, the amount was kept private. Host said his firm, "Sports Communications paid Pitino a flat fee for the endorsements" regardless of the number of products the coach hawked. By 1991, Pitino's media endorsements dominated the air waves as he endorsed potato chips, automobiles, a supermarket, a hotel and a telephone service. The newspaper accused Pitino and Newton of allowing the coach's endorsements to become a "cottage industry."[760] The newspaper only got it half right.

Pitino said, "I do whatever Jim Host says. He has the rights to me commercial-wise." Host claimed the agent arrangement served two purposes. It provided sponsors with a degree of protection as the coach wouldn't be endorsing competing products. It afforded the university a measure of control that would make Pitino less of an entrepreneur. Translated, that meant Newton and Host wanted to control Pitino's endorsements, and it certainly made more money for Host. The coach outfoxed them when he personally backed an Italian restaurant, Bravo Pitino's, where he and his New York friends could hang out.[761]

Two years later, Newton and Host finally got around to discussing the problem of Pitino's overexposure on television. Host said he was placing a restriction in future contracts on the number of times clients could run commercial spots on television featuring Pitino. "This will do a great deal," he told Newton, "toward cutting down what is perceived to be over exposure in terms of *our* (emphasis mine) coaches."[762]

From all appearances, Pitino almost left Kentucky in late 1993, and it seemed to be related to the agent clause in his contract. A March 1994 memorandum was attached to Pitino's contract that placed his media shows and endorsements inside the bids for broadcast and telecast game rights. The memorandum called for Pitino to receive an amount not less than he received from Host as his agent. "The agreements included in this memorandum," the document read, "are given as an inducement for Richard A. Pitino, to continue in the position of head basketball coach at the University of Kentucky, and that the undersigned (Newton and president Charles T. Wethington) acknowledge that Richard A. Pitino is relying on this memorandum of agreement to extend his employment contract dated June 8, 1993."[763]

Another memorandum, dated a year later, indicated the agent arrangement continued to be a problem for Pitino. This time the meaning was

quite clear. The 1994 memorandum called for Newton, as athletics director, "To verify the minimum amounts due (Pitino) from the coach's agent
in each of the seven years referred to in this memorandum."[764]

The agent deal with Host reached the height of ridicule in the fall of
1994, and must have been acutely embarrassing for the coach. Kentucky's
department of education agreed to pay Host $123,965, in federal funds
designated for promotional purposes, for a media campaign to encourage
children to eat the breakfasts provided at their schools. Host's proposal
listed a $18,000 fee for Pitino as the celebrity spokesman. State education
commissioner Thomas Boysen immediately rejected the plan. Pitino
heard about the flap in a news account. The Lexington newspaper ran an
editorial drawing portraying the gray-haired Host carrying a brief case lettered "Jim Ho$t." Host's figure in the drawing had two heads. One head
was directing Pitino toward a tiny Uncle Sam figure saying, "OK, you put
on a show to distract him, and I'll grab his lunch money." Host's second
head looked the other way, saw Boysen and said, "Uh-oh, never mind."[765]

Host's attempts to explain the $18,000 celebrity fee confirmed Pitino
was a money making machine for him. The $18,000, Host explained, was
never going directly to Pitino; it was merely the value he placed on the
coach's endorsement. "The money would have gone to Host
Communications," he commented, "just as the other $105,965 in the
contract. Host Communications had guaranteed Pitino a flat fee for
endorsements, so the money would have gone to Pitino only in the sense
that all revenues going to Host Communications helped cover Pitino's
fee." Host declined to say how much he paid Pitino for his endorsements.
"I can tell you that it is a substantial amount of money," Host said, "it is
sufficient enough that it helped attract Rick here and I think it helps keep
him here." The Associated Press estimated Pitino earned $1 million a year
from his endorsements.[766]

Host claimed Pitino's television shows weren't profitable to his company, but there was no indication that Host ever attempted to get out of
the agent deal. The show didn't lack for commercials and, at the end of

every show, a long list of additional sponsors scrolled down the screen. Host selected broadcaster Ralph Hacker to handle Pitino's shows. Later the coach did that himself, and did it very well.

The coach managed to salvage some of his rights for himself in his contracts with the school. Pitino's 1989 contract and the seven-year extension in 1993 gave him exclusive rights, with no agent involved, to enter into contracts with athletic apparel suppliers. Newton's approval of Pitino's choices couldn't be unreasonably withheld.[767]

Coaches, in high profile athletic programs making arrangements with apparel companies wasn't unusual. Universities, however, seeing their coaches pocket vast sums of money wanted in on the action, and everything began to change in the 1990s. Michigan, in 1994, signed a $7 million endorsement deal with Nike for six years, and basketball coach Steve Fisher received $200,000 for his share. North Carolina basketball coach Dean Smith's Nike contract between his DES Enterprises and the school provided him with a one-time fee of $500,000, annual payments of $300,000 and a long line of perks.[768]

Pitino changed the teams' apparel from Nike, used by Sutton, to Converse, the brand he used at Boston and Providence. In 1996, Converse showcased the Kentucky team in new uniforms and shoes of white and blue denim. Appearing at the news conference with Pitino to unveil the new apparel was Converse's national marketing director and the athletic director's son, Martin Newton. The faithful took an instant dislike to the uniforms, flooded radio call-in shows with their complaints, and they were soon changed.[769]

Soon after that appearance, Martin Newton left his thirteen-year position with Converse and joined Nike. Rumors circulated that Kentucky basketball would soon be outfitted by Nike. For once, they were right. Newton began talking about developing a national marketing concept for Kentucky athletics where all apparel contracts would be executed through the university with the coaches receiving a set amount. He added that any new plan would honor Pitino's existing contract with Converse. Allowing

Pitino to keep his Converse contract, and an all-sports deal with Nike weren't exactly compatible. By October 1996, Newton announced the school's athletic teams would be outfitted by Nike, but gave no date. That move prompted "Cat's Pause" publisher Oscar Combs to suggest if football fans really wanted Commonwealth Stadium expanded they should find Martin Newton a job with a contractor.[770]

Nepotism may have entered the picture, but Newton was attracted by the big bucks Nike was paying for college athletic programs. The giant fly in Newton's ointment was Pitino's contract with Converse that didn't expire until June 2000. Newton had his multi-million-dollar deal with Nike just sitting there, and he couldn't do anything about it because Pitino's contract with Converse didn't expire for four years. Forcing Pitino out was a questionable option since the good old boys were elated with the money the coach's endorsements brought their businesses, and the bragging rights his wins represented. They also knew it was only a matter of time until Pitino won a national championship they could brag about for years.

What Pitino did for the Kentucky program was amazing; it also showcased his coaching talents. Sutton's players deserted the ship after the scandal. LeRon Ellis, who averaged 16.0 a game transferred to Syracuse. The NCAA said Chris Mills could play for any school except Kentucky, and he chose Arizona. Pitino was left with Derrick Miller, Reggie Hanson, Deron Feldhause, John Pelphrey and Sean Woods. None were stellar stars, but Pitino made up for their lack of talent by teaching them to launch volleys of three-point shots. The team, known as "Pitino's Bambinos," played their hearts out. The season's high point was their 100-95 defeat of a LSU team which had future NBA stars Shaquille O'Neal, Chris Jackson and Stanley Roberts. Pitino hired the first female assistant coach in the history of men's Division 1 basketball, and he signed New York high school star Jamal Mashburn. [771]

Pitino's second team was built around Mashburn and a quartet of home-grown talent, John Pelphrey, Reggie Hanson, Deron Feldhause and

Richie Farmer. They had a 22-6 season. The faithful now knew, without a doubt the savior of their basketball program was Pitino. It was hard to tell who was having the most fun, Pitino, the good old boys or the average fans. The team's 14-4 record was the best in the SEC, but NCAA penalties prohibited their being conference champions. Since they couldn't celebrate a conference championship, they had their own parade. Thousands of fans cheered the team as they rode fire trucks from downtown to a Memorial Coliseum rally that ended the season.[772]

Pitino's third team with Mashburn, who'd elevated his scoring to 21.3 points a game his sophomore season, and seniors Pelphrey, Feldhause, Farmer and Sean Woods captured the coach's first SEC tournament title in 1992. That team captured the attention not only of the commonwealth but of the entire nation. With the exception of Mashburn, the others would have been bench warmers in most Division 1 programs, but Pitino was a master motivator. The team gutted out win after win to reach the Elite Eight in the NCAA tournament. Their game with Duke was one of the most exciting in the annals of college sports. A shot by Woods gave Kentucky the lead in overtime with 2.1 seconds left. Grant Hill threw a length of the floor pass to Christian Laettner who swished in a seventeen-footer as the buzzer sounded. Pitino called them "The Unforgettables," and their jerseys were retired in an emotional Rupp Arena ceremony that capped the 29-7 season.[773]

Known as the "Monster Mash," Mashburn carried the team along with native Kentuckian Travis Ford, who transferred from Missouri, to Pitino's second SEC tournament championship. Their 30-4 season carried them to the Final Four where they lost to Michigan's "Fab Five" 76-81.

Pitino's 1993-94 team, without Mashburn who was drafted by the Dallas Mavericks, posted season numbers Kentucky was accustomed to, 27-7, and again won the SEC tournament. They lost in the second round of the NCAA tournament to Marquette 63-75. Led by the amazing three-point shooting of Tony Delk, the high point of the season was their rebounding from a thirty-one point second half deficit to beat LSU

99-85. It was the greatest come-from-behind road victory in the history of men's Division 1 basketball.[774]

In the next two years, Pitino signed prep All-Americans Antoine Walker from Chicago and Ron Mercer from Nashville, and found a gold mine in Louisville native Derek Anderson who transferred from Ohio State. Delk, Walker, Mark Pope, Walter McCarty and Anthony Epps made up the team that won another SEC tournament, but ended their 28-5 season when they lost to North Carolina in the NCAA's southeast regional tournament.[775]

It was only a matter of time until Kentucky was once again the national champion of college basketball.

With Mercer added to the 1995-96 team, Kentucky opened the season with the number one ranking. Pitino's biggest problem was too much talent and too little playing time. He did a super motivational job molding the players into a team he called "The Untouchables." After a stunning 82-92 loss to Massachusetts early in the season, "The Untouchables" romped through the SEC regular season undefeated, 16-0. The first time that had happened in forty years. Mississippi State shocked them by beating them in the finals of the SEC tournament. That was the impetus they need to plow through the NCAA tournament. Many thought the first game of the Final Four, Kentucky v Massachusetts, actually decided the championship when "The Untouchables" exacted revenge 81-74. They defeated Syracuse 76-67 to win Pitino's first national championship and Kentucky's seventh.[776]

With three players going to the NBA, Walker to the Boston Celtics, Tony Delk to the Charlotte Hornets and Walter McCarty to the New York Knicks, Pitino rebuilt his 1996-97 team around Ron Mercer and Derek Anderson. ESPN commentator Dick Vitale dubbed them "The Air Pair" for their play above the basket, and they were a pleasure to watch. Scott Padgett, Allan Edwards, former walk-on Cameron Mills, Nazar Mohammed, Wayne Turner and Epps were the supporting cast. Anderson was leading the SEC in three-point shooting, going to the foul line and steals when he went down with a knee injury in January. Pitino called them "The Unbelievables" because they somehow managed to win game after game. Their dedication took them to the championship game of the Final Four where they lost to Arizona 79-84.[777]

Pitino far exceeded Roselle's expectation of taking four or five years to rebuild Kentucky basketball. In three years, Kentucky was in the Elite Eight, the next year in the Final Four, and the seventh year had won another championship.

Success like that enabled Pitino to speak out in a manner Joe B. Hall and Eddie Sutton would have probably found difficult, but then the New Yorker didn't have their history. From the beginning Pitino was critical of the dead spots in the Rupp Arena floor, and having his team playing off campus. In a manner typical of Pitino, he tackled the issue head on. In October 1996, he asked millionaire health-care executive Bruce Lunsford, from Louisville, to head a fund raising drive to build a new campus arena. "If we can build an arena, and I mean a state of the art (arena); the best in all the land college or pro, without taxing anyone and get everything going to the University of Kentucky that would be a tremendous accomplishment," Pitino said.[778]

Downtown was aghast! The very idea of the university building their own basketball arena was appalling, but even more of a blow was the school wanted to keep all the revenue from their own basketball games. Urban-county councilman Roy Durbin was shocked, "It really hurts to even think they (UK) would treat our city this way. Pitino is not a legend yet; he hasn't won 800 games." Mayor Pan Miller attempted to put a positive spin on Pitino's announcement saying she was sure the university would continue to be the city's partner in Rupp Arena. Miller, whom many called "Pothole Pam" because of the deplorable condition of some city streets, said the school moving to their own campus arena "Would be an enormous psychological loss for all the restaurants and merchants downtown."[779] It wasn't their psyche Miller was protecting; it was their pockets and her base of political support.

Guess who surfaced as chairman of the Lexington Center Corporation? It was none other than Cecil Dunn, a refugee from the 1985 basketball scandals. Dunn questioned why athletic officials had failed to complain about the Rupp Arena lease negotiations twenty-one years earlier. That was a no-brainer. Pitino wasn't coach then; Joe B. Hall, Dunn's good friend, was and he complained about moving basketball games off campus. Dunn should have asked Hall that question.[780]

The good old boys began closing their ranks to protect their investment, a share of Kentucky basketball revenue. LCC manager Tom Minter, who had held Singletary's feet to the fire over the lease in 1976, said it was clear to all parties that the arena was a joint venture. Suddenly the university, who was just one of many temporary tenants using the arena, now was a partner. Singletary even offered a tepid explanation, "It was a cooperative venture…in the sense that both we and they favored and saw the need for such a facility."[781]

Pitino opened a can of worms that couldn't be closed. The LCC officials didn't help the situation when they allowed a minor league hockey team to play in the arena for less rent than the basketball team was paying. While they refused to replace the floor for Kentucky basketball, the LCC didn't hesitate to rip up the under flooring to install equipment for the ice rink. The Lexington Center began to back pedal, and offered to negotiate a more favorable lease. The school decided to conduct their own feasibility study for a new campus arena.[782]

The feasibility study was another example of the loose management of athletic affairs. Huber, Hunt and Nicholas, the Indianapolis firm that built the stadium, had just completed a feasibility study of that structure's expansion. News of a possible new campus arena for "America's Team" drew national coverage. Associate athletics director Larry Ivy received inquiries from firms interested in the study. Ivy, from all indications, sent a letter to one inquiring firm saying, "The university had already decided on its consultant." Ivy planned to expand HHN's feasibility study to include the campus arena. Firms interested in the arena project began asking questions about a study that hadn't been put out for public bids. Vice-president for business George DeBin stopped the entire arena process cold. "If such a letter exists," DeBin said, "(Ivy) was not authorized to send one. I don't know why he would have done that." DeBin made sure that proposals for the arena study were sent to seven consultants for competitive bidding. Newton attempted to smooth things over saying it was all just a misunderstanding. A Kansas City firm, HNTR Corporation, had the best bid, and HHN came in third.[783]

DeBin caught that one, but maybe the no-bid game program rights and the verbal agreement for season video highlights escaped his notice. The success of Jerry Claiborne's football program, the extraordinarily high graduation rate of his players didn't escape Roselle's attention.

Claiborne's 1987 and 1988 teams chugged along with 5-6 seasons. His 1989 team was 6-5, but the good old boys were getting restless for the glory days of "Bear" Bryant. After still another basketball scandal and losing to Tennessee 10-31, Claiborne was on a recruiting trip to Ohio when his plane encountered rough weather. When he returned to Lexington, Claiborne said he "Started thinking this (schedule) is kind of stupid. I want to spend more time with my wife than dinner once a week." Roselle accepted Claiborne's resignation but said he could coach as long as he wanted to with 6-5 seasons and players graduating at a rate of ninety percent.[784]

Claiborne took a football program in disgrace, the laughing stock of the SEC, and restored it to respectability. He proved the school could graduate football players, remain competitive and put an average of 55,726 fans in stadium seats on game days. Sixty-eight of Claiborne's players made SEC academic honor rolls, and twenty-eight were drafted by NFL teams.[785]

The contributions Claiborne made to Kentucky football eclipsed those of all other coaches, including "Bear" Bryant. Claiborne concentrated on the reason for a college education, to prepare his athletes for the real world. The good old boys, on the other hand, forever revered Bryant because his 60-25-5 record and Kentucky's only three major bowl appearances gave them bragging rights for half a century. Bryant was fortunate at Kentucky during the point shaving scandals and the sudden death penalty that the NCAA didn't discover his violations of the rules. But, he wasn't so lucky at his next coaching stop, Texas A & M. The NCAA looked into illegal subsidization of players at A & M, and Bryant asked for a meeting before the committee on infractions. "After discussing one or two of the disputed incidents with the committee," former executive director Walter Byers recalled, "Bryant fell silent, looked at Ab Kirwan, (the committee chair from Kentucky who knew the coach well) squinted his eyes in a searching gaze and said, 'Ab, you mean to tell me that an alumnus can't give these kids money?'"[786]

Byers said Kirwan replied, "Of course he can't, Paul, he can't do that." Bryant replied, "Well, I guess I don't have anything to argue about." The coach got up, put on his hat and left.[787] Claiborne clearly possessed a different athletic philosophy although Bryant was his mentor at Kentucky, A & M and Alabama.

Roselle lauded Claiborne for running a successful program that was fair to the athletes, compliant with SEC and NCAA rules and remained competitive. "We are in his debt," Roselle said, "especially the young men who played on his teams." Even that ever vigilant watchdog of the athletics program, the Lexington newspaper, praised Claiborne. "He recruited hard-working, honest kids," their editorial said, "he coached them well. He taught them there was life after football, and made sure they were prepared for it by insisting they go to class. His students graduated. This year the team had seventeen All-Academic SEC players." The newspaper recognized the good old boys' protests that his teams didn't win enough games. "But what Jerry Claiborne did for UK was more important than victories or bowl games. Claiborne made UK football respectable, both off and on the field."[788]

In addition to his vast coaching responsibilities, Claiborne worked just as hard to raise money for a training center for his program and for the indoor practice facility. The school could have named at least one of them for Claiborne, but chose instead to name them both for a deep-pocketed alumnus.

Replacing Claiborne wasn't an easy task, but athletics director C.M. Newton apparently made up his mind early in the process. Mike Shanahan, the Forty-Niner's assistant coach who later took the Denver Broncos to Super Bowl titles, flew to Lexington for a brief look, and left. Alabama coach Bill Curry was evidently Newton's choice from the beginning. Curry played football at Georgia Tech, and was a member of coach Vince Lombardi's Green Bay Packers team that won the first Super Bowl in 1967. Traded that year to the Baltimore Colts, Curry was an All-Pro in 1971 and 1972. Curry returned to Georgia Tech as coach in 1980, and five years later his team beat Michigan State in the All-American Bowl topping a 9-2-1 season. He moved to Alabama, hungry for another national championship since "Bear" Bryant's last in 1979. [789]

The knock against Curry at Alabama was his lack of ties to the "Bear." In 1989 his Alabama team was undefeated until the last game of the season with cross-state rival Auburn. The Tide lost 20-30, but the loss forced them to share the SEC championship with the War Eagles. Angry protests rained down on Curry's head. His team compounded that Auburn loss by losing to Miami 25-33 in the Sugar Bowl. Alabama fans were despondent over a 10-2 season that Kentucky's good old boys would have bragged about for forty years. Despite being the SEC coach of the year, Curry's days at Alabama were numbered.[790]

Ten days after the Sugar Bowl loss, Curry was in Lexington meeting with interim president Charles T. Wethington, Newton and, of course, Jim Host to discuss the head football coaching position. He accepted immediately. Curry's $105,000 contract for six years had the usual perks and supplemental income clauses similar to Pitino's except for one area. Curry wasn't required to have an agent handle his endorsements and media shows. The media estimated Curry's annual income at $300,000. They were close. Clause 7-f, in Curry's contract, dealing with default and termination called for a payment of $305,000 if the school fired him without cause.[791]

Curry's selection was rapidly approved by trustees, and everybody was optimistic. The good old boys were practically salivating over Curry's record at Alabama and expecting the same at Kentucky. Newton proclaimed, "It's an exciting day for the commonwealth."[792] It turned out to be not only a dismal day, but a disappointing seven years.

That old platitude of Kentucky being the graveyard of SEC coaches rose up and ate Curry alive. His first season was 4-7, and he went 3-8 in 1991. Yet, before the 1992 season started, Newton extended Curry's contract two years, until 1997, and increased his base salary to $127,000. The next year, Curry had his best season at Kentucky, 6-6, and lost to Clemson in the Peach Bowl 13-14. After the 1994 season, Newton again extended Curry's contract to 1999, and raised his base salary to $130,861.[793]

In 1994, Curry turned in a disastrous 1-10 season. It took all of Newton's guile to stem the season ticket cancellations. The athletics director agreed to stay beyond his planned retirement date to help, or perhaps, protect his football coach. Curry's 1995 record of 4-7 was barely enough to keep his head off the chopping block.[794]

Curry's option system turned to a dull muddle of three runs and then a punt. It was incredulous that, with his running system and seasonal records of 27-44, Curry was able to sign the nation's best high school quarterback after the 1996 season. Tim Couch came from Leslie County High School, in eastern Kentucky, and could have signed with just about any high profile college football program in the country. Couch could have signed with Kentucky out of a sense of loyalty. He said he signed because of Curry. In the audience for his signing ceremony was one of the high profile good old boys, Dudley Webb. An attorney and developer Webb was alleged to have been involved in subsidizing one of coach Joe B. Hall's basketball players in 1985[795].

Couch's freshman season was a disaster for many reasons. Curry only started him twice, and endured angry screams of the fans when he took him out of games. Couch and Curry's option system didn't mesh. The offensive line, at best, was ineffective. Couch, in six games, completed 29 of 77 passes for 255 yards and one touchdown, and one interception. Curry's regular quarterback, Billy Jack Haskins, completed 85 out of 157 passes for 892 yards, four touchdowns and four interceptions. The result was another 4-7 season, and it was curtains for Curry.[796]

Newton asked for Curry's resignation in October 1996, the coach obliged but finished out the season. "For seven years," Newton said, "I watched coach Curry put his heart and soul into the project and the model program we were trying to build. The fact is (the program) has not progressed the way we felt it should." There was speculation that Couch would transfer. "After the season," Couch said, "I'll think about what I'm going to do, but right now I'm very happy here."[797] It was clear the freshman quarterback was giving himself an option.

Few could fault Curry for his players' academic achievements nor his molding them for life after football. Perhaps he cared too much, and that clouded his vision of the depth charts. When one of his offensive linemen, Trent DiGiuro, was shot in August 1994 on the front porch of the house where he lived, Curry got down on his hands and knees the next morning to clean up the blood stains. DiGiuro's murder remained unsolved until 2000, when a former student was arrested for the crime. Defensive back Ted Presley killed himself in a game of Russian roulette in the dorm in 1993, and Curry canceled the annual spring Blue-White game.[798]

For a man who played for the legendary coach Vince Lombardi and the Green Bay Packers, Curry appeared unable to motivate his players. Many faulted him for mismanagement of the game clock, and for clinging to the option system. Others speculated Curry wasn't willing to do what it took to win in the brutal world of SEC football, but he had done that at Alabama.[799]

Curry sold his ante-bellum home outside Lexington, and moved to North Carolina. ESPN hired him as a color commentator for their football telecasts, and he did an excellent job.

Newton set out to find a football coach to match his quarterback, not the other way around. He went to a Division 2 school, Valdosta State, to find his coach. Hal Mumme's wide open passing offense was perfect for Couch, a drop back passer with a rifle arm. Couch was elated, and Billy Jack Haskins asked for a fair chance to compete. He didn't get it. Mumme, who knew exactly why he was hired, told Haskins he was switching him to either a running back or wide receiver position. Haskins, after complaining he wasn't given a fair chance to compete, transferred to Rhode Island.[800]

The media talked about Mumme's four-year contract with a base salary of $150,000.[801] There was no contract, and wouldn't be for months.

Newton's combination of Couch and Mumme brought paying customers back into Commonwealth Stadium, a record average of 59,110 in 1997. The games were marketed as "Air Raid '97" based on Mumme's offensive system and Couch's arm. In his sophomore year, Couch racked up 365.4 yards a game in passing, thirty-seven touchdowns and a school record of 66.4 completion percentage. He broke seventeen SEC records and was the nation's number two quarterback. Ranked first was Tennessee' Peyton Manning.[802]

The good old boys went bonkers over Couch, predicting big time bowl games for themselves and a Heisman Trophy for the quarterback. Some went so far as to predict football would once again become the school's premier sport. Couch left school after his junior year when he was the number one draft selection of the Cleveland Browns.

# No Sudden Death

The coup of Roselle's administration was persuading trustees to allow him to prepare the university's reply to the NCAA's allegations of violations in the basketball program, and send it to Kansas City without their input. Some of the trustees were good old boys such as Tracy Farmer, a Cythianna millionaire who contributed $10,000 to the basketball lodge. Others, such as William E. Burnett, vice-chairman of the trustees and head of Kentucky Central Life Insurance Company that controlled the only radio and television stations in Lexington allowed to air basketball and football games, also fell into that category. Trustee Larry Forgy, Singletary's vice-president for business affairs who helped move the basketball team to Rupp Arena, allied himself with Roselle. When they discovered that Roselle was really going to send the school's reply to the NCAA's allegations without their input, some of the trustees became angry and demanded access to the Response before it went to Kansas City.

Gov. Wallace Wilkinson, who opposed Roselle from the beginning, threatened to make the nine volumes public if he got his hands on them. Wilkinson, a backer of coach Eddie Sutton, was in an excellent position to exploit Roselle's handling of the NCAA allegations. If he could move Roselle out, then Wilkinson could bring in his childhood friend, Charles T. Wethington, as president. Wethington, without a doubt, was one of the good old boys.

At a January 1989 trustees' meeting, Roselle told board members they would have access to the Response after he sent it to the NCAA. He assured them he would defend vigorously unsubstantiated allegation but, at the same time, would accept responsibility for any wrongdoing judged to have occurred. Therein lay the rub.[803]

Burnett protested, and announced he wasn't going to delegate his authority as a trustee to anybody, including the president. He maintained it was incumbent on trustees to know and agree with the contents of the Response before it went to Kansas City. Burnett wasn't a disinterested observer, and he certainly had a vested interest in the Response. If basketball games were banned from television, Burnett's company stood to lose millions. As it turned out it did anyway, since Burnett took Kentucky Central down the tubes anyway by losing millions in real estate loans. Burnett died shortly after his scandal-ridden firm was taken over by state insurance officials in 1994.[804]

Tracy Farmer strongly suggested trustees see the document before it went to the NCAA. Sports management consultant Billy Wilcoxson claimed he just wanted to know what the contents of the Response were. Roselle said he had no objections to trustees' having full access to the Response at a later date. He calmly reminded them of their October 1988 resolution that the Response would be free of any taint of influence. Roselle told them he was available to discuss the document, scheduled to be sent to the NCAA at the end of the month, and he expected to meet with the committee on infractions around the first of March.[805] A discussion wasn't what they wanted.

Farmer said he "Did not mean to try to influence the report one way or another unless it was totally unreasonable, and (if it was) that would have to be voted on by the entire board." Roselle held his ground saying he would be glad to convene a joint meeting of the athletics board and trustees. Framer wasn't happy with that either. He suggested trustees meet and have an informal discussion in order to avoid conflicting stories.[806]

The suggestion that trustees tell the same story smelled like there were possible plans to leak the contents to the media. The implied threat sounded like an attempt to increase the pressure on Roselle to such an extent he would resign. If that happened, trustees could control the damage they expected the Response would bring the school. Neither happened.

"Happy" Chandler wanted to be heard. He demanded Roselle tell the trustees if any efforts were made by school officials to ascertain which of the charges had any foundation. Roselle assured him all efforts were made to defend charges they felt were unsubstantiated.[807]

Chandler had been a thorn in Roselle's side from the beginning because he was selected as the president instead of Charles T. Wethington. The president handled him with diplomacy. In an earlier trustees' meeting dealing with the school's investment there was a discussion concerning South Africa. "You know," Chandler said, "Zimbabwe's all nigger now." All hell broke loose when his remark hit the media. Claud Mills called assistant coach Dwane Casey about Chandler's statement. Black students marched in protest and demanded Chandler's resignation as a trustee. The football team voted to cancel their annual spring Blue-White football game. Roselle told students Chandler's statement was wrong, but there was nothing he could do about it."[808]

The good old boys knew how to protect one of their own. Henry "Cap" Hershey, horseman and chairman of the trustees' investment committee, refused to censure Chandler, and appeared puzzled about how to handle the situation. "To make an issue out of an 89-year-old's comment that is a passing remark," Hershey said, "is inappropriate." The man who was known as the "boy governor" in the 1930s still had some plays. He called a news conference at his Versailles home with a black acquaintance in attendance. Chandler attempted to defend himself by claiming he was responsible for bringing Jackie Robinson into major league baseball. Robinson broke the color barrier in major league baseball while Chandler was commissioner, but most of the credit for the move went to Branch Rickey, president of the Brooklyn Dodgers. The pressure was so great over his remark, Chandler was forced to issue an apology, of sorts, a few days later.[809]

Shortly thereafter, students charged Chandler made a similar comment at a signing of his book, "Heroes, Plain Folks and Skunks."

Chandler denied that incident, but admitted he was unable to understand college students and athletes of the 1980s and 1990s. Roselle, despite all the problems Chandler caused him, appeared to have sympathy for the elderly trustee. Chandler wasn't as generous, "I think Roselle would have been a whole lot better off if he (had) kept his mouth shut in the first place when he popped off about repudiating anything I said. He's new on the job; perhaps he'll learn with experience."[810]

It wasn't one-sided. Roselle had his supporters among the trustees. Faculty trustee Mary S. Coleman said she trusted the investigators, and advised other trustees to stay away from the Response. Jim Rose, a coal-baron turned banker who moved to Lexington from eastern Kentucky, agreed with Coleman that trustees shouldn't tamper with the Response. What made Rose's position notable was his financial support of the basketball program. Rose contributed $30,000 for the building of Wildcat Lodge, but yet refused to adopt the good old boys line.[811]

Another effort was made by a group of trustees on February 3rd to insert their input into the Response. They attempted to rescind their October 1988 agreement not to interfere with Roselle's reply to the NCAA's allegations, and the motion barely failed to pass, 7-8, with three trustees not voting. Roselle said he was ready to discuss the Response. Attorneys handling the Response, Park, Burch and Lawson, were grilled by trustees for almost four hours about the document's contents.[812]

Roselle won his fight with trustees to preserve the integrity of the Response, but that sealed his fate. He had a document, while not perfect by any means, that was the best any school every produced in a NCAA investigation.

The NCAA withdrew three of the allegations. Two had to do with Casey's recruiting of Los Angeles high school star Sean Higgins. The other involved Ohio basketball junkie William Chupil and the recruitment of Lawrence Funderburke. After meeting with the committee on infractions,

Roselle declined to appeal their decision to the full council. In May 1989 the NCAA issued their findings in case M5.[813]

The NCAA lauded Roselle for dispelling any doubts within the university or the larger community that the basketball program was expected to operate in compliance with the rules and regulations. The president "Acted forcefully and unambiguously, moving both promptly and with consideration for the interests of the individual student athletes and staff members who might be affected by his actions," the NCAA said. They recognized Roselle's determination to discover, to the best of his ability, if the basketball program was guilty of the allegations.[814]

Infarction cases, as serious as Kentucky's, called for sudden death for two years, no expense-paid recruiting visits for two years, no off-campus recruiting for a year, termination of the coaching staff, no television or post-season appearances for two years and recertification of the program. Remember, the school was still on probation from the investigation of the 1985 newspaper articles.[815]

Roselle saved Kentucky basketball, but the faithful were never convinced. The committee took into consideration his efforts to bring the basketball program into compliance. The report said, "He was credited in acting forcefully to uncover all relevant information bearing on these matters, and set a proper direction for the future of the university's athletics program."[816]

Five mitigating factors led the committee on infractions to impose lesser penalties on the school. Roselle's willingness to conduct a full investigation. His replacing Cliff Hagan with C.M. Newton as athletics director, and the departure of the entire basketball coaching staff. Two small fry representatives of the school's athletic interests, William Chupil and Al Ross, were disassociated from the program. Wildcat Lodge was placed under the control of university housing instead of athletics.[817]

The NCAA determined, to their satisfaction but few others, that Casey sent the video tape with the money. The committee said the assistant coach "Demonstrated a knowing and willful effort on his part to operate the men's basketball program contrary to the requirements and provisions of NCAA legislation, and provided misleading information to both the university and the NCAA."[818]

Manuel, the committee determined, committed academic fraud by cheating on his ACT exam in Lexington in 1987, and he provided misleading information about the test. The school was in error for certifying him in the first place, the report said, when he should have been a partial qualifier.[819]

There were seven areas, the committee pointed out, where the university failed to exercise institutional control. Those areas clearly implicated Singletary, Hagan and Sutton since the report noted several violation after the coach's arrival in 1985. Those areas were: (1) not taking meaningful steps to insure the basketball coaching staff and related administrators understood and followed NCAA legislation that resulted in improper benefits to players; (2) inadequate endeavors made to identify representatives of the university's athletic interests, monitor their involvement and educate them about NCAA regulations; (3) failure to oversee operations of summer basketball camps and athletes' summer jobs; (4) negligence in establishing an adequate system to certify eligibility of incoming athletes; (5) ignoring the recruiting violations of William Chupil; (6) athletes living in Wildcat Lodge under credit arrangement not available to other students, and (7) assistant coach James Dickey's violation of recruiting regulations when he took prospective recruit Matt Bullard to visit All-American Dan Issel's Woodford County farm when the former Denver Nuggets player was there.[820]

The NCAA levied nine penalties against the school. Kentucky was publicly reprimanded, censured, placed on probation (again) and subjected to the repeat violations penalty for five years. To insure institutional control, the university had to report on the basketball program annually to the NCAA enforcement staff. Men's basketball had to comply with NCAA regulations, and the monitoring would continue since they were still on probation from the 1985 violations. Pre-season and post-season play, including foreign tours, and television were prohibited for two years. Elimination of expense-paid campus visits for recruits for one season were set aside. The committee on infractions initially determined Kentucky could award no grants-in-aid for the 1989-90 season, other than the one already committed to Jeff Brasso, of Plano, Texas. The last two penalties were set aside due to the school's cooperation, and they were allowed to award two more grants-in-aid. The television ban was lifted after the first year.[821]

Instead of requiring the school to return the entire proceeds from the 1989 NCAA tournament, the university only had to repay the shares allotted them by the SEC. Had Casey not resigned, the number of assistant coaches, who could recruit off campus, would have been reduced. The NCAA suspended Casey from coaching at a member school for five years. In 1993, the NCAA knocked one year off his suspension leaving him free to coach at the college level again. Casey, who was then coaching in Japan, became an assistant to George Karl, coach of the Seattle Supersonics.[822]

Kentucky was ordered to erase the three 1989 tournament games from their record. Those included the 99-84 win over Southern, the 90-81 win over Maryland and the 74-80 loss to Villanova. Sutton's 27-6 season, for the record books, was reduced to 25-5. SEC presidents voted to strip Kentucky of both the regular season and tournament championship, but the school wasn't forced to forfeit any of the regular season games.[823]

The NCAA said Kentucky escaped two years of sudden death because of Roselle's cooperation. There may have been another reason. Kentucky basketball was one of the NCAA's best "cash cows," and a two-year loss of that income would have put a serious dent in the NCAA's coffers.

That wasn't just my idea. A national news magazine had the same concept. US News and World Report pointed out how gingerly the NCAA was dealing with Kentucky while they were such a cash producer, and coming down hard on schools who returned less revenue. Robert Morris College was an example. Robert Morris authorities reported to the NCAA that a trustee co-signed a loan for an athlete, and made the payments. Robert Morris was banned from the 1990 NCAA tournament, and had to return $88,145 from the previous year's tournament. UNLV coach Jerry Tarkanian, certainly no admirer of the organization, said, "The NCAA is so mad at Kentucky they'll probably slap another two years probation on Cleveland State."[824]

"I don't think I ever convinced people the basketball program was in real jeopardy," Roselle said. Sport radio show callers labeled Roselle as the biggest threat their sporting life. Sports columnist Curry Kirkpatrick wrote, "Kentucky fans don't know what to think of Roselle. They can't figure whether he has sold the farm down the river or what."[825]

The good old boys knew exactly what they thought of Roselle and, collectively, refused to acknowledge that the penalties were light. William Burnett, the trustees' vice-chairman and insurance executive who wanted to tamper with the Response, said, "I don't see how it could have been much worse. I just thought the whole thing was very severe. I would appeal." Of course, Burnett, if it had been left to him, would have appealed since his company stood to lose considerable money with the loss of the televised games.[826]

"Happy" Chandler's convoluted reasoning for the penalties was that the university was wrong to let the NCAA dictate institutional policies. "I'm as sad as I can be over the whole thing," Chandler said, "I think generally from start to finish, from the standpoint of the NCAA and all the fellows who've filed charges, it's been badly handled...by everyone connected with it."[827] Chandler was back in the Donovan era when such glaring violations were swept under the rug whenever possible.

Another trustee, Henry "Cap" Hershey, called university officials to task for the amount of money they spent on outside counsel and investigation and demanded an accounting. Vice-president Edward Carter rather tersely replied that defending the university was a complicated process and often required outside legal expertise. He told Hershey the school spent $388,686 for outside legal assistance during the investigation.[828] When contrasted with the millions the school would have lost with a two-year sudden death, it was a good investment.

"I was very pleased to see there were no sanctions against coach Sutton," Hershey said. "Never before in the NCAA annals has any school done what we did or cooperated to the degree that we cooperated. I'd say they laid a pretty big one on us."[829]

Billy Wilcoxson, another trustee who badly wanted to see the Response before it went to the NCAA, said, "I have not thought from day one that anything we would do would affect the decision they made. It looks as if the university's cooperative attitude had no bearing at all on the severity of the penalty. I think it was severe enough to take the heart out of Kentucky. They hurt the program, the institution and a lot of young men."[830]

Blaming "They" was always the recourse of the good old boys when the athletics program was caught in wrongdoings. No matter what the program and athletic officials did, when they were caught it was never their fault. Someone else was always to blame, and such excuses had served them well for a century.

Another doomsayer was broadcaster Ralph Hacker. "I think our darker days are ahead of us," he said, "By the turn of the century we might be respectable in basketball again. I think it will take that long." [831]Hacker made the wrong call, but there appeared to be something of an acknowledgment in his statement that excesses existed in the program.

While the good old boys wanted to skewer Roselle for his cooperation with the NCAA, he had support from faculty, staff and most students. Educator Robert Sexton said, "There's a lot of irony there, because it wasn't the expectation when he (Roselle) came here he would be dealing with athletics." Cleaning up athletics, Sexton predicted, would be Roselle's greatest legacy.[832]

Kentucky's historian laureate Thomas D. Clark, an original incorporator of the UKAA and an observer of the school's athletics for seven decades, thought the scandal would return to haunt future presidents. "He (Roselle) saw the university through a very stormy period, and that in itself was a highly useful service," Clark said, "He'll be remembered for cleaning up the basketball scandal until the next one happens."[833]

Roselle knew Gov. Wallace Wilkinson would soon control the majority of trustees, and it was no secret the governor wanted his friend, Charles T. Wethington, as the university's next president. Roselle was also cognizant that increased state support for the school was questionable as long as he was president and Wilkinson was governor. His major regret, he told trustees, was the inability to provide increase funds to make the university a place where it would be less complicated for faculty and staff to accomplish their scholarship. Roselle resigned in December 1989, and the University of Delaware moved quickly to select him as their president.[834]

After Pitino and his team won the 1996 national championship, Roselle did an extensive interview with the Louisville newspaper. He spoke of the volumes of hate mail he received during the basketball program investigation. There were also death threats. "I tried not to waver in my strong belief that the University of Kentucky could have a basketball program that could win and be compliant within the rules of the NCAA," he said. "Nobody likes to take medicine," he added, "but it has always been my belief the best way to take medicine is to take it all at once."[835]

Roselle said he started cheering when the team warmed up for the championship game on Monday night, and hadn't stopped by Thursday. "I'm happy for the players, coaches, the students, the fans and the people of Kentucky," he said, "but most of all I'm happy that not only did Kentucky win but they won the right way."[836]

The right way appeared alien to Kentucky athletic management when the extension of a coach's contract was in question.

# THE MORE THINGS CHANGE, THE MORE THEY STAY THE SAME

---

Athletics director C. M. Newton extended football coach Bill Curry's contract for an additional two years based on seasons that totaled 7-15. Even after Curry's disastrous 1-10 season in 1994 Newton extended his contract for another two years, expiring in 1999.[837]

Basketball coach Rick Pitino received a contract extension in 1994 that let his agreement with the school expire in 2000, and that was coupled with a memorandum that Newton was responsible for seeing the coach's agent, Jim Host, paid Pitino what he was due from his endorsements. Although he won a national championship in 1996, his contract wasn't extended. A contract extension was the usual practice when a coach had a good season, or in the case of Curry when the numbers were in the pits. Former coach Joe B. Hall routinely received contract extensions. Winning a national championship in 1996 and being the runner-up the next year was exceptional even for Kentucky basketball. There apparently was no contract extension offer after the 1997 season either.

The fans who bled Blue thought they were set for life, and Pitino would give them one championship after another. Pitino was actually an anomaly at Kentucky. The fans accepted his New York accent, even joked with him about it; they condoned his preference for Armani suits over the traditional uniform of khaki trousers and blue blazers; admired his Catholicism in the Bible belt; tolerated his amazement at their religious-like zeal for the sport, and saw through the glitz he surrounded himself

281

with and found his deeper substance. They accepted his demanding discipline of the athletes because they knew it was for the players' best interests. They would have demanded that his new campus arena be built, but most of all they venerated his restoration of their beloved basketball tradition to respectability at the championship level once again.

Not even "Bear" Bryant enjoyed the level of popularity Pitino reached at Kentucky. The absence of a contract for Pitino and Newton's generous allowance of contract extensions with Curry and the athletics director's pursuit of a comprehensive agreement with Nike was a puzzle whose pieces eventually fell into place. Pitino spoke publicly about the absence of a formal contract extension offer.[838] It was unusual for Pitino to speak out about his business dealings with the school, even when he was being gored in the media over the actions of his agent, Jim Host.

While Newton was negotiating the multi-million-dollar Nike contract in 1996, Pitino had four years left on his agreement with Converse to provide his teams' apparel and make payments directly to the coach. Newton's arrangement with Nike channeled the payment for teams' apparel directly to the school. The athletics director said any agreement with Nike would honor Pitino's contract with Converse. It was unlikely that Pitino would give up the lucrative contract, and Nike certainly wasn't paying millions for the football, tennis or gymnastic programs. It was basketball they wanted. Some wondered if Martin Newton's job switch to Nike had anything to do with changing the teams' apparel. Newton reached mandatory retirement in 2000, and it was doubtful if Nike would wait to finalize the contract with Kentucky.

After his initial successes at Kentucky, NBA teams' courting of Pitino became an annual rite each spring. There were reports of offers from the Los Angeles Lakers, Orlando Magic, Golden State Warriors and Miami Heat. In 1996 the New Jersey Nets reportedly offered Pitino a $30 million contract that he declined after soul searching that had the faithful gnashing their teeth over his possible departure. The Nets eventually hired John Calipari, whom Pitino recommended earlier to coach his alma mater, Massachusetts, for a reportedly $15 million. In April 1997, the great Larry Bird called Pitino about again rescuing the Boston Celtics, with sixteen NBA championship banners, from a 15-67 season. The challenge of being the salvation of the great Celtic mystic was much like the situation Pitino found at Kentucky. There was every indication the coach was more than interested.[839]

Pitino continued to talk about the absence of a contract extension. "I'm interested in a commitment more than anything else; what I'm interested in is stopping this (will he, won't he speculation) from occurring next year," he said. "That's my only interest in an extension," he added. Newton claimed he'd offered Pitino a contract extension before the start of the previous season, "To let him know he was appreciated and so on." Newton claimed he made another contract extension offer after the 1997 season. Then, Newton was telling the media, "We can restructure the contract in two minutes; we can do that with a handshake and a look in the eye. That's not the issue."[840]

It was the issue. Restructuring a contract was quite different from extending Pitino's contract with its Converse clause. Newton's public announcements that he twice offered Pitino contract extensions weren't documented in any athletics board meeting minutes, where such matters are routinely discussed, from April 1996 through July 1997. In fact, there was not even a mention of Pitino's name in those minutes, and only a reference to the basketball team being invited to the White House after winning the 1996 national championship.[841]

An individual quite close to Pitino and the basketball program told me, in a privileged conversation, that athletic officials expected the coach to leave after the national championship, but he threw them a curve and remained. That made sense since Newton told the athletics board in August 1996 negotiations with Nike were complete and the contract was ready to sign, but nothing happened.[842]

A media feeding frenzy ensued while Pitino made up his mind to remain at Kentucky or go to Boston. Media equipment in front of

Memorial Coliseum resembled the Los Angeles courthouse scene during the O.J. Simpson criminal trial. While on a book-signing tour promoting his best-seller, "Success Is A Choice," Pitino told the media he would announce his decision on May 6th after meeting with Newton. "The meeting with C.M. (Newton) will not change the decision, whatever it is," Pitino said in Atlanta.[843]

The good old boys whimpered over thoughts of Pitino's departure and what the loss of his endorsements of their companies and products might mean to their corporate profits. John Paul Miller, a Lexington automobile dealer, moaned over Pitino's possible departure. Miller used a Pitino signature edition Ford Explorer to advertise his dealership. Miller hoped, if Pitino left, UK would hire the "Second best coach in the country." Lincoln Lewis, a partner in a Louisville based marketing firm, and Glen Moyes, a cell telephone executive, agreed that Pitino had more impact on sales than any other Kentucky sports personality in the last ten years. Both Lewis and Moyes planned to use the coach's successor if Pitino left.[844]

Jim Host had an answer for Pitino's popularity. "That's because in Kentucky, the aura of UK basketball is still bigger than any coach," Host claimed. He did admit that Pitino would be tough act to follow. "It's been my experience that whoever the coach is, he will have a very successful time in endorsing products," Host was quoted as saying.[845] Apparently Host forgot about coach Eddie Sutton, whose last two years were so unsuccessful, that Host claimed he lost money on his television rights contract, and persuaded athletics director Cliff Hagan to slice off more then $100,000 from his payments to the school.

Collectively the commonwealth held its breath while Pitino made up his mind. One faithful fan had her brother, stationed in Germany, call her cell telephone, using a prearranged signal, with news of Pitino's decision.

After a ninety-minute meeting with Newton in his home, Pitino arrived at Memorial Coliseum and told his players he had decided to take the Celtics job. It was an emotional moment for all concerned. That Pitino cared deeply for his players was undeniable. He guided Jamal

Mashburn's journey through the NBA's troubled waters, especially his difficult years in Dallas. He approved sophomore Antoine Walker's going to the NBA, and he was drafted sixth by the Celtics. When orthopedic surgeons gave his star, Derek Anderson, their approval to play in the 1997 NCAA tournament, Pitino declined to used the talented player, except to shoot a technical foul in one game, although it might have been the difference in winning another national championship. He feared another injury could wreck Anderson's NBA career before it began. Anderson, who lived with an uncle in Louisville, was drafted thirteenth by the Cleveland Cavaliers. Famous for his engaging smile and winning personality, Anderson was chosen by Michael Jordan to endorse Nike's "Air Jordan" basketball shoes with a multi-million-dollar contract.[846]

Former walk-on Cameron Mills, who earned a scholarship under Pitino, said he started to cry during the emotional farewell meeting. "I really wanted to thank him," Mills said, "for letting me walk on and making me a better player but I started to cry. At the end, I told him I loved him, and he said the same." Scott Padgett, who resurrected himself from dismal academic problems his freshman year to be selected to the 1997 Final Four All-Tournament team, said, "If it wasn't for coach P, I'd still be cutting grass (one of several jobs Padgett held while working himself back onto the team). He gave me a second chance when a lot of other coaches would have said, 'forget about Scott.'"[847]

Pitino, his usual witty repartee dulled with the solemnity of occasion, said he came to UK for a specific reason, "To try to rebuild a program in shambles to a championship level. We've accomplished that. I think if I didn't take this new opportunity, I would look back." He said he had never looked back at the many NBA offers he'd had over the years. "But," he continued, "I have a similar type situation at the professional level that I had eight years ago at this level, something that is full of glory and tradition." He added emotionally, "God so many great memories here at Kentucky, I don't know where to begin and where to end."[848]

Immediately after Pitino's announcement, Newton began to micro-manage the situation. He claimed to have a short list of coaches, all Pitino's former assistants coaching elsewhere, but later admitted there was only one name on his list. The four former assistants were: Orlando "Tubby" Smith at Georgia; Herb Sendeck at North Carolina State; Ralph Willard who left Western Kentucky for Pittsburgh, and Billy Donovan who was building a powerhouse at Florida. The athletics director placed the basketball players off limits to the media, and held a secret meeting in a Blue Grass Airport general aviation hanger with Smith who left a golf game to take a private jet to Lexington.

When it appeared Smith was the next Kentucky basketball coach, the newspaper's liberal, rabble-rousing columnist Merlene Davis appointed herself the commonwealth's representative on racism. She wrote Smith, who was also black, an open letter in the newspaper. Davis advised Smith to stay in Georgia. "Your mail will be hate-filled and truly evil," she told him, "the things people would feel free to say to your face would be unconscionable. Criticism will be aimed at your lack of intelligence rather than your lack of coaching skills." Davis cautioned, "I want to remind you that the first of any movement suffers the most." Claiming Kentucky had never been faced with their racism, Davis told Smith, "I sincerely fear for your safety and the safety of your family if you agree to become head coach."[849]

Davis ignited a firestorm. Radio talk shows, sports and otherwise, were flooded for days with calls from people saying Davis certainly didn't speak for them. The newspaper received letters to the editor from as far away as Canada about the column. James E. Staples, of Versailles, wrote, "Get real people! Tubby Smith will be an asset to the university, the basketball program and the community if you will just let him. Quit telling me the color of his skin, I couldn't care less. And I am betting there are thousands more just like me."[850]

Smith was no stranger to Lexington since he spent two years at Kentucky as an assistant to Pitino before leaving for Tulsa. Smith's Georgia teams played a similar pressing defense and fast-paced offense that Pitino used. In six years, Smith compiled a 124-62 record as a head coach with four NCAA appearances. Within a week, Smith was named Kentucky's head coach. The media said he had a five year contract that paid him $1.2 million a year.[851] There was no contract.

When Pitino resigned, his agreement with Converse became null and void, and cleared the way for Newton's Nike deal. Less than three weeks after Pitino's departure Newton signed a twenty-three-page, five-year Nike contract worth an estimated $23 million if the second five-year option was elected. While Newton disavowed the school would become the "University of Swoosh," his Nike contract said otherwise. According to the contract, no player, coach or staff member could wear or use any other product except in the case Nike didn't make the needed item; purchases of items not made by Nike, such as football jerseys and pants, required the company's approval; head coaches of minor sports were required to make one personal appearance on behalf of Nike while basketball and football coaches were to make four a year; women's basketball and/or soccer teams and the men's basketball team were to appear in Nike sponsored tournaments once in a three year period; Nike received eight season football tickets and were on an "as needed basis" for those scarce basketball tickets; should the school change its signage for the basketball team, the company could place a permanent sign at the scorer's table or along press row; Nike could sell their products at the football stadium and arena concessions stands, and Nike's logo went on teams' benches, seat backs and poll pads if possible. The university wasn't to disclose the financial terms of the agreement with Nike to any third party except under the Open Records Act.[852]

During each contract year, Newton as athletics director was entitled to $30,000 worth of Nike products for department and university use. Newton saw that his friend Jim Host wasn't forgotten. Nike agreed to a $75,000 annual media buy on Host's game broadcasts and telecasts. Nike was to receive, at no cost other than producing camera ready copy, a four page color spread in every game program published. Host, of course, had no-bid arrangements for both the football and basketball game programs. Clause 12-d in the contract read, "At the university's request, and as appropriate, Nike shall provide the university with consultation, through Host Communications, on university-generated sports marketing initiatives including, but not limited to, local and regional television buy-ins, special event coordination and production, media opportunities, etc." When asked about a price tag on all the services mentioned in Clause 12-d, legal counsel Richard Plymale said there was no cash estimate for the arrangement, and emphasized it was just a good faith pledge of marketing efforts.[853] Regardless of Plymale's spin, it was obviously another special favor for Host.

The Courier-Journal editorialize that Nike bought more than the right to outfit Kentucky athletes. "For all practical purposes," the editorial stated, "Nike bought the program itself. It is hardly possible to conceive of a deal in which the Nike name and trademark would be more pervasive." The editorial also mentioned Nike's involvement in alleged factory abuses such as operating "sweatshops" using child labor and paying, according to American standards, shockingly low wages. Newton was questioned about those practices on his weekly radio show in July 1997. He brushed the allegations aside saying Andrew Young, the civil rights leader, and former United Nations ambassador, found no problem with Nike during a tour of their overseas' operations. It was hardly an objective report, as Nike hired Young's consulting firm for the job. Newton also didn't address Young's failure to explain the American equivalent of $1.50 a day in wages paid in Vietnam that Bob Herbert, of the New York Times, wrote was not enough to cover the cost of food, shelter and transportation. It was also charged that Young used translators Nike furnished, spent only a few hours in each factory and dodged the issue of corporal punishment of workers who failed to meet production goals.[854]

An example of the point the newspaper's editorial made occurred at the holiday tournament in Hawaii in November 1997. Smith and his assistants appeared for their first game attired in colorful Hawaiian shirts that cost $800.00. An immediate response came from Nike. The print shirts had to go, and the coach was reminded that he should wear the golf shirt Nike furnished. Arizona coach Lute Olson, whose program Nike also bought, told Smith, "It's nice to see you got with the program." For the next game Smith and his coaching staff wore suits and ties.[855]

Now that Newton had his Nike contract, he had to determine just how much the head football and basketball coaches would get. "We'll be fair with our coaches to say the least," Newton promised. Not only did "Tubby" Smith move to Lexington for the head coaching job without a contract, but the football coach who'd been there seven months didn't have one either. Smith admitted he only had an agreement with Newton. "Hal's been here all along with a handshake and a little informal piece of paper in my handwriting that probably wouldn't hold up in a court of law," Newton said.[856]

Coaches taking jobs without contracts was further evidence that it was necessary for Pitino to leave so Newton could formalized the Nike contract. A month after Newton signed the Nike contract, Mumme had a four-year contract retroactive to December 1996, with a base salary of $150,000. Mumme sold all his endorsement rights, including media shows, calendars, personal appearance and athletic apparel, to the UKAA for the paltry sum of $160,000 a year. The UKAA turned around and assigned those rights to Jim Host for $100,000 a year, plus additional funds from a complicated percentage arrangement, in an addendum to his broadcast and telecast rights. It was Pitinoville all over again. Mumme face and voice filled the airwaves, billboards and print. Mumme was allowed to keep the revenue from his football camps, and received the usual perks of two automobiles, retirement and insurance. Mumme had to notify Host if he received any offers to publish books or produce videos. If Host didn't match the offer in thirty days, the coach was free to negotiate with the other party. Media appearances on shows, other than Host productions, were limited to five minutes.[857]

Mumme was allotted twenty season football tickets, fourteen of which were in the coach's box, but he had to provide Host with at least six of those tickets. Newton, always stingy with basketball tickets, gave the football coach four season tickets. Mumme's contract had some wiggle room for the school. His performance was evaluated on an annual basis beginning in November 1999.[858]

Mumme's contract was laced tighter than the proverbial pigskin.

Newton was more generous with Smith, but he was dealing with a proven Division 1 coach. Smith's five-year contract called for a base salary of $150,000 plus $1 million for all his endorsement rights, and the other perks the football coach received. Smith had other perks that exceeded those of Mumme: twenty lower arena season basketball tickets, but only eight were permanent and the others were on a game by game basis; eight season football tickets. If Smith's contract was terminated without cause he got $600,000 a year compared to Mumme's $150,000. Host forked over $450,000 a year to the UKAA, plus an additional percentage, for Smith's endorsement rights. The coach, however, didn't have to share his season ticket allotment with Host. [859]

# EPILOGUE

The century was ready to roll over, but Kentucky's athletics management wasn't likely to change. While subtle shifts in direction were acceptable, sudden moves were out of bounds. The style of management remained much the same.

Athletics director C.M. Newton reached the mandatory retirement age of seventy in June 2000. Newton kept the program out of any NCAA athletic scandals for more than a decade, an outstanding accomplishment. Newton's successor was purposely selected from the inside to keep the network intact, so to speak. Problems loomed ahead in defending two struggling head coaches in one of the nation's highest profile college athletics program. Deference to downtown Lexington would continue, and perhaps next manifesting itself in the purchase of Rupp Arena and its debts.

Newton, like former president Otis A. Singletary, had a talent for reaching into the deep pockets. Newton more than doubled the UKAA budget from $17 million to $37 million, and increased the number of varsity sports to twenty-two, the most of any SEC school. He used athletic funds to pay off the bonds on the new library after the legislature refused to give the school the money. Despite making every effort to increase funding for women's sports, Newton was unable to make up for the decade lost because of Singletary's stalling the implementation of Title IX.

While at Kentucky, Newton was president of USA Basketball for two terms; chairman of the NCAA Division I basketball committee; chairman of the NCAA basketball officiating committee; a member of the Federation of International Basketball Associations, and was inducted into the Naismith Basketball Hall of Fame in 2000. Newton was called the most powerful man in college basketball, and that designation was probably correct.[860]

During Newton's tenure there were some embarrassing moments, but no serious NCAA violations or allegations. He maintained the compliance program Roselle put in place, and expanded the tutorial program for athletes. Just after Newton left, questions of recruiting problems arose again with coach "Tubby" Smith's apparent illegal contact with a prized recruit, his program found a way to make a two-time North Carolina player of the year eligible after the Tar Heels turned him down and another one of his recruits had his scholarship revoked after he was arrested on marijuana charges.

An invisible asterisk will forever be attached to Smith's 1998 national championship win. He won the title with players former coach Rick Pitino recruited, conditioned and molded into an pressing defensive and fast paced offensive unit. Instead of gradually building the program up to the championship level, Smith inherited his. Career-wise, it was probably the worst thing that could happen to a first year coach at Kentucky.

Newton claimed he hired Smith because he was the best coach available. He acknowledged that hiring Kentucky's first black basketball coach would be a media event, and charges that Rupp was a racist would be rehashed.[861] He was right. There was strong support for another former Pitino assistant, Florida's Billy Donovan. Newton claimed Donovan was too young for the high pressure job. That went out the window when Donovan took Florida to the 1999 Final Four and Smith took Kentucky home after the regional tournament.

Four of Pitino's players left the program for various reasons during Smith's first two seasons. Center Nazr Mohamad was drafted by the Philadelphia Seventy-Sixers. Ryan Hogan, who was charged with driving while intoxicated, transferred to Iowa. Mike Bradley left because of tensions between Smith and his family. Myron Anthony departed after being involved in a hit-an-run accident in a vehicle belonging to guard Wayne

Turner, which he took without permission. In September 1997, Anthony crashed Turner's car into another vehicle, causing $8,000 worth of damage, and left the scene. Turner told all who would listen that he wasn't driving the car, and had no idea who was behind the wheel. He had an alibi that attracted little attention. Very few people, including the coach, appeared to be defending the player. After spending eight months twisting in the wind, Turner was persuaded to plead guilty to an amended charge of failing to file an accident report. The delay and plea were for the good of the program, especially after winning the national championship. Turner's reputation, however, had already been trashed in the national media.[862]

Anthony finally confessed to taking the car without permission. Turner's record was wiped clean, but it appeared the point guard was unable to get into Smith's good graces. The coach often benched the senior in favor of a sophomore guard, Saul Smith, his son. Smith took a lot of grief for giving his son so much playing time. The coach started another son, G.G., while at Georgia, but there was a world of difference between Athens and Lexington, where basketball was almost a religion. If Saul had been an immensely talented player there wouldn't have been a problem. He wasn't. Even the motor-mouth of college basketball, Dick Vitale, a big Smith admirer, admitted that. Vitale said if Smith put four marquee, prime-time players around his son, "They might be able to get by."[863]

Smith got by with playing his son into a 23-10 record for the 1999-2000 season, but became very thin skinned about criticism of both his son and the program.[864]

He complained about the difficult schedule Newton put together, took a lot of heat for not playing the traditional Kentucky style of "race horse" basketball, hawked everything from modular homes to hamburgers, stepped into another recruiting mess and had still another player caught in a drunk driving case.

Smith and an assistant coach, Shawn Finney, went to Bowling Green, Kentucky, in July 2000 to see high school star, Josh Carrier, work out.

NCAA rules prohibited any off-campus contact, during the month of July, with prospective recruits and their parents, but coaches can observe athletes. Smith and Finney, later named head coach at Tulane, were more deeply involved. The coaches tossed basketballs to the player and talked with Carrier and his parents. Athletic officials said if there was any violation it was of a secondary nature and the NCAA agreed. Smith maintained he did nothing wrong, and became angry at a reporter's question about the incident. That was the reason, Smith said, why he seldom allowed the media access to him or his players.[865]

Parade All-American Jason Parker, from Charlotte, North Carolina, was denied admission to North Carolina because of academics, his high school transcript and a forty-five percent increase in his most recent SAT score. Forecasted to be an immediate impact player, Parker spent the 1999-2000 season at Fork Union (Virginia) Military School, an institution noted for helping students improve their SAT scores. When Parker turned to Kentucky, athletic officials just happened to discover the NCAA clearing house apparently made an error in not recognizing an advance math class the player took in high school that was listed as regular math. Parker became a Wildcat.[866]

Sport columnist Scott Fowler wrote, "How Kentucky could get Parker eligible remains a mystery. Kentucky's athletics director Larry Ivy says some of Parker's debatable standardized-test scores are no longer 'in question' because they have been 'canceled.'" Fowler saw Parker being an immediate asset to Smith's team, and pointed out the coach was under fire for not coaching the "run and gun" offense.[867]

Smith had a scholarship to give because he revoked the grant-in-aid of another player, Michael Southall, from West Salem, Wisconsin, after he pleaded guilty to felony marijuana delivery and misdemeanor marijuana possession in June 2000. Southall's record will be wiped clean of the felony charge if he fulfills the terms of his two-year probation. Smith said revoking Southall's scholarship was one of the toughest decisions he'd ever made. Kenneth Peterson, Southall's attorney, said, "I know basketball is big down there, but this is a kid worthy of a second chance. The judge gave him a second chance and I'm just sorry Kentucky is not going to do the same."[868]

Souleymane "Jules" Camara, one of Smith's more experienced players, was arrested in September 2000 on a drunk driving charge. He wasn't given a Breathalyzer test because the unit was not operable at the time, and Camara refused to take a blood-alcohol test. The player failed a field sobriety test. The police report of the incident said there were other individuals in the car with Carama, and one fled the scene.[869] There were rumors that one of the unidentified subjects in Carama's car was one of the team's more publicized players.

Smith got a baptism of unwelcome publicity over these incidents.

Football coach Hal Mumme seemed to share Smith's problem with the media. Mumme, like Smith, was a bull in a china shop when it came to criticism. He was inept in the way he shuffled off quarterback Billy Jack Haskins in favor of Tim Couch. There was no doubt Couch was the better player, but Mumme, instead of acknowledging he was hired specifically to coach the younger player, claimed he noticed a hitch in Haskins' throw and wanted to switch him to another position. In 1999 he took a caller to his weekly radio show to task for criticizing his defensive coordinator, Mike Major. "When we get rid of him, then you'll be getting rid of me, boy, because we're a package deal and that's the way it is," Mumme said.[870]

Called the biggest gambler in the SEC for his fake punts and fourth down passes, Mumme, after spring practice in 2000, suddenly announced he was replacing junior quarterback Dusty Bonner with red-shirted freshman Jared Lorenzen, who'd never taken a snap in a college football game. Lorenzen was in the academic dog house as a freshman. Bonner, an excellent student, led the conference in passing efficiency with 65.2 percent rating despite Kentucky 6-6 record in 1999. Mumme claimed Lorenzen released the ball in half the time it took Bonner to throw.[871]

Some sports writers saw Mumme's move as being gutsy while others thought he'd gone off the deep end. Birmingham Post-Herald columnist

Paul Fienbaum referred to him as "The mophead coach," a reference to Mumme's wind blown hair style that was carefully coifed. Finebaum said "Coach Mophead made (Alabama coach Mike) DuBose (who Fienbaum often criticized) look like a whiz kid while becoming the laughing stock at the same time." Anthony Dasher of the Athens Daily News wondered if there wasn't something else behind the quarterback controversy that hadn't been told.[872] There probably was.

Another reporter accused Mumme of taking reprisals against reporters. Pat Forde, of the Courier-Journal, said Mumme was making Lorenzen available for interviews to "friendly" reporters. Mumme placed a media blackout on his players and coaches for two weeks before the game with Louisville in September 2000, that UK lost 34-40 in overtime. Lorenzen, at 6'4" and 275 pounds, looked awkward and clumsy in the backfield. [873]

Mumme's program had been under media scrutiny since 1998 when his starting center, Jason Watts, was involved in a drunk driving accident that killed another player, Artie Steinmetz, from Edgewood, and Eastern Kentucky University student Scott Brock, a childhood friend of Tim Couch. All three were thrown from the truck Watts was driving through Pulaski County on their way to hunt deer. Mumme's football players had been hanging out at a small bar in west Lexington and, apparently, drinking after hours in bar owner James Haney Jr.'s home adjoining the tavern. Watts, Steinmetz and Brock were all drunk, and Watts' blood alcohol level after the accident was 0.15. The legal blood-alcohol level limit was 0.10.[874]

There were questions of whether Mumme was aware of the players hanging out in Haney's bar and, after hours, in his house. Upon hearing the tragic news, he said he and his wife June panicked because they thought their son Matt, the back-up quarterback, might have gone on the hunting trip. Mumme had no weekend curfew for his players.[875]

Watts was given two five-year sentences for second degree manslaughter to be served consecutively. By August 1999, less than a year after the accident, Watts was released on shock probation. There were other dark stories about the bar that was decorated in the school colors of blue and white. Another student, Chad Clore, 20, of Union, was killed on nearby railroad tracks after a round of drinking at Haney's. Watts accompanied Clore to the bar the night he was killed. Haney filed for bankruptcy after the Watts incident, and listed $8,000 in gambling debts. He was fined $750 for serving minors, such as Clore, and eventually lost his liquor license.[876]

It was impossible that Mumme didn't know there were alcohol problems among his players. He appeared to run as loose a program as Chet Wynne did seventy years earlier. Watts, in July 1997, accidently shot a team mate, Omar Smith, while drinking. Smith wasn't seriously injured, and Watts' blood-alcohol level, two hours after the shooting, was 0.129. Watts was charged only with discharging a firearm inside the city limits. Cornerback Tony Woods, was charged with DUI after hitting a parked car. Robert Jones, a defensive end, was arrested in August 1998 on six criminal charges some of which involved alcohol, and was dismissed from the team. Two months later, tight end Jimmy Haley borrowed a friend's Jeep and hit a parked car. It took police so long to locate Haley after the accident that he was only charged with leaving the scene. Mumme declined to comment about his alcohol policy. Football spokesman Tony Neely said he didn't know of "A stated alcohol policy espoused by Mumme." Neely said, "Our athletes have to conform to any campus and legal regulations that apply to everybody else."[877]

Nine days after the accident that killed Steinmetz and Brock, Newton rushed a zero-tolerance alcohol abuse policy into effect. An athlete convicted of driving under the influence of alcohol would be taken off scholarship and suspended from the team. A public intoxication charge would result in probation and require counseling. Newton, while not exactly saying Mumme had a loose grip on his team, stated, "Jason Watts' making the bad choice of abusing alcohol is one issue. But, the fact that no one stopped him or kept him from getting in that truck, and there was some for sure who probably knew his situation, that's bothersome."[878]

There were some bright spots for the athletics director. Before Newton's official departure date of June 30, 2000, his good friend, Jim Host, published a puff biography written by sports columnist Billy Reed. Host was the first person Newton acknowledged in the book. He called him an old friend, confidant, consultant and advisor. Host's company, of course, published the book. How it was published was similar to the way Newton and Host handled athletic business which included verbal and no-bid contracts. The school's health care insurer, UK Health Care, paid a portion of the publishing costs. On the page dedicated to UK Health Care there was no mention of the amount.[875]

Evidently, there weren't enough deals like that out there for Host since his companies were faltering. In 1992, General Electric Capital Corporation invested in Host and held approximately 48 percent of the common stock and 100 percent of Host's preferred stock. Bull Run, an Atlanta, Georgia, corporation that also owned WKYT-TV in Lexington, in 1999 held a combined interest in Host of 32.5 percent of outstanding common stock. In 1998 Host's consolidated financial report indicated he had a $2.2 million operating loss. Host, whose sports marketing empire began with Kentucky athletics, eventually became the primary marketer for the NCAA. In 1998 the NCAA corporate sponsors made up thirty-five percent of Host's total billed accounts receivable. Other clients included coaches' and athletics directors' association, National Football Foundation and the College Football Hall of Fame. Through his Universal Sports America, operating in Dallas, Texas, Host managed events for the NBA, NFL, NHL, MLB, PGA, and was the broadcast partner for a number of leading schools and conferences. By 1997 Host's companies were stretched thin and looking for additional capital. The next year Thomas Hicks, from Dallas, proposed to merge his Southwest Sports Group with Host's holdings. When it became apparent Host's companies wouldn't be a priority of Southwest Sports, merger plans were halted.[876]

Bull Run offered Host $158 million in a combination of stock and cash for Host Communications and Universal Sports America. In their call for a stockholders' meeting, Bull Run said they didn't expect to make any sub-stantive changes in business operation or personnel.[877]

The merger required Host to vote his stock in board elections in the manner designated by Bull Run president Robert Prather and chairman of the board J. Mack Robinson. Host's employment contract, which expired in 2002, paid him $260,000 a year plus perks that included an annual performance based-bonus and a $40,000 contribution to his retirement plans, would be honored. In addition, there was a non-compete clause that Host would not compete with the company during his employment and for eight years thereafter. During such an eight year period, Host would receive $200,000 annually and would provide consulting services to the company not to exceed 200 hours per year.[878]

Days after the Host-Bull Run merger was completed, the company announced that Host would replace Doug Jarvie as president and chief operating officer of the Dallas-based Universal Sports America. Jarvie was to head USA's division of Bull Run Sports Investments that planned to air college sports over the Internet. Six months later, Host announced that his company wouldn't continue as the marketer of NCAA championships. The Lexington newspaper theorized that the likely buyer would be ISL, a Swiss marketing firm that would probably offer $800 million. Host's reported offer was approximately $500 million. Host did keep the media and marketing rights to Kentucky basketball and football for the next five years with a bid of $17.65 million, just barely eclipsing the $17 million bid of WLEX-TV and Cumulus Media.[879]

There can be no doubt of the close association between Host and Newton right down to their no-bid and verbal contracts. Only a small group of people know how intense that business relationship was and, per-haps, will continue to be. It was possible that Host advised Newton on every aspect of Kentucky athletics, including construction of athletic buildings. One of Newton's construction projects, the renovation of Memorial Coliseum, was actually finished on time and within budget. His other large projects, the indoor practice field house and expansion of

Commonwealth Stadium, fell victim to the usual method of athletic construction, late and over budget. In 1998, the General Assembly approved a $24 million bond issue to expand Commonwealth Stadium. Athletics officials decided to divide the project into twenty-two separate bids to save money. The bids came in at more than $29 million, and the school planned to ask the legislature for the difference. Apparently that didn't work out, and the program had to dip into their $28 million reserve to make up what turned out to be a $5 million difference.[880]

The expansion increased the stadium seating from 59,000 to 67,500. Forty luxury suites were included in the project that also expanded concessions and restroom facilities. Newton's zero tolerance alcohol policy applied to the athletes and other areas of the stadium, but not the luxury suites. Whiskey was still a necessity for the good old boys on games days. Four of the luxury suites, each accommodating twenty-four, rented for $52,800 a year. The thirty-six smaller suites, equipped to handle eighteen people, rented for $39,000 a year. The four larger suites were grabbed up by Ralph B. Anderson, with the Belcan Corporation in Cincinnati, Luther Deaton, head of Lexington's Central Bank; Frank Shoop, a wealthy automobile dealer-politician and the current state racing commissioner, and Jim Host, who held the media rights to Kentucky's basketball and football games plus his other private contracts with the program. Each of the climate controlled suites had a food service area, private restrooms, two television sets, a live feed of the game broadcast, parking passes, catered meals, game programs and maintenance was provided by the school.[881]

Many familiar names rushed to snap up the luxury suites. Among them were Tracy Farmer, banker and a former trustee who had wanted to see how president David P. Roselle handled the 1988 basketball scandal before his response was sent to the NCAA; William Sturgill, the strip mining mogul who was Otis Singletary's good friend from the Haggin Trust days; Dudley Webb, who figured prominently in the 1985 basketball scandal; Buddy Schneider, who attempted to use past favors to the program to get a seat on the athletics board in 1988. Sue S. Badgett, from the western Kentucky mining family of Brown Badgett, and Robert Addington, who headed a noted coal mining family from eastern Kentucky, had luxury suites. Peter Bosomworth's successor as medical center chancellor, James. W. Holsinger, Jr., also had one of the smaller suites.[882]

Newton's program wasn't without its blemishes. Newton postponed his retirement in 1996 to help Bill Curry's troubled football program, but in the end he had to fire the coach. Newton's last four years were plagued with public relations blunders and personal problems. In addition to his athletics duties, his wife, Evelyn, was terminally ill with cancer. In 1997, Federal Bureau of Investigation agents interviewed Newton and associate athletics director Larry Ivy about the UKAA's free use of the private jet of Larry Rogers, chief operating officer of PIE Mutual Insurance Company, from Cleveland, when Ohio's superintendent of insurance took control of the company. Law enforcement and Ohio insurance officials charged Rogers with misleading insurance regulators and violating the state's ethics law. Athletic officials used Rogers' jet several times to fly to the annual SEC meetings in Destin, Florida, and had the plane fly the Georgia basketball coach "Tubby" Smith to Lexington when he was offered the Kentucky coaching job left vacant by the departure of Rick Pitino. Newton brushed the involvement off by saying, "I don't remember that much about it, it was really just a brief interview."[883]

Newton managed to get himself, Pitino, the program and the university involved in a $2 million sexual discrimination suit filed by JoAnn Hauser, men's basketball trainer from 1991 to 1994. Although Newton promised Pitino he could select his own staff, he asked him to use available trainers already working within the program. Pitino wanted to and later did hire "Fast" Eddie Jamiel, who he had used at Providence, as his trainer. Newton told Hauser he was transferring her to the women's basketball team. When Hauser made noises about discrimination, Newton offered to return her to men's basketball but she refused, saying the work environment would be too hostile. The publicity was especially rough on Pitino who had hired Bernadette Locke-Mattox as an assistant coach, the only woman assistant coach in men's Division I basketball, and he was hailed for breaking the gender barrier.[884]

University attorneys tried to get the suit dismissed, but circuit judge Mary Noble ruled Hauser had a cause of action. Depositions from the athletics staff revealed there was much friction in the department. Head trainer Al Green said he heard rumors that Pitino wanted to eliminate women from his staff. Green's wife, trainer Sue Stanley, said she heard, "They really wanted women out of the program." Rena Vicini, associate athletics director for media, said she heard a similar statement from Sandy Morgan, secretary to associate athletics director Larry Ivy. Morgan, in her deposition, said she had no recollection of making that statement to Vicini. In a second deposition, Vicini testified that it was Newton who told her that he couldn't force another woman staffer on Pitino.[885]

Newton and Pitino were dismissed as defendants in the suit. A year later Hauser settled with the school for $120,000 plus $100,000 for her legal fees. The school admitted no liability, and Hauser promised to not seek any future employment with the university and waived any future claims against the institution.[886] The athletics program suffered considerable negative national publicity.

Newton caught little local flack over the Hauser affair because the media treated him with kid gloves. As it turned out, there was probably a reason. The athletics director was pretty good at holding a grudge. In a 1999 interview with Lexington sports writer John Clay, Newton reflected on his accomplishments at Kentucky. One of his legacies, he said, was rebuilding the basketball program with Pitino's help. The other accomplishment he spoke of was absolutely astounding. "The other legacy," Newton said, "from my standpoint is what we've done in sports medicine. I really feel we've been able to build a model here with Jim Madaline and Keith Webster and the doctors we have in UK Sports Medicine are the doctors out of our student health and the UK hospital and now we're getting this athletic training program in Allied Health. We've got a model that is really kind of special, and it's been a long time coming."[887]

Newton spouted Dr. Spencer Turner's line that his group of physicians in student health was UK Sports Medicine instead of the practice that Dr. Mike Ray established in the department of orthopedics in the medical center. Remember it was Newton and medical center chancellor Peter Bosomworth who insisted in the early 1990s on bringing outside orthopedists, Drs. James Andrews and Mary Lloyd Ireland, into the medical center to care for athletes in an effort to cut the throat of Ray's UK Sports Medicine practice. They placed athletes' medical care in student health, and the orthopedists had to fight to be included. Newton was parsing his words. His next statement was not only amazing but completely incorrect. "When I came here, all (medical) care of our student athletes was outside the university."[888]

When Newton came in 1988, Ray's practice was not only caring for Eddie Sutton's basketball team, but for other athletes in the school's minor and intramural sports. The battle over sports medicine had apparently been so brutal that a decade later Newton couldn't even bring himself to acknowledge there was a UK Sports Medicine practice in the department of orthopedics. After all, the chairman of the department of orthopedics, of which sports medicine was a section, had the gall to question whether the athletics director was being fair in his treatment of UK Sports Medicine physicians.

Similar incidents happened with tickets, especially the scalping of them, that put Newton in a bad light. In 1998, state senator Tim Philpot, from Lexington, tacked an amendment onto an appropriation bill calling for the legalization of ticket scalping in the commonwealth. On the last day of the legislative session when a bill could be passed, Newton began calling legislators with adamant opposition to the bill. Philpot, son of the late evangelist Ford Philpot, defended his amendment, "If we decriminalize ticket scalping more (sellers) will be involved, the price will be lower and average people...will have the opportunity to buy basketball tickets." Newton countered that ticket brokers would corner the market on UK basketball tickets, selling them to corporations and pricing ordinary fans out of the market. That was a misnomer because ordinary fans were never able to crack the market for Kentucky basketball tickets. Philpot charged UK scalped their own basketball tickets, and athletics officials gave lower arena tickets to the deep pockets who contributed $100,000 or more to the program.[889] There was a difference?

Newton said if the legislators wanted the program to stop going to major donors the state could fund Kentucky athletics. The athletics director threatened legislators by saying if they legalized ticket scalping he would raise UK ticket prices. After some swift parliamentary maneuvering, the house-senate conference committee deleted Philpot's amendment. After all, C.M. Newton had spoken. All was well, and Newton went ahead with a visit to the capitol with the 1998 national basketball champions.[890] Nobody wanted to talk about where the scalped tickets came from in the first place.

Legislators received two free season basketball tickets until 1992 when they were required to pay for them. Newton and his athletic officials were warped out of shape when Rep. Tom Riner, a Baptist minister from Louisville, sold his two 1999 Kentucky season basketball tickets to his church for face value, $620. Two other representatives also sold Riner's church their tickets, at the same price. The church then sold the six tickets to a Texas ticket broker, Golden Tickets, for $7,800. Riner's church used the proceeds from the tickets to feed 1,600 families in eleven counties. "The Salvation Army got 460 of the turkeys and the rest were distributed to churches and shelters," Riner said.[891]

That well-known commodity hit the fan. The attorney general's office investigated Riner to determine if he scalped the tickets, and turned the matter over to the Legislative Ethics Commission, who didn't think it was such a big deal. The commission's executive director, Anthony Wilhoit, said once legislators bought the tickets they were their property to do with as they chose. Keep in mind attorney general Ben Chandler's investigation didn't materialize out of thin air.[892]

Newton announced "We have a policy that tickets cannot be sold in excess of face value, and we try hard to see that policy is enforced and there's a law in this state that scalping is illegal. In cases where we find that tickets have been sold in excess of face value, we take the tickets back." Riner said that if his tickets were withdrawn a lot of people who need help would be hurt. Newton replied that "Doesn't really make a difference."[893] It was all the matter of whose ox was being gored. Various charities , service organizations and individuals in Lexington had used basketball tickets for years to raise money. The whole affair left a bad taste with many people who felt athletic officials overstepped their bounds. After all, they used the tickets to lure the deep pockets into donating large sums of money to the program.

Sen. Philpot's charge that the athletics program traded tickets for $100,000 donations was almost correct. The actual requirement for Rupp Arena tickets in the Blue White Fund section was "Approximately $100,000 minimum gift required for eligibility to obtain Blue White section seats which *may* (emphasis mine) become available." If a seat opened up, the donor had to ante up another $500.00 for a ticket.[894]

Actually Philpot's charge of the UKAA scalping its own tickets had some merit in another area of athletic management, team travel. Athletics officials had one of their tidy little arrangements with a Lexington travel agency. In 1991, the UKAA asked for proposals for handling the travel of their major teams, officials and cheerleaders. Commonwealth Travel was awarded the business, and touted itself as the program's "Official" travel agency. In the ensuing nine years, the UKAA just didn't bother to ask other travel agencies to bid for their business.[895]

In 1998, the athletics association sold 600 of their 3,500 Final Four tickets to Commonwealth Travel, the only agency allowed to buy the tickets. In return, Commonwealth gave the association discounts on team travel such as $93,000 in savings for the basketball team's travel to the 1993 Maui Classic Tournament in Hawaii. Associate athletics director

Larry Ivy had one of his usual clear explanations. "If they've been helping you along the way," he said, "why would you not give them tickets?"[896]

Other Lexington travel agencies had some sensible answers for Ivy. Trevor Conway, owner of Carlson Wagonlit Travel, called the practice between the school and Commonwealth disgraceful, and suggested the school practice more free market economics. Connie Hyde, owner of Avant Travel, said the collaboration between the university and Commonwealth Travel had become a real monopoly.[897]

The program's business with Commonwealth Travel grew from $256,144 in 1993-94 to $410,789 for the 1997-98 fiscal year.[898] When the UKAA took bids for radio and television game rights, they were purchasing a service though a competitive bidding process, which the university was supposed to use for items over $100,000. Purchasing teams' travel arrangements was also a service. The manner in which Ivy made arrangements was open to numerous interpretations, but it was business as usual at Kentucky.

Apparently Ivy's team travel arrangements weren't the norm among high profile athletic programs. Daren Lucas, ticket manager at North Carolina, said, "We would never give control of our tickets away." Tom Duddleston, at Arizona, said his program had a profit-sharing arrangement with a travel agency. "They don't get the tickets," he said.[899]

Remember it was Ivy who tried to short circuit the bidding process for the school's arena feasibility study by tacking it onto the stadium expansion analysis being conducted by the company that built the structure in 1973. It was also Ivy who handled the no-bid football game programs and who wrote about the no-bid season video highlights contracts with Jim Host. When it was time for Newton to retire, there were no questions about who the next Kentucky athletics director would be. More important than finding the best person for the job was carrying on business as usual.

President Charles T. Wethington, who attempted unsuccessfully to short circuit his own retirement process, made a show of conducting a search for a new athletics director by appointing a selection committee. Wethington quipped, "We're probably looking for someone who can walk on water."[900]

No search was ever made. Ivy was the only candidate considered. Newton practically canonized Ivy in recommendations of his associate. The local media asked no questions about Ivy's management style, and practically slathered over his appointment. No one pointed out that he cut his athletic management teeth under the direction of president Otis Singletary and athletics director Cliff Hagan when he came to the department in 1976 from student housing.[901]

Newton wasn't completely fading from the scene. He had a four-year consultant's contract that paid him $50,000 a year with other perks including the use of a free automobile.[902] He also signed a contract with the Boston Celtics to advise Pitino on player selection.

One of the search committee members, law professor Robert Lawson, had an interesting observation about the way Ivy was hired. "I think we're in the best shape we've been in during my twenty-five years here," Lawson said. "That makes the chore rather bothersome, because I guess the only thing we could do is mess up."[903]

An important item of athletic business remained on the agenda, Rupp Arena. Ivy's appointment indicated the drain of basketball revenue into downtown Lexington coffers would continue. He didn't disappoint them. Newton, however, had already established the direction the school would take after doing an about face. In 1997, Newton made it clear the idea of building a campus arena didn't depart with basketball coach Rick Pitino. "If there's a driving force (for a campus arena) it's not Rick; it's me," he told sports columnist Jerry Tipton. "I'm the one that has to fund the 22-sports program at Kentucky." Newton predicted that Pitino's replacement would also favor a campus arena.[904] That wasn't exactly how it turned out.

Obviously, the downtowners had something to say about the loss of the school's basketball revenue. Soon, not only Newton, but president Charles T. Wethington began to extol the virtues of the school continuing to play their games in Rupp Arena. Even Pitino's successor, "Tubby" Smith joined the chorus. When it took some time for the school to finalize their assessment of the situation, the LCC commissioned their own feasibility study of the program remaining in Rupp Arena.

City officials claimed the delay was making it difficult for them to set financial priorities and plan for the future. The city had already committed $10 million for a minor league baseball stadium and had used some of their bonding capacity to fund the school's new library. In January 1998, the school's arena feasibility study was complete, and provided three options to give the program the 25,000-seat arena they wanted with luxury suites and all the necessary accessories. They were: renovate Memorial Coliseum, update Rupp Arena or build a new campus arena.[905]

The Memorial Coliseum option called for the building to be demolished saving only the court and possibly the lower seating area. The consultants pointed out the lack of parking and street configurations would make controlling traffic difficult. They concluded expanding Memorial Coliseum would exceed the cost of a comparable arena on a more suitable site.[906]

There were two alternatives for the Rupp Arena option. The first called for adding luxury suites, increasing the size of the concourses, adding a club room and smoking areas. The cost would be around $20.5 million. Such a renovation, the study said, would produce a "Facility substantially below modern standards for a comparable facility" the school said they wanted. The consultants concluded that Rupp Arena "Alternative one does not appear an appropriate alternative for the University of Kentucky basketball program."[907]

Alternative two called for a reconstruction of Rupp Arena from the High Street concourse level up and out from the existing structure. The cost was estimated at $60 to $85 million. Such a renovation, the consultants said, would meet the basketball needs specified by the university. Since no financial strategies or temporary facilities were designated they were unable to determine the feasibility of that alternative since the arena would have to be closed for at least a year.[908]

The third option called for a new campus arena, adjacent to Commonwealth Stadium, which would cost an estimated $93 million. "The market analysis and financial strategy indicate this option may be viable," the consultants said. They pointed out the infrastructure and parking facilities were already in place at the stadium.[909]

Does that sound familiar? It was the same plan Lexington dentist Roy Holsclaw's Citizens Rupp Arena Committee recommended in 1971 that so affronted then president Otis Singletary. In the early 1970s the cost of a 25,000-seat arena was approximately $12 million.

In 2000, if the school built one, the cost would be eight times that.

While everybody waited for the arena feasibility study, president Charles T. Wethington soothed the downtowners's fear by promising, if an on-campus arena was built, it would be for basketball-related activities only. Rupp Arena's concert and other attractions business Singletary took away from the campus in 1976, was safe in the downtowners' hands.

After the university's consultants presented their findings, the Lexington Center Corporation decided they could give some of the school's basketball earnings back to them. The LCC, with the approval of mayor Pam Miller and the acceptance of president Wethington, restructured the lease to allow the program to keep $485,000 of their own basketball revenue, but the school had to agree to a six year lease, instead of the original two year term, with an option to renew for a two year period. None of the revenue, however, came from parking, concessions or the game programs. Singletary had given the game programs to the LCC which only allowed UKAA rights holder Jim Host to handle them without competitive bidding. It was a great deal for the LCC. They kept the estimated $3.2 million fans spent downtown each year at the basketball games for shopping, lodging, restaurants and parking in circulation. The school got almost a half-a-million-dollars of their own basketball revenue back.[910]

There were strong hints from the downtowners that perhaps the best idea would be for the university to buy Rupp Arena. The mayor was all for that. "Selling Rupp Arena to UK is one of the best options for meeting the needs of the community and the university together," she said.[911] Not only would the LCC be unloading a twenty-two-year old facility needing renovation, but a portion of the bond debts, used to build the facility in the 1970s, went with the arena.

The entire LCC complex, the arena, convention hall, retail section and hotel plus the Opera House, cost $53.4 million in 1977. Here's the kicker. In 1998, the LCC still owed approximately $23 million on the thirty-year revenue bonds. Of course the city was sweating, but if officials could persuade the university to buy Rupp Arena they could get rid of some, if not a major portion, of the debt. Former councilman and LCC board member Barkley Blevins said, "Selling Rupp to the university solves everybody's problems. The university would have its own arena, the city would get out from under some debt and basketball would stay downtown. It's just that simple."[912] It was always simple when the downtowners skinned the university.

Two refugees from the 1985 basketball scandal, Cecil Dunn and Dudley Webb, got into the act. Dunn, LCC chairman who was purported to have paid inflated prices for a player's season tickets, favored the school buying the arena. Webb thought it was a great idea. Webb was said to have been one of the "Sugar Daddies" in coach Joe B. Hall's basketball program. Dunn told Wethington, if the university bought the arena, the LCC would lease it back from them for concerts and other events. "It makes perfect sense," Webb said, "more than anything it make business sense. And you can be sure the numbers will make much more sense than UK building an arena of its own." Webb added that the deal could be worked out by separating the debt for the arena from the remainder of the complex. He said, "UK could buy the arena for the value of the debt and include any improvements it wants when it refinances the debt."[913]

Mayor Miller asked Gov. Paul Patton for $45 million to expand the LCC's convention facilities and Rupp Arena in 1999. Newton, who apparently had been waiting for the dust over the arena dispute to settle, said the university would extend their Rupp Arena lease if the project funding came through. It did. Newton said the team would keep playing in the municipal arena if the city fixed it up, and Ivy later agreed.[914]

Seems the mayor wanted $30 million to update convention facilities and $15 million for the Rupp Arena upgrade. It was the same old story from the early 1900s, but this time there was more money involved than the proceeds from a used book store. The LCC wasted no time, and by June 2000 had selected HOK Sports Facilities Group, from Kansas City, to design the expansion. The Rupp Arena portion of the plan called for new seats, a new scoreboard, giant television screen, reconfiguring the concourses and concession stands. Ivy said the plan would make the arena more fan friendly. What, no luxury suites?

If the university decides to buy Rupp Arena from the city, rest assured the school will, as usual, get the short end of the deal.

# BIBLIOGRAPHY

*Acts of the General Assembly of the Commonwealth of Kentucky.* Frankfort, Ky.: 1952.

Baily, John W. *Handbook of Southern Intercollegiate Track and Field.* Starkville, Miss.: University of Mississippi Press, 1924.

Baily, Rex L., ed. *Report of the Committee on Intramural and Intercollegiate Athletics.* Lexington, Ky.: University of Kentucky, 1982.

Barker, Henry S. Papers, Special Collections, M. I. King Library. University of Kentucky.

*Baton Rouge Sunday Advocate.*

*Board of Regents of the University of Oklahoma and the University of Georgia Athletics Association v National Collegiate Athletic Association.*

*Bright et al v Nunn et al.*

Carolyn Brooks. Interview.

Bryant, Paul W. and Underwood, John. *Bear, The Hard Life and Good Times of Alabama's Coach Bryant.* Boston: Little Brown and Company, 1975.

Byers, Walter. *Unsportsmanlike Conduct: Exploiting College Athletes.* Ann Arbor, Mich.: University of Michigan Press, 1995.

Bull Run Corporation's 1998 Annual Stockholder Report.

Burch, Joseph. Biographic File, Special Collections, M. I. King Library. University of Kentucky.

*CFA Sidelines.* Boulder, Col.: College Football Association, 1983.

Chandler, A. B. *Heroes, Plain Folks and Skunks.* Chicago: Bonus Books, 1989.

Chandler, A. B. Medical Center. Documents and records from the offices of the dean of medicine and the chancellor. University of Kentucky.

*Chronicle of Higher Education.*

*Cincinnati Enquirer.*

Clark, Thomas D. Interview.

*Compact Edition of the Oxford English Dictionary.* London, England: Oxford University Press, 1989.

Cone, Carl. *The University of Kentucky: A Pictorial History.* Lexington, Ky.: University Press of Kentucky, 1989.

*Courier-Journal.*

Darsie, John. Biographic File, Special Collections, M. I. King Library, University of Kentucky.

Daugherty, Nathan. *Education and Athletes*. Knoxville, Tenn.: University of Tennessee Press, 1981.

Dealy, Francis X., Jr. *Win At Any Cost: The Sell Out of College Athletics*. New York: Carol Publishing Group, 1990.

Delinger, Kenneth and Shapiro, Leonard. *Athletes For Sale*. New York: Thomas Y. Crowell Company, 1975.

Denton, Sally A. *Bluegrass Conspiracy*. New York: Avon Books, 1990.

DeVenzio, Dick. *Rip-Off U., The Annual Theft and Exploitation of Major College Revenue Producing Athletes*. Charlotte, N.C.: The Fool Court Press, 1986.

Dickey, Frank G. Papers, Special Collections, M. I. King Library, University of Kentucky.

_____. Biographic File, Special Collections, M. I. King Library, University of Kentucky.

Donovan, Herman L. Papers, Special Collections, M. I. King Library, University of Kentucky.

_____ Biographic File, Special Collections, M. I. King Library, University of Kentucky.

Dove, Edward. Interview.

*Dwane Casey v Emery Air Freight et al.*

*Dun and Bradstreet's Million Dollar Directory.* Bethlehem, Pa.: Dun and Bradstreet Information
Service, Inc., 1994.

Ellison, Betty B. "In The Beginning: Athletic Administration of James K. Patterson." University of Kentucky Graduate History Seminar Paper Prepared Under the Direction of Dr. Humbert S. Nelli. Lexington, Ky.: 1989.

_____. "Nothing Short of Disaster: Athletic Administration of Henry S. Barker." University of Kentucky Graduate History Seminar Papers Prepared Under the Direction of Dr. Humbert S. Nelli. Lexington, Ky.: 1990.

_____. "Coming Of Age: Athletic Administration of Frank L. McVey." University of Kentucky Graduate History Seminar Paper Prepared Under the Direction of Dr. Humbert S. Nelli. Lexington, Ky.: 1991.

_____. "From The Clouds To An Abyss: Herman L. Donovan, Architect of Twentieth Century Kentucky Athletics." University of Kentucky Graduate History Seminar Paper Prepared Under the Direction of Dr. Humbert S. Nelli. Lexington, Ky.: 1991.

_____. "Still In The Shadows: Frank G. Dickey and the UKAA." University of Kentucky Graduate History Seminar Paper Prepared Under the Direction of Dr. Humbert S. Nelli. Lexington, Ky.: 1992.

_____. "Too Much To Do, Too Little Time For John W. Oswald To Clean Up UK Athletics." University of Kentucky Graduate History Seminar Paper Prepared Under the Direction of Dr. Humbert S. Nelli. Lexington, Ky.: 1992.

*Encyclopedia Britannica.* Chicago: Encyclopedia Britannica, Inc., 1957.

*Eric Manuel v University of Kentucky et al.*

ESPN.

Estes, Lane. Interview.

*Facts On File Yearbook.* New York: Facts On File, Inc., 1952.

Falla, Jack. *NCAA, The Voice of College Sports.* Mission, Kan.: National Collegiate Athletic Association, 1981.

Feinstein, Milton D. *The History and the Development of Football at The University of Kentucky 1877-1920.* M.A. Thesis, University of Kentucky, 1941.

Fleisher III, Arthur A., Goff, Brian L. and Tollison, Robert D. *The National Collegiate Athletic Association, A Study in Cartel Behavior.* Chicago: University of Chicago Press, 1992.

Funk, Gary D. *Major Violation, The Unbalanced Priorities in Athletics and Academics.* Champaign, Ill.: Leisure Press, 1991.

"Great Moments in Kentucky Basketball With Adolph Rupp." Lexington, Ky.: Committee of 101, nd.

HealthSouth Corporation 1998 Annual Report.

Hisle, J. R. Interviews.

*Inside Outside, A Behind Scenes Look at Kentucky Basketball.* Lexington, Ky.: Host Communications, Inc., 1995.

Ireland, Robert M. *Little Kingdoms, The Counties of Kentucky 1850-1891.* Lexington, Ky.: University Press of Kentucky, 1977.

James, David N. and Andre, Judith, eds. *Rethinking College Athletics.* Philadelphia, Pa.: Temple University Press, 1991.

Jokl, Ernst. Interview.

*Kentucky Alumnus.*

*Kentucky Basketball 1994-95.* Minister, Ohio.: Post Publishing Co., 1994.

*Kentucky Kernel.*

*Kentucky Post.*

Kerr, Charles. *History of Kentucky.* Chicago: American Historical Society, 1922.

Kirwan, A. D. Papers, Special Collections, M. I. King Library, University of Kentucky.

Kindred, Dave and Luster, Bill. *A Year With the Cats, From Breathitt County to the White House.* Lexington, Ky.: Lexington Productions, Inc. 1978.

Kleber, John, ed. *The Kentucky Encyclopedia*. Lexington, Ky.: University Press of Kentucky, 1992.

Knight Foundation. *Keeping The Faith With the Student Athlete: A New Model for Intercollegiate Athletics*. Charlotte, N.C.: Washburn Graphics, 1991.

Lancaster, Harry C. *Adolph Rupp As I Knew Him*. Lexington, Ky.: Lexington Productions, Inc., 1979.

Lawrence, Paul R. *Unsportsmanlike Conduct, The National Collegiate Athletic Association and The Business of College Football*. New York: Praeger Publishers, 1987.

Lawson, Robert. Biographic File, Special Collections, M. I. King Library, University of Kentucky.

Ledford, Cawood. *Heart of Blue*. Lexington, Ky.: Host Communications, Inc., 1995.

*The Legacy and The Glory, Greatest Moments in Kentucky Basketball*. Louisville, Ky.: Adcraft Sports Marketing, 1995.

Lexington Ball 1971 Program.

Lexington Center Corporation Archives.

*Lexington City Directory*. Cincinnati: R. L. Polk Co., 1958-1990.

*Lexington Daily Press*.

*Lexington Daily Transcript.*

Lexington-Fayette Urban County Government Archives.

*Lexington Herald.*

*Lexington Herald-Leader.*

*Lexington Leader.*

*Lexington Morning Herald.*

Lipsey, Richard. *Sports Marketplace.* Princeton, N. J.: Sportsguide, 1998.

*Louisville Times.*

McCallum, John D. *College Football USA.* Greenwich, Conn.: McGraw-Hill,

McVey, Frank L. Papers, Special Collections, M. I. King Library, University of Kentucky.

_____. Dairies. Special Collections, M. I. King Library, University of Kentucky.

*Memphis Commercial Appeal.*

*Memphis Press-Scimitar.*

Michener, James A. *Sports In America.* New York: Random House, 1976.

Nail, Jeremy. Interview.

Nash, Francis M. *Towers Over Kentucky: A History of Radio and Television in The Bluegrass State.* Lexington, Ky.: Host Communications, Inc., 1995.

*NCAA Infractions Committee Reports.*

*NCAA News.*

Nelli, Humbert S. *The Winning Tradition: A History of Kentucky Wildcat Basketball.* Lexington, Ky.: University Press of Kentucky, 1984.

_____, ed. *Sports In Society Past and Present University of Kentucky.* Lexington, Ky.: Kentucky Humanities Council, 1980.

*New York Times.*

Newton, C.M. Interview.

*1967 University of Kentucky Football Facts.* Lexington, Ky.: University of Kentucky, 1967.

*1979 University of Kentucky Football Facts.* Lexington, Ky.: University of Kentucky, 1979.

*1989-90 Kentucky Wildcats Basketball.* Lexington, Ky.: Host Communications, 1989.

*1989 Kentucky Wildcats Football.* Minister, Ohio: Post Publishing, 1989.

*1991 Kentucky Wildcats Football.* Minister, Ohio: Post Publishing, 1991.

*1992 Kentucky Wildcats Football.* Minister, Ohio: Post Publishing, 1992.

*1994 Kentucky Wildcats Football.* Minister, Ohio: Post Publishing, 1994.

*1991 Kentucky Revised Statutes.* Charlottesville, Va.: The Michie Co., 1991.

Nunn, Louie B. Interview.

Oswald, John W. Papers, Special Collections, M. I. King Library, University of Kentucky.

_____. Biographical File, Special Collections, M. I. King Library.

*Paducah Sun Democrat.*

Patterson, James K. Papers, Special Collections, M. I. King Library, University of Kentucky.

*People of New York v Alex Groza, Ralph Beard, Dale Barnstable.*

Pitino, Rick and Weiss, Dick. *Full Court Pressure, A Year In Kentucky Basketball.* New York.: Hyperion, 1992.

_____ and Reynolds, Bill. *Success Is A Choice, Ten Steps To Overachieving In Business and Life.* New York.: Broadway Books, 1997.

Reed, Billy. *Hello Everybody, This Is Cawood Ledford.* Lexington, Ky.: Host Communications, 1992.

_____. *Newton's Laws, The C.M. Newton Story.* Lexington, Ky.: Host Communications, 2000.

*Report of the Committee on Intramural and Intercollegiate Athletics.* Lexington, Ky.: University of Kentucky 1982.

*Response of the President of the University of Kentucky to the National Collegiate Athletic Association.* Lexington, Ky.: University of Kentucky, 1989.

Rice, Russell. *The Wildcats, A Story of Kentucky Football.* Huntsville, Al.: The Strode Publishers, 1975.

_____. *Joe B. Hall, My Own Kentucky Home.* Huntsville, Al.:The Strode Publishers, 1981.

_____. *Kentucky Basketball's Big Blue Machine.* Huntsville, Al.: The Strode Publishers, 1978.

_____. *Adolph Rupp, Kentucky's Basketball Baron.* Champaign, Il.: Sagamore Publishing, 1994.

_____. *Wildcat Legacy.* Virginia Beach, Va.: JCP Corp., 1982.

Roland, Charles, P. Interview.

Roselle, David P. Papers, Special Collections, M. I. King Library, University of Kentucky.

_____. Biographical File, Special Collections, M. I. King Library, University of Kentucky.

Rosen, Charles. *Scandals of '51, How Gamblers Almost Killed College Basketball.* New York: Holt, Rinhart and Winston, 1978.

Rupp, Adolph F. *Rupp's Championship Basketball for Player, Coach and Fan.* Englewood Cliffs NJ: Prentice Hall, 1957.

_____. Biographical File, Special Collections, M. I. King Library, University of Kentucky.

Savage, Howard J. *American College Athletes.* New York: The Carnegie Foundation for Advancement of Teaching. Bulletin No. 23, 1929.

Singletary Otis A. Papers, Special Collections, M. I. King Library, University of Kentucky.

_____. Biographical File, Special Collections, M. I. King Library, University of Kentucky.

Slone, Kay Collier. *Football's Gentle Giant, The Blanton Collier Story.* Lexington, Ky.: Life Force Press, 1985.

Smith, Dean. *A Coach's Life, My Forty Years In College Basketball.* New York: Random House, 1999.

Smith, Ronald A. *Sports and Freedom, The Rise of Big Time College Athletics.* New York: Oxford University Press, 1990.

Smotick, Derek. Interview.

*Sports Illustrated.*

Stange, Frank. Interview.

Stebleton, Larry. Interview.

Stoldt, Clay. Interview.

Talbert, Charles A. *The University of Kentucky: The Maturing Years.* Lexington, Ky.: University Press of Kentucky, 1965.

Thelin, John. *Games Colleges Play: Scandal and Reform in Intercollegiate Athletics.* Baltimore, Md.: John Hopkins University Press, 1994.

Tidwell, Treva. Interview.

*University of Kentucky All-Sports Media Guide 1984-85.* Lexington, Ky.: University of Kentucky, 1985.

*University of Kentucky Alumni Directory.* nc: Publishing Concepts, 1988.

University of Kentucky Athletics Association Board of Directors' Meeting Minutes, 1946-1997.

*University of Kentucky Athletics Association and Dwane Casey v Emery International.*

University of Kentucky Athletics Association Records and Documents.

University of Kentucky Board of Trustees' Meeting Minutes, 1963-1998.

*University of Kentucky Bulletin 1991-1992.* Lexington, Ky.: University of Kentucky, 1992.

University of Kentucky. Controller's Office Documents.

University of Kentucky. Faculty Senate Minutes.

University of Kentucky. Legal Counsel's Office.

University of Kentucky. Purchasing Department Records.

University of Kentucky. Sports Information.

*University of Kentucky Wrestling Wildcats.* Lexington, Ky.: University of Kentucky Athletics Association, 1981.

*US News and World Report.*

*Washington Post.*

*Washington Times.*

Wetherby, Lawrence. Interview.

Wethington, Charles T. Papers, Special Collections, M. I. King Library, University of Kentucky.

*Who Was Who.* Chicago, Il.: A. N. Marquis Co., 1942.

Wolff, Alexander and Keteyian, Armen. *Raw Recruits, The High Stakes Games Colleges Play To Get Their Basketball Stars And What It Costs To Win.* New York: Pocket Books, 1990.

*The Woodford Sun.*

WKYT-TV.

WVLK Radio.

# ENDNOTES

1. *The Kentucky Encyclopedia* (Lexington, Ky., 1992), 266-67, 103-04.

2. *Encyclopedia Britannica* (Chicago, 1957), XXII: 315-16. *The Compact Edition of the Oxford English Dictionary* (New York, 1989), 1113. Tom White, *A Century of Racing, The Red Mile 1875-1975* (Lexington, Ky., 1975), 21. *The Kentucky Encyclopedia*, 961.

3. *The Kentucky Encyclopedia*, 961.

4. *Lexington Daily Press*, 10 October 1889. *Lexington Daily Transcript*, 8 May 1892. *The Lexington Leader*, 7 June 1891. *University of Kentucky All-Sports Media Guide* (Lexington, Ky., 1985), 5.

5. *University of Kentucky All-Sports Media Guide 1984-85*, 19.

6. *Lexington Daily Press*, 20 December 1891. Russell Rice, *The Wildcat Legacy* (Virginia Beach, Va., 1982), 17.

7. Milton David Feinstein, "The History and Development of Football at the University of Kentucky 1877-1920." Master Thesis, University of Kentucky, 1941, 12.

8. Faculty Senate Minutes, 6 December 1895. Board of Trustees' Metting Minutes, 11 December 1895.

9. Nathan Daugherty, *Educators and Athletes* (Knoxville, Tenn., 1981), 33.

10. Daugherty, *Educators and Athletes*, 19-20, 32-35.

11. The Papers of James K. Patterson, Special Collections, M.I. King Library, University of Kentucky. Faculty Senate Meeting Minutes, 8 March 1898.

12. Ibid. Russell Rice, *The Wildcats: Kentucky Football* (Huntsville, Ala., 1975), 30-34.

13. *Lexington Morning Herald*, 2 June 1901.

14. Faculty Senate Meeting Minutes, 27 April 1904.

15. *Lexington Morning Herald*, 10 April 1904.

16. *Lexington Morning Herald*, 30 April 1902.

17. *Lexington Morning Herald*, 11 January 1903.

18. *Lexington Morning Herald*, 19 November, 26 November, 10 December 1903.

19. Board of Trustees' Meeting Minutes, 10 June 1904.

20. Rice, *The Wildcats: Kentucky Football*, 39. *1989 Kentucky Football Media Guide* (Minister, O., 1989), 199.

21. *Lexington Herald*, 2 December 1904. *1989 Kentucky Wildcats Football*, 157. Telephone interview with Lane Estes, SEC research librarian, in Birmingham, Alabama.

22. Patterson Papers. Richard C. Stoll file, Special Collections, M.I. King Library. Faculty Senate Meeting Minutes, 5 April 1895, 6 April 1895.

23. Board of Trustees' Meeting Minutes, 30 May 1905.

24. Nick Falla, *NCAA: The Voice of College Sports* (Mission, Kansas, 1981), 8-12.

25. *1989 Kentucky Football Media Guide*, 157. *1994-95 Kentucky Basketball* (Minister, O., 1994), 205.

26.Faculty Senate Meeting Minutes, 5 December 1905.

27.Faculty Senate Meeting Minutes, 26 May 1905.

28.Board of Trustees' Meeting Minutes, 12 December 1905.

29.*1989 Kentucky Football*, 157. *1989-90 Kentucky Basketball* (Minister, O., 1989), 163. UK Sports Information, 8 June 1992.

30.Board of Trustees' Meeting Minutes, 5 June 1906, 5 June 1907, 10 December 1907, 14 December 1909. Faculty Senate Meeting, 3 December 1909. *1989 Kentucky Wildcats Football*, 157.

31.*1989 Kentucky Wildcats Football*, 147. *The Kentuckian* (Lexington, Ky., 1910), 232.

32.*University of Kentucky All-Sports Media Guide 1985*, 51. Rice, *The Wildcats: Kentucky Football*, 52.

33.Board of Trustees' Meeting Minutes, 14 December 1909, 2 June 1909. Patterson worked hard lobbying the legislature and Congress for education funds. He lost control to the good old boys of the 330,000-acres of land Congress set aside in 1862 when the Morrill Act establishing land grant colleges was passed. The 1909 yearbook had some choice words about that land. "Here it may be worthwhile to note that the magnificent donation of lands by Congress was virtually sacrificed through the culpable negligence of the Commonwealth." Management of the land was turned over, by the legislature, to Lexington businessman, Madison C. Johnson, one of the early good old boys, who carelessly placed the land with a New York broker to sell without placing a price reserve on the sale. The land sold for fifty-cents an acre. The school saw the $165,000 dwindle after the broker and Johnson's cuts were subtracted. Johnson's cut of the sale may have helped build his classic home, Botherum, that still stands in downtown Lexington.

34.Board of Trustees' Meeting Minutes, 12 December 1911.

35.Faculty Senate Meeting Minutes, 1 June 1912.

36.*Lexington Leader*, 12 March 1911, 5 June 1912.

37.*Kentucky All-Sports Media Guide 1984-85*, 20.

38.Charles G. Talbert, *The University of Kentucky: The Maturing Years* (Lexington, Ky., 1965), 12. *Lexington Herald*, 31 October 1912.

39.*Lexington Herald*, 24 November 1912.

40.Ibid.

41.*Lexington Herald*, 25, 27 29 November 1912.

42.*Lexington Herald*, 8 December 1912.

43.*Lexington Herald*, 10, 12 December 1912.

44.Ibid.

45.John W. Bailey, *Handbook of Southern Intercollegiate Track and Field 1894-1924* (Starkville, Mississippi, 1924), 7.

46.Ibid.

47.*Lexington Herald*, 18, 22, 24, 25, 28 December 1912.

48.*Lexington Herald*, 4, 7, 9, 11, 16, 23 January 1913. *1994 Kentucky Football Media Guide* (Minister, O., 1994), 189.

49.*Lexington Herald*, 13, 15, 16, 17 January 1913.

50.Ibid. Rice, *The Wildcats: Kentucky Football*, 75-77.

51.Taubert, *The University of Kentucky: The Maturing Years*, 12-13. Papers of Henry S. Barker, Special Collections, M.I. King Library, University of Kentucky.

52.Faculty Senate Meeting Minutes, 3 June 1913.

53.UK Sports Information, 22 May 2000.

54.Faculty Senate Meeting Minutes, 4 December 1915; 5 February 1916.

55.Faculty Senate Meeting Minutes, 1 May, 1 June 1914. Board of Trustees' Meeting Minutes, 1 November 1916. Barker Papers. *Lexington Herald*, 27 June 1943.

56. Barker Papers. *1989 Kentucky Wildcats Football*, 155. Rice, *The Wildcats: Kentucky Football*, 58.

57.*The Kentuckian 1906*, (Lexington, Ky., 1906), 111. *1989 Kentucky Wildcats Football*, 147.

58.John D. McCallum, *Southeastern Conference Football*, (New York, 1980), 40. John A. Garraty, editor, *Dictionary of American Biographies* (New York, 1981), 7:745.

59.Barker Papers.

60.*The Kentucky Encyclopedia*, 600-01.

61.Thomas D. Clark interview, 9 October 1991.

62.The Papers of Frank L. McVey. Special Collections, M.I. King Library, University of Kentucky.

63.McVey Papers.

64.Ibid.

65.Ibid.

66.Ibid.

67.Ibid.

68.Ibid. Taubert, *The University of Kentucky: The Maturing Years*, 63.

69.McVey Papers. *1989 Kentucky Football Media Guide*, 158.

70.McVey Papers.

71.Board of Trustees' Executive Committee Meeting Minutes, 26 January 1923. McVey Papers.

72.Board of Trustees' Executive Committee Meeting Minutes, 23 March 1923.

73.Board of Trustees' Meeting Minutes, 20 July 1923.

74.Board of Trustees' Meeting Minutes, 20 July 1923.

75.Board of Trustees' Meeting Minutes, 2 October 1923.

76.Board of Trustees' Executive Committee Meeting Minutes, 15 October 1923.Faculty Senate Meeting Minutes, 1 May, 1 June 1914. Board of Trustees' Meeting Minutes, 1 November 1916.

77.Ibid.

78.Board of Trustees' Meeting Minutes, 19 December 1923.

79.Board of Trustees' Executive Committee Meeting Minutes, 7 January 1924. Board of Trustees' Meeting Minutes, 31 May 1924, 2 February 1927.

80.Board of Trustees' Executive Committee Meeting Minutes, 7 April 1924. McVey Papers.

81.McVey Papers.

82.Board of Trustees' Executive Committee Meeting Minutes, 1 May 1924.

83.*Lexington Herald*, 10 March 1931.

84.Board of Trustees' Executive Committee Meeting Minutes, 1 May 1924.

85. Board of Trustees' Meeting Minutes, 9 December 1924.

86. Board of Trustees' Meeting Minutes, 11 November, 9 December 1924.

87. Trustees' board minutes, 10 May 1924. McVey Papers.

88. Board of Trustees' Executive Committee Meeting Minutes, 19 February 1926. McVey Papers.

89. McVey Papers. McVey's Diary, 21 October 1931.

90. Rice, *The Wildcats: Kentucky football*, 95-102. It was said that Redd rode into the lobby of the Lafayette Hotel every Fourth of July shouting the same comments.

91. McVey Diary, 13, 16 December 1932. Clark interview.

92. University Senate Meeting Minutes, 17 April 1933.

93. McVey Papers.

94. Ibid. UK Sports Information, 22 May 2000.

95. McVey Papers.

96. McVey Papers. *The Kentucky Encyclopedia CD-ROM*.

97. McVey Papers.

98. *Courier-Journal*, 2 September 1970.

99. Ibid.

100. *Courier-Journal* 22 March 1941, 2 September 1970.

101. *Courier-Journal*, 2 September 1970.

102. *Courier-Journal*, 13 March 1941. Adolph F. Rupp biographic files, Special Collections M.I. King Library, University of Kentucky. In the 1980s a person connected to the athletics program spread the story that Rupp had no personal friends, that all his life centered on basketball. That

wasn't correct, and I doubt if the coach would have had a social contact with this person if he had been alive. I've heard long-time alumni secretary Helen King; Helen Fishback, football housemother for a number of years; my in-laws, George and AnnaBelle Ellison, and Willie Shinnick talk about social outings with the Rupps.

103.Ibid.

104."Great Moments In Kentucky Basketball With Adolph Rupp," An undated recording of Rupp's recollections of his career produced by the Committee of 101, Lexington, Ky.

105. *The Kentucky Encyclopedia*, 787.

106.Ibid.

107. *1989-90 Kentucky Wildcats Basketball* (Lexington, Ky., 1989), 101.

108.Ibid., 164-70. UK Sports Information.

109. *Courier-Journal*, 7 December 1996. Telephone interview with Gary Johnson at NCAA headquarters, Kansas City, Kansas, 18 March 1997. *1994-95 Kentucky Basketball*, 116, 121- 26, 151, 208-10. Dean Smith, *A Coach's Life* (New York, 1999), 288.

110. *The Kentucky Encyclopedia*, 787. Rupp biographic files.

111. *Lexington Herald*, 10 May 1935. *Lexington Leader*, 30 March 1949. Adolph F. Rupp, *Rupp Championship Basketball for player, Coach and Fan* (New York, 1949), 24.

112.Rupp, *Rupp's Championship Basketball for Player, Coach and Fan*, 24.

113. *Courier-Journal*, 1 February 1998.

114.Russell Rice, *Adolph F. Rupp, Kentucky's Basketball Baron* (Champaign, Illinois, 1994), 20-30.

115.*Inside NBA Stuff,* May 1998, 7:3, 12.

116.*Courier-Journal,* 10 January 1960.

117.Rice, *Adolph Rupp, Kentucky's Basketball Baron,* 20-30.

118.*Lexington Herald,* 9 February 1942. *Courier-Journal,* 14 January 1951.

119.Interview on 9 October 1991 with Thomas D. Clark, Kentucky's historian laureate who came to UK one year after Rupp's was hired, and who was certainly no great admirer of the coach.. *Courier-Journal,* 24 August 1994.

120.Betty B.Ellison, "Coming of Age: The Athletic Administration of Frank L. McVey." A University of Kentucky graduate history seminar paper prepared under the direction of Dr. Humbert S. Nelli. Lexington, Kentucky, 1991.

121.Ibid. Rice, *The Wildcats: Kentucky Football,* 118-19.

122.McVey Papers.

123.Ibid. *Rice, The Wildcats: Kentucky Football,* 120.

124.Rice, *The Wildcats: Kentucky Football,* 173-74.

125.Bryant, *Bear, The Hard Life and Good Times of Alabama's Coach Bryant* (Boston, 1975). 118-20.

126.1994-95 *Kentucky Basketball,* 123, 208.

127.*Courier-Journal,* 1 February 1998, 21 September 1995.

128.*Courier-Journal,* 19 March 1998.

129.*Courier-Journal,* 2 January 1998. *1994-95 Kentucky Basketball,* 141, 147.

130. *Courier-Journal*, 2 January 1998.

131. *The Kentucky Encyclopedia*, 303.

132. 1994-95 *Kentucky Basketball*, 208. *Courier-Journal*, 2 January 1998.

133. Ibid. Rupp biographic files.

134. *1994-95 Kentucky Basketball*, 208, 124. "Great Moments in Kentucky Basketball With Adolph Rupp."

135. *Courier-Journal*, 28 February 1951.

136. *1994-95 Kentucky Basketball*, 209. "Great Moments in Kentucky Basketball With Adolph Rupp."

137. *1994-95 Kentucky Basketball*, 209.

138. *1994 Kentucky Football*, 149-50. Kentucky football clip files in Special Collections. The Papers of Herman L. Donovan, Special Collections, M.I. King Library, University of Kentucky.

139. Interview with former governor, Lawrence Wetherby, in Frankfort, 16 March 1991.

140. *New York Times*, 4 March 1951.

141. Donovan Papers. *Acts of the General Assembly for the Commonwealth of Kentucky* (Frankfort, Ky., 1951), 1-3.

142. Donovan Papers. Clark Interview.

143. Charles Rosen, *Scandals of '51, How Gamblers Almost Killed College Basketball* (New York, 1975), 188. *New York Times*, 21 October 1951. Donovan Papers.

144. Ibid.

145. *The People of New York v Alex Groza, Ralph Beard, Dale Barnstable.* Donovan Papers.

146. Ibid.

147. Harry C. Lancaster, *Adolph Rupp As I Knew Him* (Lexington, Ky.,1979), 47. Rosen, *Scandals of '51, How the Gamblers Almost Killed College Basketball,* 183.

148. Lancaster, *Adolph Rupp As I Knew Him*, 47. Donovan Papers.

149. Donovan Papers.

150.Ibid. Rosen, *Scandals of '51, How Gamblers Almost Killed College Basketball,* 183-87.

151. Donovan Papers.

152. Ibid. *The People of New York v Alex Groza, Ralph Beard, Dale Barnstable.*

153. *Herald-Leader,* 20 January 2000.

154. Ibid. Donovan Papers.

155. Ibid. Donovan Papers.

156. Ibid. *Facts On File Yearbook* (New York, 1951), 232.

157. Donovan Papers. Clark Interview.

158.Donovan Papers.

159. Ibid.

160. Ibid.

161. *Lexington Herald,* 5 November 1952.

162.*Courier-Journal,* 22 February 1953. Donovan Papers.

163. *Courier-Journal*, 4 November 1952.

164. Walter Byers, *Unsportsmanlike Conduct, Exploiting College Athletes* (Ann Arbor, Michigan, 1995), 57. Donovan Papers.

165. Confidential interview in Lexington, 3 October 1989.

166. Donovan Papers.

167. Bryant, *The Hard Times and Good Life of Alabama's Coach Bryant*, 120-21.

168. *Courier-Journal*, 17 August 1953. Rice, *Wildcat Legacy* (Virginia Beach, Va., 1982), 93.

169. "Great Moments in Kentucky Basketball With Adolph Rupp."

170. Ibid.

171. *Courier-Journal*, 25 February 2000.

172. Bryant, *The Hard Life and Good Times of Alabama's Coach Bryant*, 119.

173. The Papers of Frank G. Dickey. Special Collections, MI. King Library, University of Kentucky.

174. *Courier-Journal*, 6 December 1957.

175. Ibid. Dickey Papers.

176. Dickey Papers.

177. Ibid.

178. Ibid. Clark Interview.

179. Dickey Papers.

180. Ibid.

181. Ibid.

182. Ibid.

183. Clark interview.

184. Ibid.

185. John W. Oswald Papers. Special Collections, M.I. King Library, University of Kentucky.

186. Dickey Papers.

187. Ibid.

188. Ibid.

189.1994 *Kentucky Football Media Guide*, 135, 201. Rice, *The Wildcats: Kentucky Football*, 307.

190. Rice, *The Wildcats: Kentucky Football*, 306-11.

191. Oswald Papers.

192. Ibid. *The Kentucky Encyclopedia*, 914.

193. Oswald Papers. Rice, *Adolph Rupp, Kentucky's Basketball Baron*, 153.

194. Oswald Papers.

195. Ibid.

196."Great Moments In Kentucky Basketball With Adolph Rupp."

197. James A. Michener, *Sports In America* (New York, 1975), 146-49.

198. Telephone interview with Derek Smolick, UTEP assistant SID, in El Paso, Texas, 24 February 1997.

199. UK Alumni Records.

200. *Herald-Leader*, 19 December 1991. *Courier-Journal*, 11 February 1997.

201.Telephone interview 7 March 2000, with Jeremy Noel in ACC media relations, Greensboro, NC. Dean Smith, *A Coach's Life* (New York, 1999), 288.

202.Smith, *A Coach's Life*. 288.

203.*Herald-Leader*, 14 March 1993.

204. Oswald Papers.

205.*Courier-Journal*, 15 April 1968.

206. Oswald Papers. The Papers of A.D. Kirwan, Special Collections, MI. King Library, University of Kentucky.

207. Ibid. Board of Trustees' Meeting Minutes, 29 January 1969.

208. *The Kentucky Encyclopedia*, 823-24. *Herald-Leader*, 1 March 1987.

209. Ibid.

210. *Herald-Leader*, 1 March 1987.

211. Ibid. *Courier-Journal*, 15 April 1973.

212. The Papers of Otis A. Singletary. Special Collections, M.I. King Library, University of Kentucky. *Bright et al v Nunn et al.* No. 21002, United State Court of Appeals for the Sixth District.

213. *Bright et al v Nunn et al.*

214. Ibid.

215. Singletary Papers. UKAA Board Meeting Minutes, 10 March 1970, 29 April 1970.

216. Singletary Papers.

217. *Herald-Leader*, 1 March 1987. *The Kentucky Encyclopedia*, 740-41.

218. UKAA Board Meeting Minutes, 20 October 1970. Singletary Papers.

219. *Lexington Leader*, 2 April 1969. Kirwan Papers. Russell Rice, *Joe B. Hall, My Own Kentucky Home* (Huntsville, Ala., 1981), 75-76, 159-60.

220. Singletary Papers. UKAA Board Meeting Minutes, 20 January 1971.

221. Singletary Papers.

222. Ibid..

223. Ibid. *Louisville Times*, 11 February 1971.

224. *Louisville Times*, 11 February 1971.

225. UKAA Board Meeting Minutes, 20 October 1971.

226. Singletary Papers.

227. Ibid.

228. Ibid.

229. *Courier-Journal*, 4 February 1972.

230. *Lexington Leader*, 28 January 1972.

231. Ibid.

232. Ibid.

233. Rupp biographic file.

234. *Courier-Journal*, 28 March 1972. *The Kentucky Encyclopedia*, 796. UKAA Board Meeting Minutes, 27 March 1972.

235. UKAA Board Meeting Minutes, 27 March 1972.

236. *Lexington Herald*, 29 March 1972.

237. Singletary Papers. UKAA Board Meeting Minutes, 31 March 1972.

238. Singletary Papers.

239. Ibid.

240. Interview with former Gov. Louis B. Nunn, 22 January 2000, Louisville, Kentucky.

241. Singletary Papers.

242. Ibid.

243. *Memphis Press-Scimitar*, 18 January 1973.

244. Singletary Papers.

245. Ibid.

246. Ibid.

247. Ibid.

248. Ibid. The Papers of David P. Roselle, Special Collections, M.I. King Library, University of Kentucky.

249. Singletary Papers.

250. Dave Kindred, *A Year With The Cats, From Breathitt County To The White House* (Lexington, Ky., 1978), 21-22.

251. Ibid.

252. Rupp biographic file.

253. Singletary Papers.

254. *Herald-Leader*, 12 February 1997.

255. UK news release, 1 September 1966. *Lexington Herald*, 17 June 1966. Board of Trustees' Meeting Minutes, 17 June, 13 December 1966. UKAA Board Meeting Minutes, 7 October 1969.

256. Lexington Fayette Urban-County Government Archives.

257. Ibid.

258. UKAA Board Meeting Minutes, 12 June 1971.

259. UKAA Board Meeting Minutes, 20 January 1971. *Lexington Leader*, 25 February 1971.

260. LFUCG Archives. UKAA Board Meeting Minutes, 29 April 1971. Singletary Papers.

261. Roselle Papers. *1994-95 Kentucky Basketball*, 109.

262. Singletary Papers.

263. Ibid.

264. Ibid. *Courier-Journal*, 14 June 1971.

265. UKAA Board Meeting Minutes, 19August 1971.

266. Ibid.

267. *Courier-Journal*, 16 September 1971. *Kentucky Post*, 16 September 1971.

268. Singletary Papers.

269. Ibid.

270. Ibid.

271. Ibid.

272. Byers, *Unsportsmanlike Conduct, Exploiting College Athletes*, 57.

273. Donovan Papers.

274. *The Kentucky Encyclopedia,* 397.

275. Singletary Papers.

276.Ibid. Telephone interview with archivist Frank Stanger, 17 April 1996.

277. Singletary Papers.

278. Ibid.

279. *Courier-Journal,* 17 October 1987.

280. *Lexington Herald,* 17 October 1980. Singletary Papers.

281. Singletary Papers.

282. Ibid.

283.Ibid.

284. Ibid.

285. UKAA Board Meeting Minutes, 19 December 1972. Singletary Papers. *Herald-Leader,* 16 August 1981.

286.*Courier-Journal,* 18 June 2000.

287.LFUCG archives.

288.*Lexington Morning Herald,* 11 April 1902.

289.*Herald-Leader,* 1 March 1987.

290.Singletary Papers. *The Kentucky Encyclopedia,* 209-11, 639-40.

291.Singletary Papers.

292.Ibid.

293.Ibid. LFUCG archives.

294.UKAA Board Meeting Minutes, 11 September 1971. Interview with UKAA board member Charles P. Roland.

295.Singletary Papers.

296.Ibid.

297.Ibid. LFUCG archives.

298.Singletary Papers.

299.Ibid.

300.*Lexington Herald*, 21 November 1973; 17 March, 7 November 1974; 13 March 1975. *The Kentucky Encyclopedia*, 493.

301.Singletary Papers.*Lexington Leader*, 14 April 1975.

302.*Lexington Herald*, 10 Arpil 1975. *Courier-Journal*, 11 April 1975. Singletary Papers.

303.Ibid.

304.Singletary Papers. Rice, *Joe B. Hall, My Own Kentucky Home*, 156.

305.Singletary Papers.

306.Ibid.

307.Ibid. Clipping Files, Special Collections, M.I. King Library, University of Kentucky.

308.UKAA Board Meeting Minutes, 2 April 1976. LFUCG archives. Legal counsel's office. Singletary Papers.

309.Singletary Papers. Lexington Center Corporation archives. Legal Counsel's Office.

310.Ibid.

311.Interview with LCC accounting manager Carolyn Brooks, 12 July 1993. Singletary Papers. LCC archives.

312.UKAA Files.

313.Ibid.

314.Ibid. LFUCG archives. LCC archives.

315.Singletary Papers. LCC archives.

316.UKAA Files.

317.Singletary Papers.

318.Interviews with LCC controller Larry Stebleton, 4 June 1993; UKAA accounting director J.R. Hisle, 27 September 1993. Singletary Papers.

319.LFUCG archives.

320.UKAA Files.

321.Tour of the Blue Room, 12 July 1993.

322. Board of Trustees' Meeting Minutes, 6 May 1975. *Lexington Herald,* 8 May 1975.

323. *Kentucky Alumnus,* July 1987.

324. Board of Trustees' Meeting Minutes, 6 May, 26 June 1975.

325. Singletary Papers.

326. Legal Counsel's Office.

327. *The Kentucky Encyclopedia,* 292-93. Charles Kerr, *History of Kentucky* (Chicago, 1922), IV: 570.

328. Ibid. 1971 Lexington Ball Program. *Who Was Who* (Chicago, 1942), 500.

329. Margaret Voorhies Haggin Indenture, 14 July 1938. McVey Papers.

330. Legal Counsel's Office. Singletary Papers.

331. McVey Papers. Dickey Papers.

332. Singletary Papers.

333. Ibid.

334. Ibid.

335. Ibid. *Herald-Leader*, 1 March 1987.

336. Singletary Papers.

337. Ibid. Legal Counsel's Office.

338. Ibid.

339. McVey Papers. Dickey Papers.

340. 1971 Lexington Ball Program.

341. Singletary Papers.

342. Legal Counsel's Office.

343. *1994 Kentucky Football*, 149, 202.

344. Singletary Papers.

345. Ibid.

346. Ibid.

347. Ibid.

348. *Courier-Journal*, 30 November 1975.

349. Singletary Papers.

350. Ibid.

351. *1994-95 Kentucky Basketball*, 211-14.

352. *Courier-Journal*, 8 December 1975.

353. Ibid.

354. Singletary Papers. *Courier-Journal*, 8 December 1975.

355. *Courier-Journal*, 8 December 1975.

356. Ibid.

357. Ibid.

358. Singletary Papers.

359. Ibid.

360. Ibid.

361. Ibid.

362. Ibid.

363. Ibid.

364. Ibid.

365. Ibid.

366. Ibid. Sally A. Denton, *The Bluegrass Conspiracy* (New York, 1990), 150-81, 293-95, 303- 05.

367. Ibid.

368. Singletary Papers.

369. Ibid.

370. Ibid.

371. Ibid.

372. Ibid.

373. *Lexington Herald*, 6, 8 March; 12, 13 April 1979.

374. *Kentucky Kernel*, 22 February 1980. *Lexington Herald*, 20 May 1981.

375. *Lexington Herald*, 21 May 1981. *Lexington Leader*, 11 July 1981.

376. Ibid. *Courier-Journal*, 15 July 1981.

377. UKAA Board Meeting Minutes, 16 December 1981. *Lexington Herald*, 25 November 1981.

378. Ibid.

379. UKAA Board Meeting Minutes, 16, 21 December 1981. *Lexington Leader*, 16 December 1981. *Courier-Journal*, 17 December 1981. Singletary Papers.

380.Singletary Papers.

381.Ibid.

382.Ibid.

383.*Herald-Leader*, 9 July 1978.

384.Singletary Papers.

385.Byers, *Unsportsmanlike Conduct, Exploiting College Athletes*, 101-02.

386.Singletary Papers.

387.Ibid.

388.Ibid.

389.Byers, *Unsportsmanlike Conduct, Exploiting College Athletes*, 101-02.

390.Singletary Papers.

391.Ibid.

392.Ibid.

393.Ibid.

394.Singletary Papers. Donovan Papers.

395.Singletary Papers.

396.Ibid.

397.Ibid.

398.Ibid. UKAA Financial Report 1980-81.

399.Singletary Papers.

400.*Report of the Committee on Intramural and Intercollegiate Athletics* (Lexington, Ky., 1982), 29.

401.*Herald-Leader*, 19 June 1984. UKAA Annual Financial Report 1983-84.

402.*Cincinnati Inquirer*, 13 April 1998.

403.*Herald-Leader*, 30 November 1978.

404.*Herald-Leader*, 23 March 1991, 14 March 1992.

405.Roselle Papers.

406.Board Trustees' Meeting Minutes, 24 June 1984; 23 June and 15 September 1987; 23 June 1988. Singletary Papers. Roselle Papers.

407.Singletary Papers.

408.Ibid.

409.Ibid.

410.Ibid.

411.Ibid.

412.Ibid.

413.Ibid.

414.*The Kentucky Encyclopedia*, 974.

415.Singletary Papers. *Herald-Leader*, 9 March 1997.

416.Singletary Papers.

417.Ibid.

418.Francis M. Nash, *Towers Over Kentucky, A History of Radio and Television in the Bluegrass State* (Lexington, Ky., 1995), 237-38.

419.Ibid.

420.Singletary Papers. UKAA files.

421.Singletary Papers.

422.Ibid.

423.Singletary Papers. UKAA records. UKAA Board Meeting Minutes, 4 June 1977.

424.Singletary Papers. UKAA records.

425.Singletary Papers.

426.Ibid. *1991 Kentucky Wildcat Football*, 136-37, 200.

427.Singletary Papers.

428.Ibid.

429.Ibid.

430.Ibid.

431.Ibid.

432.Ibid.

433.The Papers of David P. Roselle and Charles T. Wethington. Special Collections, M.I. King Library.

434.Singletary Papers.

435.Ibid. UKAA Board Meeting Minutes, 26 June 1980.

436.Ibid.

437.Singletary Papers.

438.Ibid. UKAA Board Meeting Minutes, 30 September 1982.

439.Singletary Papers.

440.Ibid.

441.UKAA files. *Lexington Herald*, 24 May 1980. *Herald-Leader*, 16 June 1983.

442.UKAA files.

443.Singletary Papers. UKAA files. *Herald-Leader*, 16 June 1983.

444.Singletary Papers.

445.Telephone interview with Treva Tidwell, LSU's athletics department's electronic media division, Baton Rouge, Louisiana, 2 September 1991.

446.Singletary Papers. *Herald-Leader*, 29 June 1983.

447.Singletary Papers. UKAA Board Meeting Minutes, 29 June 1983. UKAA files.

448.Singletary Papers. UKAA files.

449.Singletary Papers.

450.Tidwell interview. UKAA Annual Financial Report 1988-89.

451.LCC archives. Singletary Papers.

452.Ibid. Brooks interview.

453.LCC archives.

454.Singletary Papers. UKAA files.

455.UKAA files.

456.Donovan Papers. Dickey Papers. UKAA files.

457.Singletary Papers.

458.Ernst Jokl biographic file. Special Collections, M.I. King Library, University of Kentucky.

459.Ibid.

460. Ibid. *Lexington Herald*, 1 March 1958.

461.Ernst Jokl interview, Lexington, Ky., 28 September 1994.

462.Dickey Papers.

463.Ibid. UKAA Board Meeting Minutes, 2 October 1962.

464.Oswald Papers. *Lexington Leader*, 29 October 1964.

465.Medical Center Chancellor and Dean of Medicine's files.

466.Ibid.

467.Ibid.

468.Ibid. Singletarys Papers.

469.Dean of Medicine files.

470.Board of Trustees' Meeting Minutes, 5 March 1985.

471.Medical Center Chancellor and Dean of Medicine's files.

472.Ibid.

473.Ibid.

474.Ibid. UKAA files.

475.Healthsouth Corporation's Annual 1999 Report (SECform 10-k). healthsouth.com/sports/index.

476.UKAA Report of Medical Services, 15 December 1987.

477.Ibid.

478.Medical Center Chancellor's files.

479.Ray was my orthopedic surgeon for a number of years but, to keep an objective perspective, there was no discussion of his relationship with Andrews, Ireland or Bosomworth. The doctor-patient relationship had no bearing on how I handled the sports medicine sections of this book. That determination came from documents obtained by the Open Records Act from the medical center chancellor and dean of medicine's offices and UKAA records.

480.Singletary Papers.

481.Ibid. Francis X. Dealy, *Win At Any Cost: The Sell Out Of College Football* (New York, 1990), 193-96.

482.Legal Counsel's Office, Singletary's amended 1985 employment contract.

483.*Herald-Leader*, 27 October 1985.

484.Singletary Papers. UKAA Board Meeting Minutes, 2 April 1984.

485.*Herald-Leader*, 27 March 1985.

486.Singletary Papers. UKAA Board Meeting Minutes, 2 April 1985.

487.*Herald-Leader*, 27 October 1985. *Sports Illustrated*, 11 November 1985.

488.*Herald-Leader*, 27 October 1985.

489.Ibid.

490.Ibid. Singletary Papers.

491.Singletary Papers.

492.*Herald-Leader*, 20 October 1996.

493.Ibid.

494.*Herald-Leader*, 27 October 1985. Singletary Papers.

495.*Herald-Leader*, 27 October 1985.

496.Ibid.

497.Ibid.

498.Ibid.

499.Ibid.

500.Ibid.

501.Ibid.

502.*Herald-Leader*, 29 October 1985. *Kentucky Kernel*, 29 October 1985.

503.*Herald Leader*, 30, 31 October 1985.

504.*Sports Illustrated*, 11 November 1985.

505.Singletary Papers.

506.Ibid. *Herald-Leader* 12 November 1985.

507.*Herald-Leader*, 15 December 1985.

508.Ibid.

509.Ibid.

510.Ibid. *Courier-Journal*, 8 December 1985.

511.Ibid.

512.Ibid. UKAA Annual Financial Report 1985-86.

513.Trustees' Executive Committee Meeting Minutes, 17 January 1986. *Herald-Leader*, 28 January 1986.

514.National Rifle Association annual meeting, Charlotte, North Carolina, 20 May 2000, CSPAN. Singletary Papers.

515.Singletary Papers. NCAA news release, 3 March 1988.

516.Documents obtained from the Legal Counsel's Office.

517.Roselle Papers.

518.Board of Trustees' Meeting Minutes, 21 January, 14 October, 9 December 1986. *Herald-Leader*, 24 December 1986.

519.Board of Trustees' Meeting Minutes, 21 January 1986; 15 June 1987.

520.*Herald-Leader*, 31 July 1990.

521.*Courier-Journal*, 10 May 1987.

522.David P. Roselle biographic file, Special Collections, M.I. King Library, University of Kentucky. Board of Trustees' Meeting Minutes, 3 March 1987.

523.Roselle Papers.

524.Ibid.

525.Ibid.

526.Board of Trustees' Meeting Minutes, 3 March 1987. *Herald-Leader*, 4 March 1987.

527.Roselle Papers.

528.Ibid.

529.*Herald-Leader*20 July 1987.

530.Ibid.

531.Roselle Papers. Singletary Papers.

532.Roselle Papers.

533.Ibid.

534.Roselle Papers. UKAA files.

535.Ibid.

536.Ibid.

537.Roselle Papers.

538.Alexander Wolffe and Armen Keteyian, *Raw Recruits, The High Stakes Games College Play To Get Their Basketball Stars And What It Costs To Win* (New York, 1990), 148-49.

539.Roselle Papers.

540.Ibid.

541.Ibid.

542.Ibid.

543.Ibid.

544.Ibid.

545.Ibid. Legal Counsel's Office.

546.Byers, *Unsportsmanlike Conduct, Exploiting College Athletes*, 128-29.

547.Roselle Papers.

548.Ibid.

549.Ibid.

550.Ibid.

551.Singletary Papers. Roselle Papers.

552.Roselle Papers.

553.Ibid.

554.Ibid.

555.Ibid.

556.Ibid.

557.Ibid. *Sports Illustrated*, 11 February 1991, 166-67; 29 May 1989, 24-34. *Herald-Leader* 26 July 1988.

558.*New York Times*, 27 November 1989. *Response of the President of the University of Kentucky To The National Collegiate Athletic Association* (Lexington, Ky., 1989), D-143, E-18. *Herald-Leader*, 13 November 1988.

559.Roselle Papers.

560.Ibid. *Herald-Leader*, 9, 11 April 1988.

561.Roselle Papers.

562.Ibid.

563.Singletary Papers. Roselle Papers.

564.Ibid.

565.Ibid. Board of Trustees' Metting Minutes 10 July 1986 to 4 March 1988.

566.Singletary Papers. Roselle Papers. Telephone interview with UKAA accounting director J. R. Hisle, 10 December 1993.

567.*Kentucky Kernel*, 6 March, 9 March 1989.

568.UKAA Board Meeting Minutes, 8 April 1988.

569.Roselle Papers.

570.Ibid.

571. Ibid.

572.UKAA Board Meeting Minutes, 8 April 1988.

573.Ibid.

574.Ibid. *Herald-Leader*, 9 April 1988.

575.*Herald-Leader*, 18 August 1988. UKAA files.

576.*Herald-Leader*, 18 August 1988.

577.Roselle Papers.

578.*Herald-Leader*, 11 November 1988.

579.Ibid.

580.Roselle Papers. Legal Counsel's Office.

581.*Herald-Leader*, 12 November 1988.

582.*Herald-Leader*, 16 November 1988.

583.Ibid.

584.Board of Trustees' board Meeting Minutes, 24 January 1989. *1989-90 Kentucky Wildcat basketball, 133.*

585.*Herald-Leader,*13 December 1990. Legal Counsel's Office.

586.Ibid.

587.Ibid. *Courier-Journal,* 29 January 1997.

588.Roselle Papers.*1994-95 Kentucky Wildcats Basketball,* 167.

589.Roselle-Wethington Papers.These papers were a combination of Roselle's last months in office and Charles T. Wethington's early weeks as president. The papers have now probably been separated into each of the presidents' documents.

590.Roselle-Wethington Papers. UKAA files.

591.Roselle-Wethington Papers.

592.*1991 Kentucky Wildcats Football,* 139, 154-58. *Herald-Leader,* 30 October 1991. *Kentucky Kernel,* 29 April 1993.

593.*Courier-Journal,* 3 January 1997. *Herald-Leader,* 5 January 1997.

594.Legal Counsel's Office.

595.Dean of Medicine's records.

596.Ibid.

597.*Herald-Leader,* 18, 20 April 1987. UKAA files. *Scott Graham Hartman v University of Kentucky Athletics Association et al,* US District Court for the Eastern District of Kentucky, 88-120. Legal Counsel's Office.

598.Dean of Medicine's records that included a copy of the *Woodford County Sun* with an article about the board of education meeting.

599.Ibid.

600.Ibid.

601.Ibid. Singletary Papers.

602.UKAA files. Dean of Medicine's records.

603.Dean of Medicine's records. UKAA files.

604.Roselle Papers. Dean of Medicine Medical Center Chancellor's records.

605.Ibid.

606.Ibid.

607.Dean of Medicine and Medical Center Chancellor's records.

608.Ibid.

609.Ibid.

610.Ibid.

611.Ibid.

612.Ibid.

613.Ibid.

614.Ibid.

615.Ibid. UKAA files.

616.Medical Center Chancellor's recordss.

617.Ibid.

618.UKAA files. Al Green to author, 23 June 1994.

619.Medical Center Chancellor and Dean of Medicine's records.

620.Medical Center Chancellor's records.

621.Ibid.

622.UKAA files. Dean of Medicine's records.

623.Dean of Medicine's recordss.

624.Ibid.

625.Ibid.

626.Legal Counsel's Office.

627.*Courier-Journal,* 15 June 1995, 22 March 1998. Bull Run Corporation's 1997 Annual Stockholders' Report.

628.Lexington Center Corporation archives.

629.UKAA files.

630.Ibid.

631.LCC archives.

632.Roselle Papers.

633.Ibid.

634.Ibid.

635.Ibid.

636.Ibid.

637.Ibid.

638.Ibid. UK Sports Information.

639.UKAA files.

640.Ibid. UKAA Annual Financial Reports 1979-1989. Legal Counsel' Office.

641.George J. DeBin to author, 3 December 1996.

642.UKAA files.

643.Richard A. Lipsey, ed, *Sports Marketplace* (Princeton, NJ, 1995), 704-05.

644.Lipsey, *Sports Marketplace*, 704-05.

645.UK Project Report 1991 Basketball Highlights Video. UKAA files.

646.UKAA files.

647.Ibid.

648.Ibid.

649.UKAA files. Associate athletics director Larry Ivy to author, 25 January 1994.

650.*Herald-Leader*, 13 April 1996. UKAA files.

651.*Herald-Leader*, 13 April 1996.

652.Ibid.

653.Ibid. *Herald-Leader,* 21 April 1996. *Journey to Greatness* (Louisville, Ky., 1996). *Bravo Blue* (Lexington, Ky., 1996).

654.*Herald-Leader*, 13, 21 April 1996.

655.*Sports Illustrated*, 17 April 1996.

656.Tour of Joseph Beth Bookstore.

657.*Herald-Leader*, 26 April 1996.

658.UKAA files.

659.*Herald-Leader*, 13 December 1996.

660.*Herald-Leader*, 13 December 1997, 7 July 1997.

661.UKAA files.

662.Ibid.

663.Contracts from the UK Division of Purchasing.

664.Ibid.

665.Ibid. UKAA files.

666.UKAA files, John Darsie to Bernard L. Vonderheide, 30 November 1988.

667.*Herald-Leader*, 27 November 1997.

668.UKAA files.

669.*Herald-Leader*, 27 November 1997. UKAA files.

670.Corporate Records section, Kentucky Secretary of State's office, 13 December 1994. *Courier-Journal*, 22 July 1993. UKAA files.

671.*Courier-Journal*, 22 July 1993. *Herald-Leader*, 25 July, 31 August 1993.

672.*Herald-Leader*, 10 March 1996.

673.*Herald-Leader*, 27 April 1996.

674.*Los Angeles Daily News*, 14 April 1988. *Response.*

675.Ibid.

676.Ibid.

677.*Dwane Casey v Emory Air Freight et al.* United Stated District Court for the Eastern District of Kentucky, 88-234.

678.Ibid.

679.Ibid.

680.*Herald-Leader*, 15 April, 4 May 1988; 3 November 1976. *Herald*, 13 November 1959.

681.Biographic files of John Darsie, Robert Lawson, Joe Burch. Special Collections, M.I. King Library, University of Kentucky.

682.Roselle Papers.

683.*Dwane Casey v Emory Air Freight et al.*

684.*University of Kentucky Athletic Association and Dwane Casey v Emery International.* United States District Court for the Eastern District of Kentucky. 88-146.

685.*Response.*

686.Ibid.

687.Ibid.

688.Ibid.

689.Ibid.

690.Ibid.

691.Ibid.

692.Ibid.

693.Ibid.

694.Ibid.

695.Roselle Papers. *Herald-Leader*, 26 July 1988.

696.Roselle Papers. *Response.*

697.*Response.*

698.Roselle Papers.

699.Wolff and Keteyian, *Raw Recruits, The High Stakes Games Colleges Play To Get Their Basketball Stars and What It Costs To Win*, 257-58.

700.Ibid. *Dwane Casey v Emery Air Freight et al.*

701.IN RE: NCAA Committee on Infractions Report No. 28, University of Kentucky Investigation Report, Request for Reconsideration on Behalf of Dwane Casey.

702.Ibid.

703.Legal Counsel's Office.

704.Ibid.

705.Ibid.

706.*Response.*

707.Ibid. *Supplemental Response. Dun and Bradstreet's Million Dollar Directory* (Bethlehem, PA., 1994) 4348.

708.*Response.*

709.Ibid.

710.Ibid.

711.*Dwane Casey v Emery Air Freight et al.* Marta McMackin's deposition.

712.Ibid. Eddie Sutton's deposition.

713.*Response.*

714.*Response.*

715.Ibid.

716.Ibid.

717.Ibid.

718.Ibid.

719.Ibid.

720.Ibid.

721.*Herald-Leader,* 13 November 1988. *New York Times,* 27 November 1988. *Kentucky Kernel,* 2 November 1988.

722.Ibid.

723.*Response.*

724.Ibid.

725.*Sports Illustrated,* 11 February 1991. Telephone interview with Clay Stoldt, OCU sports information director, 3 November 1994.

726.*Response.*

727.Ibid.

728.Ibid.

729.Ibid. *Herald-Leader,* 4, 5 August 1988.

730.Ibid.

731.*Response.*

732.Ibid.

733.Ibid.

734.Ibid.

735.Ibid.

736.*Sports Illustrated,* 11 February 1991. *Eric Manuel v University of Kentucky et al,* US District Court for the Eastern District of Kentucky, 89-33. US Code 20 1232 G. *Herald- Leader,* 1 October 1988.

737. Interview with Edward Dove, 4 November 1994. *Response. Sports Illustrated*, 11 February 1991.

738.Dove interview. *Response. Sports Illustrated*, 11 February 1991.

739.*Herald-Leader*, 3 June 1991.

740.*Response.* Dove interview. *1994-95 Kentucky Basketball*, 133.

741.*Response.*

742.Ibid.

743.Ibid.

744.*Herald-Leader*, 20 March 1989. *Response.*

745.*Response.*

746.Ibid.

747.*Courier-Journal*, 29 May 1991. *Herald-leader*, 5 May 1993.

748.*Response.*

749.Cawood Ledford and Billy Reed, *Hello Everybody, This Is Cawood Ledford* (Lexington, Ky., 1992), 215.

750.Roselle-Wethington Papers. *Sports Illustrated*, 29 May 1989.

751.*Herald-Leader*, 21 March 1991.

752.*Herald-Leader*, 4 March 1991.

753.*Herald-Leader*, 23, 24 May 1989.

754.Ibid.

755.Rich Pitino, *Full Court Pressure, A Year In Kentucky Basketball* (New York, 1992), 38-39.

756.Ibid.

757. Legal Counsel's Office.

758. Ibid.

759. Ibid. Roselle-Wethington Papers.

760. *Herald-Leader*, 3 February 1991.

761. Ibid.

762. UKAA files.

763. Legal Counsel's Office.

764. Ibid.

765. *Herald-Leader*, 1, 11 September 1994.

766. *Herald-Leader*, 1 October 1994. *Kentucky Kernel*, 12 April 1996.

767. Legal Counsel's Office.

768. *Courier-Journal*, 21 October 1994. *Herald-Leader*, 10 March 1996.

769. *Herald-Leader*, 10 March 1996.

770. *Herald-Leader*, 10 March 23 October 1996.

771. 1994-95 *Kentucky Basketball. Courier-Journal*, 7 May 1997. *Herald-Leader*, 9 May 1997.

772. Ibid.

773. Ibid.

774. Ibid.

775. Ibid.

776. Ibid.

777. Ibid.

778.*Herald-Leader*, 30 June, 6 and 12 October 1996.

779.Ibid.

780.Ibid.

781.Ibid.

782.*Herald-Leader*, 17 October 1996; 9 January 1997.

783.*Herald-Leader*, 9, 18 January, 13 February 1997. *Courier-Journal*, 19 January 1997.

784.*Herald-Leader*29 November 1989.

785.*1991 Kentucky Wildcats Football*, 137, 146.

786.Byers, *Unsportsmanlike Conduct, Exploiting College Athletes*, 62.

787.Ibid.

788.*Herald-Leader*, 30 November 1989.

789.*Courier-Journal*, 9 January 1990. *1994 Kentucky Football*, 22-23, 25-28.

790.Roselle-Wethington Papers. *Courier-Journal*, 9 January 1990. *1991 Kentucky Wildcats Football*, 25, 28.

791.Legal Counsel's Office. *Herald-Leader*, 19 September 1990.

792.Board of Trustees' Meeting Minutes, 24 January 1990. *Herald-Leader*, 25 January 1990.

793.Legal Counsel's Office. *1994 Kentucky Wildcats*, 202.

794.*Courier-Journal*, 22 October 1996. *1994 Kentucky Wildcats Football*, 202.

795.*Courier-Journal*, 22 October 1996.

796.Ibid.

797.Ibid.

798.*Courier-Journal,* 22 October 1996.

799.Ibid.

800.*Courier-Journal* 3 December 1996. *Cincinnati Enquirer,* 5 January 1997.

801.Ibid.

802.*Herald-Leader,* 12 April 1998.

803.Board of Trustees' Meeting Minutes, 24 January 1989.

804.Ibid. *Courier-Journal*24 January, 10 February 1994; 23 July 1998.

805.Board of Trustees' Meeting Minutes, 24 January 1989.

806.Ibid.

807.Ibid.

808.Ibid. *Response. Herald-Leader,* 8 and 12 April 1988.

809.Ibid.

810.A.B. Chandler, *Heroes, Plain Folks and Skunks* (Chicago, 1989), 292-296.

811.Board of Trustees' Meeting Minutes, 24 January 1989. Singletary Papers.

812.Board of Trustees' Meeting Minutes, 3 February 1989.

813.*Response.*

814.NCAA Committee on Infractions Report No. 28, 18 May 1989.

815.Ibid.

816.Ibid.

817.Ibid.

818.Ibid.

819.Ibid.

820.Ibid.

821.Ibid.

822.Ibid. *Herald-Leader*, 4 May 1994.

823.Infractions Report No. 28. *1994-95 Kentucky Basketball*, 214.

824.*US News and World Report*, 13 April 1992. Dealy, *Win At Any Cost: The Sell Out of College Athletics*, 194-96.

825.*Sports Illustrated*, 20 May 1989.

826. *Herald-Leader*, 20 May 1989

827.Ibid.

828.Legal Counsel's Office.

829.*Herald-Leader*, 20 May 1989.

830.Ibid.

831.Ibid.

832.Ibid.

833.Ibid.

834.Board of Trustees' Meeting Minutes, 28 December 1989.

835.*Courier-Journal*, 5 April 1996.

836.Ibid.

837.Roselle-Wethington Papers. Legal Counsel's Office.

838.*Herald-Leader*, 3 May 1997.

839.Ibid.

840.Ibid.

841.UKAA Board Meeting Minutes, April 1996 through July 1997.

842.Ibid.

843.*Courier-Journal, Herald-Leader*, 7 May 1997.

844.*Courier-Journal*, 7 May 1997.

845.Ibid.

846.Ibid. *Herald-Leader*, May 1997.

847.Ibid.

848.Ibid.

849.*Herald-Leader*, 9 May 1997.

850.*Herald-Leader*, 18 May 1997.

851.Legal Counsel's Office.

852.Legal Counsel's Office.

853.Ibid.

854.*Courier-Journal*, 29, 30 June 1997. "The C.M. Newton Show," WVLKRadio, 7 July 1998.

855.*Herald-Leader*, 30 November 1997.

856.*Herald-Leader*, 4 June 1997.

857.Legal Counsel's Office.

858.Ibid.

859.Ibid.

860.Billy Reed, *Newton's Law, The C.M. Newton* Story (Lexington, Ky., 2000), 299. *San Antonio Express*, 26 March 1998.

861.Billy Reed, *Newton's Law, The C.M. Newton Story*, 216.

862.*Courier-Journal*, 13 May 1998. *Sports Illustrated*, 11 May 1998.

863.Ibid. *Herald-Leader*, 26 January 1999.

864.ukathletics.fansonly, 17 July 2000.

865.*Courier-Journal*, 14, 17 July 2000.

866.*Courier-Journal*, 11 June 1000.

866.*The Charlotte Observer*, 29 August 2000.

867.*The Charlotte Observer*, 30 August 2000.

868.*Herald-Leader*, 8 June 2000.

869.*Herald-Leader*, 27 September 2000.

867.Ibid. UK Stats.

868.*Herald-Leader*, 18 June 2000.

869.*Courier-Journal*, 17 July 2000. *Herald-Leader*, 23 August 2000.

870.*Herald-Leader*, 17 November, 16 December 1998.

871.*Herald-Leader*, 17 November 1998.

872.*Courier-Journal*, 21 November 1998, 23 March, 1999, 20 July 1999, 2 September 1999.

*873.Herald-Leader,* 24 November 1998.

*874.Courier-Journal,* 13 December 1998.

875.Reed, *Newton's Law, The C.M. Newton Story,* acknowledgments.

*876.*Bull Run Corporation Notice of Special Meeting of Stockholders, 11 August 1999, 5, 23-25, 56, F-106.

*877.*Ibid., 25, 35.

*878.*Ibid., 38-39.

*879.Herald-Leader,* 12 October, 24 December 1998.

*880.Herald-Leader,* 22 October 1998. *Courier-Journal,* 9 July 2000.

*881.Herald-Leader,* 22 October 1998.

*882.*Ibid.

*883.Courier-Journal,* 22 November, 8 December 1998.

*884.Courier-Journal,* 5 December 1996.

*885.*Ibid.

*886.Courier-Journal,* 11 November 1997.

*887.Herald-Leader,* 22 December 1999.

*888.*Ibid.

*889.Courier-Journal,* 30 March 1998.

*890.*Ibid.

*891.Courier-Journal,* 1, 10, 15 January 1999.

892. Ibid.

893. Ibid.

894. HNTB's University of Kentucky Basketball Arena Study, Appendix B.

895. Ibid.

896. Ibid.

897. Ibid.

898. Ibid.

899. Ibid.

900. *Courier-Journal*, 4 February 1998.

901. *Herald-Leader*, 10 January 1998.

902. *Herald-Leader*, 20 December 1997.

903. Ibid.

904. *Herald-Leader*, 10 November 1999.

905. *Herald-Leader*, 17 May 1998.

906. Ibid.

907. Ibid.

908. Ibid.

909. Ibid.

910. *Herald-Leader*, 16 January 1999.

911. *Herald-Leader*, 21 March 2000.

912. Legal counsel's office.

913. *Herald-Leader*, 16 January 2000.